Temples
TO DOT THE EARTH

Richard O. Cowan

ISBN: 1-55517-339-x

v.2

Published and Distributed by:

Page Layout and Design by Corinne A. Bischoff
Printed in the United States of America

Contents

Preface

When I was growing up in southern California, the local Saints were eagerly anticipating the time when the long-awaited temple would be built there. As young people my friends and I enjoyed the annual "temple excursions" to St. George or Mesa, where we could perform sacred ordinances. Hence temples and temple service early became an important focus in my life.

As I joined the faculty at Brigham Young University in 1961, I was invited to concentrate my research and teaching in the areas of the Doctrine and Covenants and in recent Latter-day Saint history. From the modern revelations I learned of the Lord's restoring temple worship and of the importance he attached to these sacred structures. As a student of recent Church developments, I have followed with great interest the explosion in temple building around the world during the 1980s. I felt a compelling desire to share the information and the inspiring insights this interest and study had brought to me.

May I express appreciation to Derek F. Metcalfe of the Temple Department and Elder Boyd K. Packer, who encouraged my interest. I am indebted to Frank Bruno, who spent endless hours sifting through materials in several libraries and from a multitude of sources as we researched this topic. James and Tamera Palmer have provided substantial help in preparing this manuscript for publication. I am grateful to the leaders of Religious Education at BYU who made such help available. While I gratefully acknowledge the varied assistance received, however, I alone am responsible for the content of this book.

It is my hope that all who read the book will gain a broader understanding of the history and functions of temples and there a deeper appreciation of the place temples can occupy in our lives. Learning how the ancients regarded temples as holy places closest to heaven should enhance our awareness of their sacred nature today. As we read of the sacrifices required to build temples and of the heartfelt gratitude of the Saints at finally having a temple built within their reach, we may well resolve to participate more regularly and frequently in temple service. My prayer is that all who read this book will experience an enhancement of their temple experience that will enable them to share even more fully in the blessings available in the House of the Lord.

Chapter One

Background from Former Dispensations

Temple worship certainly is not unique to the present dispensation. Church leaders have repeatedly affirmed the antiquity of temples and temple ordinances. The Lord "has had His endowments long ago," Elder Wilford Woodruff testified; "it is thousands and millions of years since He received His blessings...."[1] From the beginning of this earth's history, mortals have felt the need of establishing sacred sanctuaries where they can get away from worldly concerns and receive instruction pertaining to the eternities. Elder John A. Widtsoe believed that "all people of all ages have had temples in one form or another." There is ample evidence, he was convinced, that from the days of Adam "there was the equivalent of temples," that in patriarchal times "temple worship was in operation," and that even after the Flood, "in sacred places, the ordinances of the temple were given to those entitled to receive them."[2] Elder Joseph Fielding Smith likewise explained that the Lord taught the fulness of the gospel to Adam and his posterity and gave them the law of sacrifice as a means of pointing their attention forward to his own infinite atonement.

As men spread over the earth, however, they began to depart from the truth and to pervert the ordinances originally revealed to Adam. "Human

sacrifice was substituted for the sacrifice of goats and lambs."
Nevertheless, Elder Smith concluded, "heathen temples" and their ceremonies did grow out of the true concepts the Lord earlier had revealed
through His prophets.[3] Thus a study even of these temples may provide
some valuable insights into the true nature of temples and temple worship.

What is a temple? Dr. Hugh Nibley, a noted Latter-day Saint scholar,
has spent years researching what various ancient religions understood
temples to be. That which makes a temple different from other buildings is
not just its sacredness, he concluded, but rather its unique function. The
earliest temples were regarded as "meeting-places at which men at specific
times attempted to make contact with the powers above...." In this respect
they resembled sacred mountains, which originally had been similar places
of "contact between this and the upper world." These ancient peoples
thought of the temple as being the highest point in the human world, the
best place to observe and learn the ways of the heavens. Consequently
many ancient temples were built atop mountains, but even if they were
physically in the valley they were still regarded as spiritual peaks where
one could be closest to God. In a very real sense the temple represented a
halfway place between heaven and earth.[4]

Ziggurats in Mesopotamia, as well as Mayan pyramids in ancient
America, had the function of supporting the temples built on top of them
and elevating them close to heaven. Consequently the prominent stairways
up their sides symbolized the pathway leading from the human to the divine
world. Perhaps the best known of these Mesopotamian ziggurats was the
Tower of Babel (Genesis 11:1-9). Although the builders' motives were
materialistic and selfish, the name of this tower does reflect a true function
of temples: in the ancient Babylonian language (as well as in modern
Arabic) the first syllable *Bab-* meant gate, while the suffix *-el* was a widely
recognized reference to deity. Hence the name "Babel" literally means
"gate of God."

In his book, *The House of the Lord*, Elder James E. Talmage affirmed
that temples have two essential functions: "A temple...is characterized not
alone as the place where God reveals Himself to man, but also as the House
wherein prescribed ordinances of the Priesthood are solemnized."[5]

Old Testament Sanctuaries

From the beginning of scriptural history, God instructed his people to sacrifice "the firstlings of their flocks." An angel informed Adam that these offerings were "a similitude of the sacrifice of the Only Begotten of the Father" (Moses 5:5-7). Other Old Testament patriarchs, including Noah, Abraham, Isaac, and Jacob, continued the practice of erecting altars and offering sacrifices (see Genesis 8:20; 12:7-8; 13:18; 26:25; 33:20; 35:7). When Jacob saw his dream of the ladder reaching into heaven and received great promises from the Lord, he named the place Bethel (which in Hebrew literally means "the house of God") and referred to it as "the gate of heaven" (Genesis 28:10-19). The Lord specified to Moses that such altars should not be constructed of hewn stones (see Exodus 20:24-25). Because these altars were places of contact between heaven and earth, they may appropriately be regarded as forerunners of the holy houses in which the Lord promised to communicate with his people. Even though some temple ordinances were known from the days of Adam, there is no definite record of actual temple buildings before the time of Moses.

The Tabernacle of Moses

While the children of Israel were still in the wilderness of Sinai, Jehovah directed that they should construct a sanctuary where they might worship him. Because of their migratory status, this structure was to be portable. Nevertheless, it was to be made of the finest materials and workmanship available. It was to be the house of the Lord, comparable to our modern temples. To this end, the Lord directed Moses to call on the people for an offering of such materials as gold and silver, fine linens, and precious stones. (See Exodus 25:1-7.) God's people must always be willing to sacrifice in order to provide these holy sanctuaries. (See D&C 109:5; 124:26-27.)

The tabernacle the Lord commanded Moses to build was to serve both purposes mentioned by Elder Talmage: (1) The Lord directed his people to "make me a sanctuary that I may dwell among them." (The Hebrew actually says "tent among them.") He promised to reveal himself there and give instructions to them (Exodus 25:8, 22). He subsequently kept the promise (see Exodus 33:9-11). (2) Specifically, the Lord intended to reveal sacred

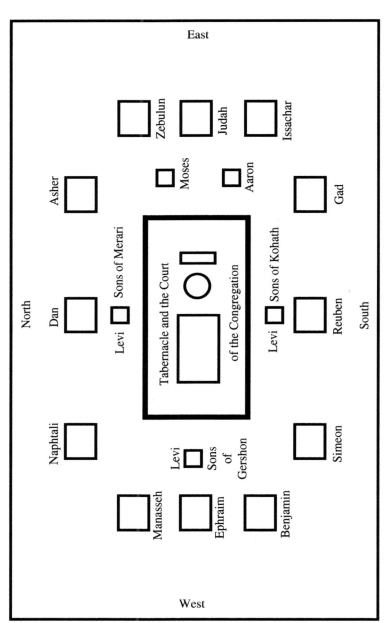

Plan of the Camp of Israel

ordinances to his people (D&C 124:38). Hence "the Tabernacle was but a forerunner of a temple," Elder Mark E. Petersen explained, because "sacred ordinances were performed therein."[6]

In all ages the Savior has revealed the patterns according to which his sacred houses were to be built (compare Exodus 25:9 with D&C 95:13-17). Exodus chapters 25-30 contain the divine revelation of the tabernacle's design and functions. The layout of the tabernacle grounds emphasized its sacredness and separation from the world. As the Israelites pitched their camp, the twelve tribes were arranged around the tabernacle as if to provide a protective shield from the outside world. Innermost was located the tribe of Levi, which included those with priestly authority. (See Numbers 2-3.) The court of the tabernacle, measuring approximately 75 by 150 feet (assuming that the biblical cubit was equal to about one and one-half feet), represented an additional protection.

The tabernacle's furnishings and ordinances further taught the children of Israel how they must prepare in order to return to the presence of God. The altar of sacrifice was the most prominent object in the tabernacle's courtyard. Constructed of acacia wood and overlaid with bronze ("brass" in the King James Version), it stood nearly five feet tall and measured nearly

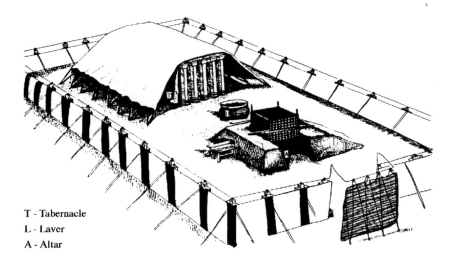

T - Tabernacle
L - Laver
A - Altar

eight feet square at the base. It was here that the people complied with the Lord's commands to make animal and other sacrifices that served as a reminder of his great future atoning sacrifice and reemphasized the vital principles of obedience and sacrifice. Between the altar and the tabernacle was the laver, or large bronze water basin, in which the priests washed their hands and feet before entering the tabernacle or before officiating at the altar. (See Exodus 30:18-21.) Becoming clean is a key step in our progress back to God's presence.

The tabernacle itself was a tent measuring about fifteen by forty-five feet. Its framework was of the most precious wood available, overlaid with gold, and covered by fine linens and costly skins. Inside the tabernacle's entrance, which faced toward the east, was the main room measuring twenty cubits, or about thirty feet, in length. This room, the "holy place," could be entered only by the priests. In it were three significant items of furniture: (1) The table of "shewbread," on which loaves of bread were changed each Sabbath day. The Hebrew *lehem panim* literally means "bread of the faces," a reference to the blessing of coming into the presence of God and beholding his face; hence "shewbread" is translated "bread of the presence" in some modern Bible versions. (2) The seven-branched lampstand (*menorah* in Hebrew) gave light that may have served as a reminder of the importance of spiritual as well as physical illumination. (3) The altar of incense symbolized the importance of prayer in one's spiritual quest; in the ancient world the ascending smoke from burning incense was a common symbol of prayers to heaven. Like the veil, the cloud of incense was also a protective screen preventing unauthorized persons from accidentally beholding the Lord. (See Leviticus 16:13.)

The innermost room of the tabernacle, the "most holy place," also known as the "Holy of Holies," was a perfect cube which measured approximately fifteen feet in height, width, and depth. It was separated from the "holy place" by a beautiful veil of pure white "fine twined linen" adorned with cherubim and other figures embroidered in blue, purple, and scarlet. A latter-day revelation (D&C 132:19) speaks of angels as guardians along the way to exaltation in the kingdom of God. Hence the veil may have symbolized the division between God and man.

Into this most sacred room was placed the ark of the covenant, a chest of acacia wood overlaid with gold, which measured about three feet nine inches in length and two feet three inches in height and width. It contained the tablets of the law given to Moses on Mount Sinai and so was a tangible reminder of God's covenant with his people. It also held a pot of manna and Aaron's rod that had bloomed miraculously—two other reminders of God's special blessings. The lid, made of solid gold, was overshadowed by two cherubim. The Hebrew name of this lid, *kapporeth*, is related to the verb, *kappar*, meaning cover, expiate, atone, or forgive, and is translated as "mercy seat" in the King James Bible. The Greek Old Testament calls this object the *hilasterion* (meaning "the place of atonement"). This is the same word which is used in the New Testament (Romans 3:25) to refer to Christ as the "propitiation" (or reconciliation) for sin. Hence the ark with its "mercy seat" powerfully represented God's atoning love, and the Lord specifically promised to manifest himself there (see Exodus 25:22).

The feeling of reverence in this inner chamber was enhanced by the use of gold in contrast to the bronze employed in the outer court. Nevertheless, Elder Boyd K. Packer reminded us, "it is not the building itself but the visitations of the Spirit that sanctify. When the people stray from the Spirit their sanctuary ceases to be the house of the Lord." Similarly, Elder Packer noted, Moses was commanded to remove his shoes at the burning bush because the place where he stood was holy (Exodus 3:5). "Perhaps it was not so much the ground itself as it was the nature of the interview that sanctified it."[7]

Admission to these holy precincts was progressively more restricted as one approached the ark. While the worthy Israelites as a whole could enter the outer court, only the priests were permitted in the tabernacle's main room. Only one man, the high priest, was permitted to enter the "most holy place," and then only once each year—on the Day of Atonement or *Yom Kippur* (see Leviticus 16:29-34). The Apostle Paul later explained that these regulations in the tabernacle foreshadowed the Savior's atoning sacrifice:

> Into the second [room of the earthly tabernacle] went the high priest alone once every year not without blood, which he offered for himself, and for the errors of the people....
>
> But Christ being come an high priest of good things to come, by a greater and more perfect tabernacle, not made with hands, that is to say, not of this building;

Neither by the blood of goats and calves, but by his own blood he entered in once into the holy place, having obtained eternal redemption for us. (Hebrews 9:7, 11-12; see also v. 24.)

Interestingly, the phrase "Holy of Holies" does not occur anywhere in the standard works. The King James Bible's "most holy place" is translated from the Hebrew *qodesh haqadashim*, which is related to the verb *qadash*, meaning to separate, reserve, or set apart for sacred purposes. Hence *qodesh ha-qudashim* is a Hebrew "construct" (or phrase) which literally means "holy of the holies." This type of construction implies the superlative as in Christ's title "King of kings." Thus the intended meaning is "holiest of all that is holy," or "the most holy place." Wycliffe's 1382 Bible used the phrase "holi of halowes," while Milton was first to use the present wording "holy of holies" in 1641, thirty years after the King James Bible had been published.[8] In recent years the New English Bible and the Jewish Publication Society's Old Testament have employed the phrase "holy of holies" rather than "most holy place."

The Temple of Solomon

After the tribes of Israel became established in the promised land, King David's thoughts turned to building a permanent temple to the Lord. "I dwell in an house of cedar," the king pointed out, "but the ark of God dwelleth [only] within curtains" (2 Samuel 7:2). The Lord, however, declined David's offer. "Thou shalt not build a house for my name, because thou hast been a man of war, and hast shed blood." Nevertheless the Lord assured David that his son Solomon, who would succeed him as king, would be permitted to build the temple. (1 Chronicles 28:3, 6.)

Construction of the temple commenced during the fourth year of Solomon's reign. Like the portable tabernacle in the wilderness, the permanent structure in the promised land was made with the finest possible materials and craftsmanship. Because Israel lacked experience in erecting such a magnificent structure as the temple was to be, Solomon turned to King Hiram of Tyre, who supplied architects, artisans, and cedar wood. Steps were taken to preserve the spirit of reverence surrounding the temple's construction. Limestone was prepared at the quarry so that no sound of hammers or other iron tools would need to be heard at the building

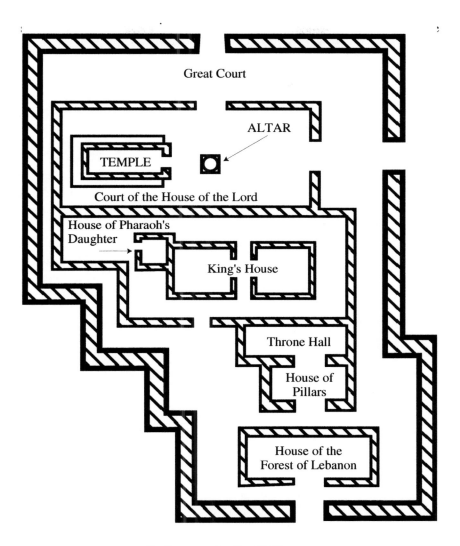

Great Court

ALTAR

TEMPLE

Court of the House of the Lord

House of Pharaoh's
Daughter

King's House

Throne Hall

House of
Pillars

House of the
Forest of Lebanon

Solomon's Buildings

(1 Kings 6:7). This specific precaution may hark back to the Lord's instructions that altars be made of unhewn stones. (Exodus 20:24-25.)

The temple was set apart from the outside world by a "great court" and by an "inner court of the house of the Lord" (1 Kings 7:12). At least one passage (2 Kings 20:4) also mentions a "middle court." With the aid of Hiram's craftsmen, several large objects of bronze were prepared for the area immediately in front of the temple. The altar was twenty feet high and was more than thirty feet square at its base. The "molten sea" of bronze measured over thirty feet in diameter, weighed over twenty-five tons, and had a capacity of at least twelve thousand gallons. It may have been cast in the clay beds of the Jordan River Valley. It was mounted on the backs of twelve oxen, three facing toward each of the cardinal points of the compass. These twelve oxen were symbolic of the twelve tribes of Israel.[9] Finally, two bronze columns about forty feet tall stood just outside of the temple's main entrance. (2 Chronicles 4:1-6; 1 Kings 7:15-26.) Their names "Jachin" and "Boaz" denoted "He will establish" and "In him is strength," respectively.[10]

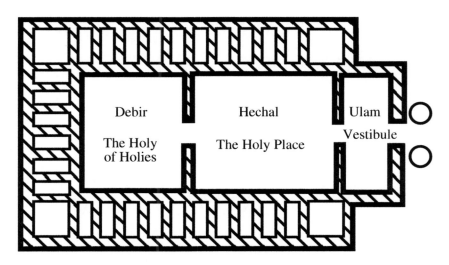

Solomon's Temple

The temple itself had the same major divisions as the tabernacle but was exactly twice as large (1 Kings 6:2-20; 2 Chronicles 3:3-8). Corresponding to the outer room or "holy place" was the main hall of the temple. Its Hebrew name, *"hechal,"* means palace or temple. Behind this room was the Holy of Holies. We are specifically told (1 Kings 6:16) that this was the *"qodesh ha-qadashim"* of the temple. Its Hebrew name *"debir"* may shed light on the nature of this holiest place. Some Bible commentators have linked this name with the Hebrew *"dabar,"* meaning "word," perhaps referring to the fact that this was the place in the temple where the Lord would speak to his people. This may be why the King James translators called this room the *"oracle"* (meaning place of revelation). Others have associated *"debir"* with a Semitic root referring to the back or rear part, hence the translation "inner sanctuary" in the revised Standard and New International versions.[11]

Surrounding the temple on three sides was a series of small chambers on three levels. These rooms could have been used for various unspecified sacred purposes as well as for storage of clothing and other items used in temple service.

In the midst of the temple construction the Lord reminded Solomon that if he would keep the commandments the Lord would dwell among the people and never forsake them (1 Kings 6:11-13; compare Exodus 25:8). After seven and one-half years the temple was completed. Its dedication was a milestone in the history of Israel and a spiritual feast for the people. King Solomon and the leaders of all the tribes gathered in the court directly in front of the temple. As the ark of the covenant was taken into the most holy place, God's glory filled the house like a cloud. As the people offered sacrifices, the king blessed them. (1 Kings 8:1-11.) "I have surely built thee an house to dwell in," he prayed, "a settled place for thee to abide in forever." King Solomon concluded his dedicatory prayer by petitioning: "The Lord our God be with us, as he was with our fathers: let him not leave us, nor forsake us: that he may incline our hearts unto him, to walk in all his ways, and to keep his commandments." (1 Kings 8:13, 57-58.)

Ancient Temple Ordinances

Modern revelation affirms that both the tabernacle of Moses and the temple of Solomon were built so that "those ordinances might be revealed which had been hid from before the world was" (D&C 124:38). Hence the Lord's people in these Old Testament times had access to at least some temple ordinances. "One has only to read the scriptures carefully, particularly the modern scriptures," stated Sidney B. Sperry, a respected Latter-day Saint scholar of the scriptures, "to discover that temples [or other holy sanctuaries] must have been built and used in great antiquity, even in the days of the antediluvian patriarchs." He reasoned that the Lord's requirements for exaltation, and therefore the need for temples, were the same then as they are now.[12]

Although vicarious service for the dead was not inaugurated until New Testament times, ordinances for the living were available during earlier dispensations. The Old Testament states that the smaller lavers at Solomon's Temple were provided to rinse the burnt offerings, but that the larger "sea" was designed "for the priests to wash in" (2 Chronicles 4:6). Elder Joseph Fielding Smith was convinced that these "washings" included baptism.[13] Speaking at the opening of the St. George Temple, President Brigham Young declared that Solomon had built his temple "for the purpose of giving endowments," but acknowledged that "few if any" of these ordinances were actually received at that time.[14] Finally, a revelation given through Joseph Smith indicates that the ancient patriarchs and prophets held the sealing power (D&C 132:39). He taught that Elijah was the last to hold these keys before the coming of the Savior.[15]

The nature and extent of these ancient ordinances and exactly where in the temple buildings they were performed has been the subject of much fruitless speculation. The Old Testament describes in detail the sacrifices and other performances associated with the lesser priesthood and the Mosaic law, but says nothing about any higher ordinances. "Because such ordinances are sacred and not for the world," Elder Joseph Fielding Smith explained, no detailed account of them has been made available. "There are, however, in the Old Testament references to covenants and obligations under which the members of the Church in those days were placed, although the meaning is generally obscure."[16]

The scriptures do emphasize, however, that those who participated in temple worship needed to be prepared. Specifically, the priests who officiated had to be ordained or consecrated. Each time they entered the temple, they were washed with water and clothed in "holy garments." On certain occasions they were also anointed with oil. (Exodus 28:40-41; 29:4-7.) The "holy garments" worn by the priests included white linen breeches, a "coat" and a "girdle" (translated as "tunic" and "sash" in many modern English versions), and "bonnets" ("hats" or "caps" in Hebrew). In addition, the high priest wore a breastplate containing the Urim and Thummim, an ephod (long, intricately woven apron), a robe, and a mitre (crown or turban). (Exodus 28:4, 39-42.)[17]

Temples in Other Ancient Cultures

A similar arrangement to Solomon's temple can be seen in temples of other nearby ancient cultures. The noted Egyptian temple at Karnak (commenced a thousand years before Solomon's) was also entered through a large walled court; one then needed to pass through the many-columned "Hypostyle Hall" (corresponding to the outer "holy place") before reaching the sacred shrine of the god Ammun (paralleling the Holy of Holies). Greek temples, such as the world-famed Parthenon built several centuries later, were similarly divided into these two rooms.

Latter-day Saints have always taught that the temple endowment is not of modern origin. Hugh Nibley has shown that evidence from ancient papyri confirms the antiquity of the endowment and demonstrates that sacred ordinances were an essential feature of Egyptian temple worship. Following the traditional initiation of washing, clothing, and anointing, one would enter the temple itself. Progressing from room to room symbolized one's increasing understanding and progress into the presence of God.[18]

Descriptions of Idealized Future Temples

The prophet Ezekiel saw in vision the future gathering of Israel and a great temple which would be built at Jerusalem (see Ezekiel chapters 40-42). He envisioned a temple similar to that built by Solomon. Two features for the plan are particularly instructive: (1) The temple was to be surrounded by an outer court and an inner court, with the sacrificial altar at the center of the latter. Each court was to be a perfect square. This symmetry reflected divine order. (2) These two courts and the ten-foot-thick walls

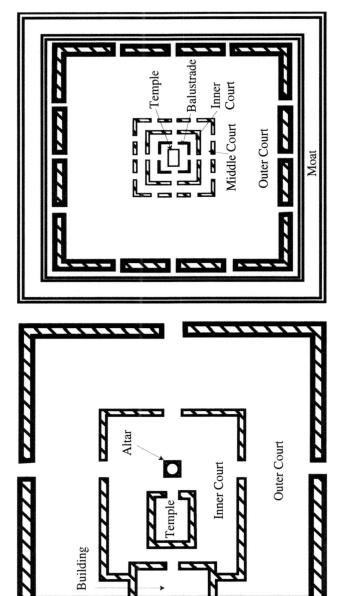

**Ezekiel's Vision
of the Temple**

Building

Altar

Temple

Inner Court

Outer Court

The Temple Scroll

Temple

Balustrade

Inner Court

Middle Court

Outer Court

Moat

which surrounded them emphasize the temple's being removed from the outside world and worldliness.

A similar plan for a future ideal temple is found in the "Temple Scroll," which dated from just before the time of Christ. Measuring twenty-eight feet in length, this was the longest of the Dead Sea Scrolls discovered beginning in the late 1940s. It was held back by an antiquities dealer until being seized during the Six-Day War of 1967; only then did it become available for study. Though this scroll is not to be regarded as inspired scripture, it does to some degree reflect concepts revealed in earlier centuries concerning temples. The Temple Scroll's plan provided for an even more total separation of the temple from the world. The temple was to be surrounded by a protective wall or balustrade, an inner court, a middle court, an outer court (the latter being nearly a half-mile square), and finally by a 150-foot-wide moat. The scroll's greatest emphasis is on the need for personal purity on the part of all who would enter the temple. Elaborate laws of purification governed the temple and its surroundings. Even the whole city where the temple was located was to be kept holy and pure.[19] This was consistent with the Lord's desire that his people should be "a kingdom of priests, and an holy nation" (Exodus 19:6).

The New Testament Period

The Temple of Herod

The "first temple," built by Solomon, stood until about 587 B.C., when the Babylonians captured Jerusalem, plundered and destroyed the temple, and carried the people off captive. In 539, however, Cyrus the Great of Persia defeated Babylonia, and he permitted the exiles to return to their homeland. Under the leadership of Zerubbabel the governor, and with the urging of the prophets Haggai and Zechariah, the temple was rebuilt on the original site. This second temple followed the general pattern of the earlier structure but was much less ornate, having been built by poor refugees. It stood for nearly five hundred years until being thoroughly rebuilt by Herod just before the time of Christ.

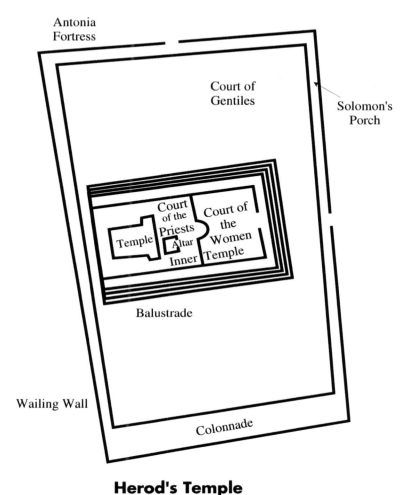

Herod's Temple

Like its predecessors, Herod's temple featured a series of courts to which admittance was increasingly restricted as one approached the holy sanctuary. All nationalities were permitted in the Court of the Gentiles, but within it was a balustrade containing warnings to those not of Israel to go no farther. The Court of Women was so named because both sexes were permitted there, while only men were allowed in the next area. Finally, the temple was immediately surrounded by a court open only to the priests; here also was located the huge altar for sacrifices. Stairs led up from court to court; this heightened the sense of the temple's sacredness. The temple itself had essentially the same floor plan as had Solomon's, but Herod's structure was one hundred rather than thirty cubits tall and was much more lavish.

The New Testament is not our primary source of information concerning the physical plan of the temple and its surroundings. Most of this data comes from the writings of Flavius Josephus, the Jewish historian who lived only a few years after the time of Christ, and from a treatise in the Mishna entitled "*Middoth*" ("Measurements") written in about A.D. 200. The New Testament does, however, reflect how the Master felt about the temple. Although the priests who officiated there had generally become corrupt, the Lord nevertheless regarded the temple as "my house"

Model of Herod's Temple

(Matthew 21:13). The Greek words *naos* (referring to the sacred building itself) and *hieron* (referring to the whole sacred area including the whole series of courts) are both translated "temple" in our New Testament. This may lead to some confusion. Christ walked and taught in the *hieron*, as only the priests were allowed in the *naos*. The "pinnacle" mentioned in relation to Christ's temptations was of the *hieron*, probably the southeast corner of the temple court which even today rises high above the Kidron Valley. On the other hand, the veil which was rent at the time of the crucifixion was in the *naos*.

After only a few decades of splendor, Herod's Temple was completely destroyed in A.D. 70 when Roman armies under Titus captured the city of Jerusalem. Thus the Master's prophetic declaration was fulfilled—that "there shall not be left one stone upon another" (Mark 13:2). All that remained were the huge retaining walls erected by Herod to form the platform on which the temple stood. The western wall, closest to the Holy of Holies, is the most sacred shrine in Judaism today. This is popularly known as the Wailing Wall because of the vocal form of worship used by faithful Jews who regularly gather there. The Temple Mount is sacred not only to Christians and Jews but also to Moslems. In A.D. 691 the Moslems built the beautiful Dome of the Rock on the spot where, according to their tradition, Mohammed had ascended into heaven. Most people have assumed that this mosque was located on the exact site of the ancient temple, but some recent discoveries suggest that the temple may actually have been located about three hundred feet further north.[20]

Early Christian Temple Worship

Interestingly, the temple ordinances received during the New Testament period were not given at Herod's Temple. Elder Joseph Fielding Smith believed that Peter, James, and John received their endowment on the Mount of Transfiguration.[21] President Heber C. Kimball likewise stated that the early Apostles received these blessings at the hands of the Savior himself.[22] The New Testament confirms that some sacred truths taught to the faithful disciples were not appropriate for the world to have. Jesus specifically charged the three Apostles to speak to no one concerning what had transpired on the mount (Matthew 17:9).

In recent decades a large body of apocryphal literature dating from early Christian times has been discovered and published. Particularly significant was the uncovering at Nag Hammadi, a settlement on the Nile River in central Egypt, of a library of documents written by fourth- or fifth-century Christians. Much of this material focuses on Christ's "forty-day ministry," especially on events in Galilee. According to these nonscriptural texts, the Lord performed sacred ordinances and gave his disciples special teachings. In the middle of the fourth century, Cyril of Jerusalem described how the faithful who "entered the Annex of the baptistery, removed [their] street clothes," which represented "putting off the old man and his works."[23]

The early Christians united in circles to pray.[24] References in the New Testament itself describe how even in public worship the disciples, in the spirit of unity, prayed with uplifted hands (1 Timothy 2:8) and also how women prayed with their heads covered, or veiled (1 Corinthians 11:5, Revised Standard Version).

The writer of the "Gospel of Philip," one of the apocryphal documents in the Nag Hammadi library, believed that the most sacred part of the temple was what he called the "bridal chamber," where a "woman is united to her husband..." and "will no longer be separated." If a person does not receive these blessings in this world, he asserted, they cannot be received elsewhere. (Compare D&C 132:15-18.)[25]

A significant development during the New Testament period was the beginning of temple ordinances for the dead. "The inauguration of [missionary] work among the dead," declared Elder James E. Talmage, "was wrought by Christ in the interval between his death and resurrection."[26] During the three days his body lay in the tomb, the Lord went and organized the work of preaching the gospel in the spirit world (see 1 Peter 3:18-20; 4:6). During his brief stay there the Savior did not preach to everyone personally, but rather from among the righteous spirits he authorized messengers to carry the gospel truth to all. (D&C 138:28-30.)

Even though it thus became possible to hear and accept the gospel in the spirit world, such essential ordinances as baptism could not be received there. It was necessary for living proxies to receive them on earth in behalf of those who had died without the opportunity. Just as the Savior had atoned vicariously for the sins of mankind, the early Christians, in the same spirit of love, performed the saving ordinances in behalf of the dead. Paul used the accepted practice of baptizing in behalf of the dead as an argument in favor of there being a resurrection. Why do you baptize for the dead, he asked, if the dead will not live again? (1 Corinthians 15:29.) Sidney B. Sperry suggested that these Saints must have had temples where such ordinances could be properly performed, but such sacred structures presumably would have been small, and nothing is known about them.[27]

Temples among the Lord's people were not limited to the Old World. The Book of Mormon contains the history of a righteous colony which left Jerusalem several years before the Babylonians captured the cry and destroyed the temple there. Within a few years of arriving in their new promised land in the Western Hemisphere, these people erected a temple in the Land of Nephi. This edifice was constructed "after the manner of the temple of Solomon, save it were not built of so many precious things," which were not available in that land. Nevertheless, "the workmanship thereof was exceeding fine." (See 2 Nephi 5:16; Jacob 1:17, 2:2, 2:11.) Some four centuries later, another temple in the land of Zarahemla filled a similar function (Mosiah 1:18). Then, some time after the three days of terrible destruction at the time of the Savior's crucifixion, "a great multitude" of the righteous survivors gathered around yet another temple in the land Bountiful (3 Nephi 11:1). Here the resurrected Lord met, instructed, and blessed them.

These Book of Mormon temples may have set the pattern for temples built during later centuries by the inhabitants of ancient America. Mayan temples, for example, were located at the center of their cities. Like Mesopotamian ziggurats, these early American structures provided elevated platforms which raised sacred places of worship closer to heaven.

Because temple worship and ordinances were important in former dispensations, they would be a necessary part of the latter-day "restitution of all things."

Chapter Two

The Kirtland Temple and the Restoration of Temple Worship

As the nineteenth century entered its fourth decade, the early Latter-day Saints eagerly proclaimed their faith that the long-anticipated "times of restitution of all things" (see Acts 3:21) had finally arrived. The Aaronic and Melchizedek priesthoods had been restored by means of divinely authorized heavenly messengers, and on April 6, 1830, the Church of Jesus Christ was once again organized among men. During the early 1830s a flood of revelations restored various elements of Church organization and unfolded gospel truths to the Saints' understanding. In these same years, the Saints gathered at Kirtland, in northeastern Ohio, where they would build the first latter-day temple. Even though the fulness of temple ordinances would not be restored until later on, the Lord's house in Kirtland would nevertheless provide the setting for remarkable spiritual experiences and for the communication of vital priesthood keys.

The School of the Prophets

Forerunners to temple worship can be seen in the School of the Prophets, which opened three years before the dedication of the Kirtland Temple. An 1832 revelation instructed Church leaders to convene this school, which was described as a "solemn assembly" designed to prepare and sanctify those who would go forth to preach. (D&C 88:70, 74.) Only the worthy were to attend: "He that is found unworthy...shall not have place among you; for ye shall not suffer that mine house shall be polluted by him" (D&C 88:134). Subsequent revelations would use almost identical language concerning those who should or should not be permitted to enter the temples. (Compare D&C 88:134 with 97:15-17, for example.)

Rules adopted for the school specified that those attending should come bathed and in clean linen.[1] This physical cleanliness was not enough; it needed to be accompanied by spiritual purity which was symbolized in sacred ordinances. "Purify your hearts, and cleanse your hands and your feet before me," the Lord instructed, "that I may make you clean...from the blood of this wicked generation" (D&C 88: 74-75). As each student entered the school, the president or teacher would greet him formally "with uplifted hands to heaven" and ask: "Art thou a brother...? I salute you in the name of the Lord Jesus Christ...in a determination...to be your friend and brother through the grace of God in the bonds of love, to walk in all the commandments of God blameless, in thanksgiving, forever and ever." (D&C 88:128-133.)

Later revelations would describe temples as places of inspiration and spiritual outpouring. The same certainly could be said of the School of the Prophets. March 18, 1833, for example, was the day when Sidney Rigdon and Frederick G. Williams were set apart as counselors to Joseph Smith in the First Presidency. Joseph had instructed the brethren to prepare for a day of "revelation and vision." "The promise was verified," the meeting's minutes recorded, "for many present had the eyes of their understanding opened by the Spirit of God, so as to behold many things.... Many of the brethren saw a heavenly vision of the Savior, and concourses of angels...."[2]

In addition to these spiritual experiences, meetings of the School of the Prophets frequently included advanced discussion of gospel doctrines. Those participating accepted a commitment "not to willfully divulge that which is discussed in the school."[3] Hence several policies and procedures which would later be applied to temple service were anticipated in the functioning of the School of the Prophets. The school met in a room measuring about twenty feet square above Newel K. Whitney's store. During the school's first season, however, the Saints were already looking forward to building the temple in order to provide a permanent home for the school.

Design and Construction of the Kirtland Temple

Over a period of about three years the Saints eagerly devoted their time and energies to building the "Lord's house" (the word *temple* not generally being used at this time). This project had its genesis in the December 1832 revelation which had directed the brethren to form the School of the Prophets. The Lord also commanded them to "establish a house, even a house of prayer, a house of fasting, a house of faith, a house of learning, a house of glory, a house of order, a house of God" (D&C 88:119).

During the winter of 1833 Church leaders decided that the best location for the temple would be on the crest of the bluff just to the south of the Kirtland flats. From this site there was a magnificent view of the Chagrin Valley and the village of Kirtland below, and the blue waters of Lake Erie could be seen in the distance. Part of the property was already owned by Frederick G. Williams, a member of the First Presidency; the remainder was purchased from Peter French in April.

On June 1, 1833, the Lord admonished the Saints to move forward with the building of the temple in which, he said, "I design to endow those whom I have chosen with power from on high" (D&C 95:8). The Prophet asked a conference of high priests two days later how the temple should be built. Some favored constructing it of logs, while others preferred a frame building. "Shall we, brethren," said he, "build a house for our God, of logs?" the Prophet challenged. "No, I have a better plan than that. I have a plan of the house of the Lord, given by himself; and you will soon see by this, the difference between our calculations and his idea."[4] The June 1 revelation had specified that the temple was not to be built "after the manner of the world," but according to a plan which the Lord promised to reveal (D&C 95:13-14). "Joseph not only received revelation and commandment to build a Temple," President Brigham Young later testified, "but he received a pattern also as did Moses for the Tabernacle, and Solomon for his Temple; for without a

Kirtland Temple

pattern, he could not know what was wanting, having never seen [a temple], and not having experienced its use."[5]

Even though the temple's exterior would look much like a typical New England meetinghouse, its interior was to have some unique features. The Lord specified that the building should include two large rooms, one above the other, each measuring fifty-five by sixty-five feet. The lower hall was to be a chapel used for praying, preaching, and administering the sacrament. The upper hall was for educational purposes. (D&C 95:8, 13-17.) An unusual feature of the temple would be the placing of pulpits at both ends of the two main halls. Those on the west were for the use of the Melchizedek Priesthood, while those on the east were for the Aaronic. At each end there were four levels, one behind the other, with the lowest level in front and three pulpits on each level. Initials were placed on each pulpit, representing the priesthood office held by the individual occupying it. These arrangements would help Church members to understand the relative authority of various groups of priesthood leaders.[6]

The main floor of the room would be divided into thirty-eight boxes. Each contained a long backless bench which could be moved from one side of the compartment to the other, allowing worshippers to face either the east or west pulpits. During cold winter months these compartments would also conserve warmth in the unheated building. Canvas "veils" or partitions could be lowered by means of a system of pulleys and rollers in the ceiling in order to divide the hall into four quarters or to seclude the pulpits from the rest of the room.

The Lord not only revealed the size and use of the temple's main two rooms, Elder Orson Pratt affirmed, but he also revealed "the order of the pulpits, and in fact everything pertaining to it was clearly pointed out by revelation…. God gave a vision of these things not only to Joseph, but to several others, and they were strictly commanded to build according to the pattern revealed from the heavens."[7]

Truman O. Angell, one of the supervisors of temple construction, testified that the Lord's promise to show the building's design to the Prophet was literally fulfilled. On an occasion when Joseph Smith invited his counselors in the First Presidency to kneel with him in prayer, the building appeared before them in a vision. "After we had taken a good look at the

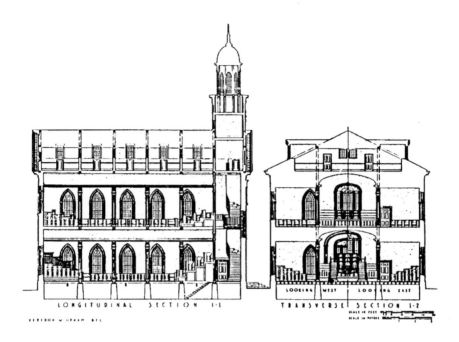

Cross-section of the Kirtland Temple showing the different
levels of the pulpits at each end of the two halls.

exterior, the building seemed to come right over us." Later while speaking
in the completed temple, Frederick G. Williams testified that the hall in
which they were convened coincided in every detail with the vision given
to the Prophet.[8]

Actual construction on the Kirtland Temple began in June of 1833. On
the sixth of that month, in response to the Lord's admonition given five
days earlier (D&C 95), a council of high priests directed the building committee to immediately procure materials so the work could begin. Initially,
the plan was to build the structure of bricks produced in a kiln on the
French property, but these proved to be too soft.[9] Joseph Smith therefore

personally led a group in search of suitable stone for the temple. A source was found two miles south of the building sight, and they immediately quarried a wagon load.

Eager to get started, Hyrum Smith and Reynolds Cahoon went to work digging by hand the trench for the foundation. The Saints were so impoverished at this time, an early member later recalled, that "there was not a scraper and hardly a plow that could be found."[10] Nevertheless, the Prophet observed, "our unity, harmony and charity abounded to strengthen us to do the commandments of God."[11]

Almost all able-bodied men, except those away on missions, worked on the temple. Joseph Smith set the example, serving as foreman in the quarry. "Come, brethren," he admonished, "let us go to work in the stone-quarry, and work for the Lord." On Saturdays a number of men brought teams and wagons, quarried the rock, and hauled enough to the building site to keep the masons busy during the coming week. The women, under Emma Smith's direction, "made stockings, pantaloons and jackets" for the benefit of the temple workmen. "Our wives were all the time knitting, spinning and sewing," Elder Heber C. Kimball recalled years later, and "were just as busy as any of us."[12]

On Wednesday, July 23, 1833, cornerstones for the Kirtland Temple were laid "after the order of the Holy Priesthood." Twenty-four elders officially took part. The Prophet and five others laid the southeast cornerstone, and other groups of six elders placed the stones at the southwest, northwest, and northeast corners.[13]

Work on the temple went forward, but not without difficulty. Under the cover of darkness, vandals attempted to destroy the walls then under construction. Because of further threatened mob violence, those who worked on the temple by day guarded it at night to protect what they had built. Night after night for many weeks, Heber C. Kimball recalled, "we...were not permitted to take off our clothes, and were obliged to lay with our fire locks in our arms."[14] President Sidney Rigdon later described how the Saints "had wet those walls with their tears, when, in the silent shades of the night, they were praying to the God of heaven to protect them, and stay the unhallowed hands of the ruthless spoilers, who had uttered a prophecy...that the walls should never be erected."[15] Another interruption came during the summer of 1834. At the time of the year when the weather was most favorable for construction, few workmen were available because many had joined the Zion's Camp march to Missouri. Furthermore, funds that normally would have gone toward the temple were instead sent to aid the distressed Saints in "Zion."

Following the return of Zion's Camp, work on the temple went forward more rapidly. In October of 1834, Joseph Smith recalled, "great exertions were made to expedite the work of the Lord's house, and notwithstanding it was commenced almost with nothing, as to means, yet the way opened as we proceeded, and the Saints rejoiced."[16] At this time the temple walls were four feet high, and they rose quickly during the winter of 1834-1835. By November of 1835 the exterior plastering commenced. Crushed glassware was mixed with the stucco to give the walls a glistening appearance. Under Brigham Young's direction finishing touches were given to the temple's interior during February of 1836. The women continued to have an important role, making curtains and carpets for the Lord's house.

During this period the Church was in constant financial distress. Funds were needed to support the temple workers, so Saints in the United States and Canada were invited to make contributions as they could. Vienna Jaques, a single sister, was one of the first to donate, giving much of her material resources. John Tanner lent money to pay for the temple site, and then sold his twenty-two-hundred-acre farm in New York State in order to give three thousand dollars to buy supplies. He continued to give "until he had sacrificed nearly everything he owned."[17] In the midst of their difficulties the Saints spent from forty to sixty thousand dollars (equivalent to well over half a million dollars today) and were forced to borrow to complete the project.

A Rich Outpouring of Spiritual Blessings

Great spiritual blessings followed this period of sacrifice. The weeks preceding and following the Kirtland Temple dedication witnessed remarkable spiritual manifestations to an unusual degree. These "pentecostal" experiences began just three days after the School of the Elders had moved into the attic of the nearly completed temple on January 18. Saints reported seeing heavenly messengers in at least ten different meetings.

At five of these meetings individuals even testified that they had beheld the Savior himself. Many received visions, prophesied, or spoke in tongues.[18]

On Thursday afternoon, January 21, 1836, the First Presidency met in the room above the printing office and were washed "in pure water." That evening "at early candle-light" the Presidency met with the patriarch Joseph Smith Sr. in the west room of the temple attic, where they anointed one another with consecrated oil and pronounced blessings and prophecies. Then "the heavens were opened," the Prophet recorded, and he "beheld the celestial kingdom of God, and the glory thereof…" He saw "the blazing throne of God" and the "beautiful streets of that kingdom, which had the appearance of being paved with gold." (D&C 137:1-4.) Joseph Smith also saw many prophets, both ancient and modern. When he saw his brother Alvin in the celestial kingdom he "marveled," because Alvin had died before the gospel was restored and consequently had not been baptized. But the Lord declared: "All who have died without a knowledge of this gospel, who would have received it if they had been permitted to tarry, shall be heirs of the celestial kingdom of God." The Prophet was also shown that all "children who die before they arrive at the years of accountability are saved in the celestial kingdom of heaven." (D&C 137:6-7, 10.)

Concerning this occasion, the Prophet testified:

> Many of my brethren who received the ordinance (of washing and anointing) with me saw glorious visions also. Angels ministered unto them as well as to myself, and the power of the Highest rested upon us, the house was filled with the glory of God, and we shouted Hosanna to God and the Lamb…. Some of them saw the face of the Savior…[and] we all communed with the heavenly host.[19]

Just over two weeks later, on February 6, various priesthood quorums met in the small rooms in the temple's attic story and experienced another spiritual feast. The seventies "enjoyed a great flow of the Holy Spirit. Many arose and spoke, testifying that they were filled with the Holy Ghost, which was like fire in their bones, so that they could not hold their peace, but were constrained to cry hosanna to God and the Lamb, and glory in the highest." Others "were filled with the Spirit, and spoke with tongues and prophesied." Joseph Smith's history declared that "this was a time of rejoicing long to be remembered."[20] In later years, Elder Orson Pratt looked back with similar feelings on these sacred experiences in the temple:

> God was there, his angels were there, the Holy Ghost was in the midst of the people, the visions of the Almighty were opened to the minds of the servants of the living God; the veil was taken off the minds of many; they saw the heavens opened; they beheld the angels of God; they heard the voice of the Lord; and they were filled from the crown of their heads to the soles of their feet with the power and inspiration of the Holy Ghost, and uttered forth prophecies in the midst of that congregation, which have been fulfilling from that day to the present time.[21]

Some of the most memorable spiritual experiences occurred on Sunday, March 27, the day the temple was dedicated. Hundreds of Latter-day Saints from Missouri and other parts of North America crowded into Kirtland and surrounding areas, anticipating the great blessings the Lord had promised to bestow upon them, including a special gift or endowment of power from on high. Early that morning hundreds gathered outside of the temple, hoping to attend the dedicatory service. The doors were opened at 8:00 A.M., and the First Presidency assisted in seating the congregation of nearly a thousand people, about double the building's usual capacity. With the leaders seated in the elevated pulpits and benches at each end of the hall and all the available seats in the temple filled, the massive doors were closed. Hundreds still remained outside, including many who had sacrificed much for the temple's construction and had come long distances to attend the dedication. Sensing their disappointment the Prophet directed them to hold an overflow meeting in the schoolhouse just to the west. (The dedicatory service would be repeated the following Thursday for their benefit.)

The service commenced at 9:00 A.M. A choir, seated in the four corners of the hall, provided music. President Sidney Rigdon then spoke eloquently for two and a half hours declaring that the temple was unique among all the buildings erected for the worship of God, having been "built by divine revelation." After he concluded, the choir next sang Elder W. W. Phelps' hymn, "Now Let Us Rejoice." Following a twenty-minute intermission, the officers of the Church were sustained by the congregation, with the various priesthood quorums voting individually. Joseph Smith then prophesied that if the Saints would "uphold these men in their several stations,…the Lord would bless them; yea, in the name of Christ, the blessings of heaven should be theirs."[22]

The climax of the day was the dedicatory prayer, which had been given to the Prophet by revelation. After expressing gratitude for God's blessings, the Prophet, with hands raised to heaven and tears flowing freely, prayed that the Lord would accept the temple which had been built "through great tribulation…that the Son of Man might have a place to manifest himself to his people." Thus the Kirtland Temple, like holy sanctuaries in former dispensations, was to be a place of revelation from God to man. Joseph petitioned that the blessings promised in the Lord's 1832 command to build the temple (see D&C 88:117-120) might now be realized. The prayer also asked that Church leaders, members, and the leaders of nations might be blessed, and that the promised gathering of "the scattered remnants of Israel" might be accomplished. (See D&C 109.) This prayer would become a pattern for other temple dedicatory prayers.

Following the prayer the choir sang "The Spirit of God," a hymn written by Elder Phelps in anticipation of the temple's dedication. After the sacrament was administered and passed to the congregation, Joseph Smith and others testified that they saw heavenly messengers present during the service. The dedication concluded with the entire congregation standing and rendering the sacred "Hosanna Shout": "Hosanna, hosanna, hosanna to God and the Lamb, amen, amen, and amen," repeated three times. Eliza R. Snow felt that the shout was given "with such power as seemed almost sufficient to raise the roof from the building."[23] After seven hours, the service concluded at 4:00 P.M.

That evening more than four hundred priesthood bearers met in the temple. Joseph Smith instructed the brethren that they should be prepared to prophesy when directed by the Spirit. The Prophet recorded:

> Brother George A. Smith arose and began to prophesy, when a noise was heard like the sound of a rushing mighty wind, which filled the Temple, and all the congregation simultaneously arose, being moved upon by an invisible power; many began to speak in tongues and prophesy; others saw glorious visions; and I beheld the Temple was filled with angels, which fact I declared to the congregation.[24]

David Whitmer testified that "he saw three angels passing up the south aisle."[25] People living in the area heard "an unusual sound" coming from the Lord's house and saw "a bright light like a pillar of fire resting upon the Temple." Others reported seeing angels hovering over the temple and hearing heavenly singing.[26]

A transcendently important spiritual manifestation occurred on Sunday, April 3, just one week following the temple's dedication. After the close of the afternoon worship service, Joseph Smith and Oliver Cowdery retired to the Melchizedek Priesthood pulpits in the west end of the lower room of the temple. The "veil" (canvas partition) was lowered so that they might pray in private. Joseph Smith testified that "the veil was taken from our minds" and that he and Oliver beheld a series of remarkable visions.

The Lord Jesus Christ himself appeared, accepted the temple, and promised to manifest himself therein "if my people will keep my commandments, and do not pollute this holy house." Moses then appeared and bestowed "the keys of the gathering of Israel from the four parts of the earth, and the leading of the ten tribes from the land of the north." Elias next conferred "the dispensation of the gospel of Abraham." Finally, in fulfillment of Malachi's prophecy (see Malachi 4:5-6) and Moroni's promise (see D&C 2), Elijah committed "the keys of this dispensation" in preparation for the "great and dreadful day of the Lord." (D&C 110.) Through the sealing keys restored by Elijah, priesthood ordinances performed on earth can be "bound" or "sealed" in heaven; also, Latter-day Saints can perform saving priesthood ordinances in behalf of loved ones who died without the opportunity of accepting the gospel in person. In this way the hearts of the children are turning to their fathers.

There is significance in the specific day when these messengers appeared. The third day of April in 1836 was Easter Sunday. There could be no better evidence that Jesus arose from the grave than the actual appearance of the resurrected Lord himself. Furthermore, this same weekend was the Jewish Passover. For centuries Jewish families had placed an empty chair at their Passover feasts, understanding that Elijah's return would occur at that season. He did return at this time, not to a Passover feast but rather to the Lord's temple in Kirtland.

Remarkable spiritual experiences associated with the Kirtland Temple did not cease after the week of dedication. "Not only did the Almighty manifest his acceptance of that house at its dedication," Eliza R. Snow recalled, "but an abiding holy Heavenly influence was realized; and many extraordinary manifestations of his power were experienced on subsequent occasions. Not only were angels often seen within, but a pillar of light was several times seen resting down upon the roof."[27]

Nature of the Kirtland Temple and Its Ordinances

Though accompanied by marvelous spiritual experiences, the ordinances as administered in the Kirtland Temple were not as complete as they would be in later times. Speaking in 1853 at the cornerstone-laying ceremonies for the Salt Lake Temple, President Brigham Young declared that in Kirtland the "first Elders" received only a "portion of their first endowments or we might say more clearly, some of the first or introductory, or initiatory ordinances, preparatory to an endowment."[28] "It should be remembered," Elder Bruce R. McConkie concurred, "that the endowment given in the Kirtland Temple was only a partial endowment, and that the full endowment was not performed until the saints had established themselves in Nauvoo."[29] "The prime purpose in having such a temple," Elder Harold B. Lee stated, "seems to have been that there could be restored the keys, the effective keys necessary for the carrying on of the Lord's work." He therefore concluded that the events of April 3, 1836 (as recorded in D&C 110), were "sufficient justification for the building of [this] temple."[30]

Thus, "the design and construction of the Kirtland Temple," Elder Boyd K. Packer explained, "was different from that of all other latter-day temples because its purpose was different. While already in 1836 certain ordinances had been introduced in a limited way which later would form part of the regular temple ordinances, the sacred ordinances and ceremonies performed in today's temples were not done in this first temple."[31] Specifically, President Brigham Young pointed out, the Kirtland Temple "had no basement in it, nor a font, nor preparations to give endowments for the living or dead."[32]

The temple was more of a multi-purpose building intended for general functions. It served as a meetinghouse and an educational center, and also provided limited office space for Church leaders. Here the Saints

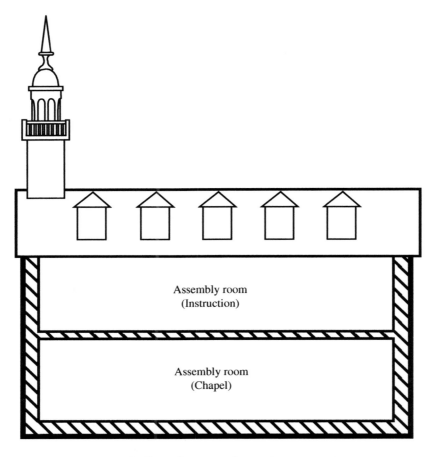

Kirtland Temple (1836)

conducted their weekly worship service as well as monthly fast meetings. During some of the latter occasions the "veils" were lowered, enabling four testimony meetings to proceed concurrently. Hence, as Elder Packer wrote in summary:

The design of the temple was preliminary. It was built as a house wherein the Lord could reveal Himself to His servants, where other heavenly beings could restore priesthood keys essential to the salvation of mankind, and where the faithful Saints would be blessed with an increase of spiritual power and enlightenment.[33]

The glorious period in Kirtland was not to last long, however. By 1837, just one year following the temple's dedication, the spirit of apostasy had divided the Saints. The dissenters claimed to be the true owners of the temple and frequently held their meetings there.

In contrast to her accounts of spiritual blessings, Eliza R. Snow also described a frightful scene occurring in the temple during one of the regular Sunday services: A group of the apostates "armed with pistols and bowie-knives" entered and occupied the Aaronic priesthood pulpits. As one of the brethren arose and began to speak from the Melchizedek priesthood pulpits on the west, "one on the east interrupted him. Father Smith, presiding, called for order—he told the apostate brother that he should have all the time he wanted, but he must wait his turn." The apostates then drew their pistols and knives and rushed from the stand down into the congregation. Many worshippers were "terribly frightened" and some attempted to escape by jumping out of the windows. "After a short, but terrible scene to be enacted in a temple of God," Eliza's account concluded, "order was restored, and the services of the day proceeded as usual."[34] The safety of the faithful Saints was increasingly threatened, and by January of 1838 Joseph Smith and his associates were forced to flee for their lives. Joseph Smith established his home in Missouri, which had been another center of Latter-day Saint activity for the previous seven years.

Temples in Missouri

Almost from the beginning the Saints were fired with the vision of establishing Zion on earth. They learned from the Book of Mormon that the New Jerusalem would be built on the American continent (see Ether 13:2-3). In December of 1830, when the writings of Enoch were revealed, Church members not only were thrilled with descriptions of the power and glory of the ancient city of Zion, but they also learned that in a future era of righteousness the elect would be gathered into a similar "Holy City" to be known as Zion or the New Jerusalem (see Moses 7:13-19, 62).

Three months earlier the Lord had revealed that the latter-day City of Zion would be located "on the borders by the Lamanites" and had called a group of missionaries to carry the gospel to the Indians (see D&C 28:8-9). Oliver Cowdery and his fellow missionaries reached the "Indian frontier" just west of Independence, Missouri, in 1831, after trudging hundreds of miles through the winter snows. More specific information about the location of the New Jerusalem came during the summer, when Joseph Smith and a large group of elders were directed to go to Missouri, preaching the gospel along the way. Upon arriving there, the Prophet learned by revelation that Missouri was "the land of promise" which the Lord had "consecrated for the gathering of the Saints," that Independence was to be the "center place," and that the temple lot was to be situated just west of the courthouse (D&C 57:1-3).

On Wednesday, August 3, 1831, Joseph Smith and a small group of elders went to a knoll about a half-mile west of the Independence courthouse, turned south from the old road, and made their way about two hundred feet through the thick forest. The Prophet then indicated the specific spot where the temple was to stand, and placed a stone to mark the northeast corner of the future structure. Relevant scriptures were read, and Sidney Rigdon offered the dedicatory prayer in accordance with previously revealed instructions (D&C 58:57). "The scene was solemn and impressive."[35] In December of that same year, Bishop Edward Partridge purchased in behalf of the Church some 63.27 acres, which included the spot dedicated for the temple.

Enthusiasm for building the temple in Missouri was renewed in June of 1833 when the Prophet Joseph Smith issued his proposed plan for the future City of Zion. This plan set forth the pattern of wide streets crossing at right angles, which would in later decades become a familiar and welcome characteristic of Mormon settlements. Just seven weeks before drawing up this plan for the City of Zion, Joseph had received a revelation (D&C 94) specifying that the Kirtland Temple, a building for the Presidency, and the printing office were to be located adjacent to one another at the center of Kirtland. Each structure in this complex was to have the same dimensions and was to be preserved as holy and undefiled.

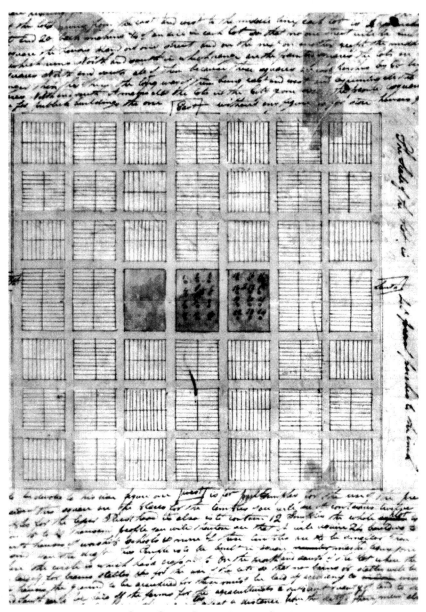

Plat for the City of Zion

The envisioned plan for Zion expanded this concept from three to twenty-four buildings. These "temples" were to be assigned to the various priesthood quorums and were to serve a variety of functions. The Prophet anticipated that the city would have a population of from fifteen to twenty thousand, so that twenty-four buildings would be needed as "houses of worship, schools, etc."[36] Because all inhabitants of the city would be expected to be living on a celestial level (D&C 105:5), all these buildings could be regarded as "temples"—places of communication between heaven and earth—even though their functions were not restricted to ordinance work.

Joseph Smith described the main temple as a building very much like the Kirtland Temple, but slightly larger. The main hall, measuring sixty-one by seventy-seven feet, would have the familiar two sets of pulpits, although in this case the Melchizedek Priesthood would be located at the east end of the room. Apparently these plans, like those for the Kirtland Temple, followed the pattern shown in vision to the First Presidency.[37] Several sketches were prepared for the proposed temple. Interestingly, some of these drawings were not rediscovered until 1967, when they were found as irregularly cut pieces of paper to which papyrus fragments had been glued for preservation.[38]

Unfortunately, plans to build the City of Zion and its temple were not to be carried out at that time. On July 20, 1833, less than a month after Joseph Smith had drawn up his plan for the city, a mob attacked the Saints' settlement at Independence and destroyed the press on which their newspaper and a book of revelations were being printed. In a revelation given just over two weeks later, the Lord insisted that Zion must be "THE PURE IN HEART"; and, speaking of coming difficulties, he declared that Zion would escape only "if she observe[d] to do all things whatsoever I have commanded her" (D&C 97:21, 25). Specifically, he directed that "a house should be built unto me in the land of Zion, like unto the pattern which I have given unto you. Yea, let it be built speedily...for the salvation of Zion." It was to be a place of thanksgiving and instruction, that those called into the Lord's work might be perfected in their understanding "in theory, in principle, and in doctrine, in all things pertaining to the kingdom of God on the earth." (D&C 97:10-14.)

Work on the temple did not commence, however. Persecutions increased during the following months, culminating with the Saints' being forced to flee from Jackson County despite the bitterly cold November weather. A revelation given the next month acknowledged that the Saints had been permitted to suffer because of their own transgressions, but affirmed that "there is none other place appointed" for the City of Zion (D&C 101:2, 20).

The exiled Saints located temporarily in Clay County, but by 1838 they were gathering in Caldwell County, which had been formed in northern Missouri especially for them. Their principal settlement was named Far West, and it was here that Joseph Smith joined them following his flight from Kirtland.

Soon after his arrival, Joseph received a revelation once again directing the Saints' attention to the building of a temple: "Let the city, Far West, be a holy and consecrated land unto me…. Therefore, I command you to build a house unto me, for the gathering together of my saints, that they may worship me." Thus, this building, like the Kirtland Temple, was for general purposes rather than specifically for ordinances. The Lord again specified that the temple should be built according to a pattern he would show to the First Presidency. (D&C 115:7-8, 14-16.) Work on the temple was to commence on July 4, 1838, and then recommence (following a winter break) on April 26, 1839. The Twelve were directed to gather on the latter date at the building site of the temple and then to depart on an overseas mission. (D&C 115:9-11; 118:4-5.)

In accordance with these instructions, cornerstones of the Far West Temple were laid on July 4, as follows: southeast by the stake presidency, southwest by the elders presidency, northwest by the bishop, and northeast by the teachers presidency; each group was assisted by twelve men. The building would measure 110 by 80 feet (outside dimensions), making it larger than both the Kirtland Temple and that planned for Zion. Following a parade and an oration by President Sidney Rigdon, the congregation joined in a shout of "Hosanna."[39]

A series of tragic events during the fall of 1838 culminated with Governor Lilburn W. Boggs's order that the Mormons be exterminated or driven from the state of Missouri. The city of Far West was captured by the mob militia, Joseph Smith and other Church leaders were imprisoned in Richmond and Liberty, and the Saints were forced once again to abandon their homes. It appeared very unlikely that the Twelve could meet their appointment in Far West on April 26 the following spring. Joseph's enemies openly boasted that the commandment would not be fulfilled: "There being a date fixed to this revelation, if Joseph Smith never was a false prophet before, we will make him one now."[40] It was obvious that the lives of the Twelve would be in peril were they to attempt returning to Missouri. John Taylor recalled that they would have to "go among a people who would kill every one of us as quickly as they would rattlesnakes." Many agreed with the patriarch Joseph Smith Sr. that "the Lord would take the will for the deed." Nevertheless, Elder George Q. Cannon later testified, "the Spirit rested upon President [Brigham] Young and his brother apostles, and they determined to go."[41]

The Apostles entered Missouri individually and traveled by different routes in order to avoid attracting attention. Shortly after midnight on the appointed day, they met at Far West, offered prayer, sang a hymn, ordained Wilford Woodruff and George A. Smith to the apostleship, and prepared to depart for their mission. "Elder Alpheus Cutler, the master workman of the house, then recommenced laying the foundation" by rolling a stone into place next to the southeast corner. "In consequence of the peculiar situation of the Saints," Joseph Smith recorded, further work on the temple was suspended until a time "when the Lord shall open the way" for its completion.[42] Hence violent opposition from their enemies prevented the Saints from building both of the contemplated temples in Missouri.

Subsequent History of These Sites

Following the Saints' exodus from Kirtland, the temple fell into the hands of people who did not appreciate its sacred purpose, A door was cut into the wall "through which cattle, sheep, and swine could be driven into the basement to share its warmth." Some older residents of Kirtland later recalled that even the main hall on the ground floor "was transformed into a stable to shelter the livestock of the neighborhood. The low benches were removed...and used for firewood, while sheep were herded into the small pews in the sacred room where the voices of angels had been heard but a short season before." Furnishings were removed from the large room on the second floor, which was then used for dances, theatrical productions, or for other public functions. The building also served as the public school for the area; one of the young pupils was James A. Garfield, a future president of the United States.[43]

Title to the temple was eventually acquired by Joseph Smith III, son of the Prophet, who claimed to be legal heir. From him it passed in 1880 to the Reorganized Church of Jesus Christ of Latter Day Saints. This group, based at Independence, Missouri, provides a guide service to conduct visitors through the building, which they use for occasional conferences and other meetings. In more recent years, The Church of Jesus Christ of Latter-day Saints has acquired the Newel K. Whitney Store in Kirtland, where so many glorious events associated with the School of the Prophets took place. In 1984 it was dedicated as a visitors' center.

Newel K. Whitney Store

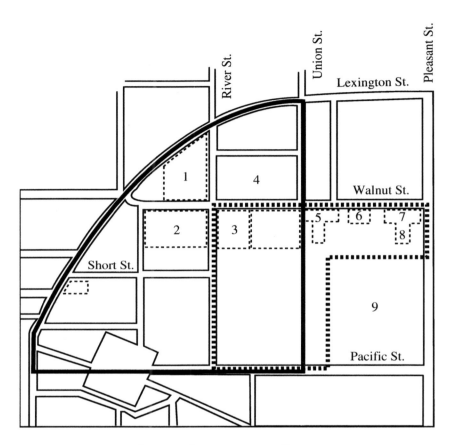

Independence Temple Area

1 Church of Christ (Temple Lot)
2 Reorganized LDS Auditorium
3 LDS Visitors' Center
4 RLDS Temple

5 New Independence, Mo. Stake Center
6 Mission Home Residence
7 LDS Chapel (Dedicated 1914)
8 Mission Office
9 RLDS "The Campus" Property

LDS Church ownership ▪▪▪▪▪▪▪▪▪▪▪▪▪▪▪▪▪▪

63+ acres, included in the Saints' original 1831 purchase ▬▬▬▬▬▬

Following their expulsion from Missouri, the Latter-day Saints relinquished title to lands there. In 1867 a group of former Church members under the leadership of Granville Hedrick returned to Independence and began purchasing the temple lot. A few years later, members of the Reorganized Church also returned and established their headquarters there. During the 1890s the Reorganized Church unsuccessfully sued the Church of Christ (as the Hedrickites were officially known) for title to the temple lot. In 1904 The Church of Jesus Christ of Latter-day Saints began purchasing property in Independence, eventually acquiring nearly twenty of the original sixty-three acres, adjacent to the lot held by the Hedrickites. In 1971 the Church dedicated there a visitors' center designed to highlight the significance of Independence, both in the past and in the future. The Far West temple property was purchased by the Church in 1909, and in 1968 it was landscaped to highlight the cornerstones and to make this an attractive spot for visitors. Construction of the temples at Independence and Far West, however, must await divine direction in the future.

Chapter Three

The Nauvoo Temple and the Restoration of Temple Ordinances

As the Latter-day Saints fled from their persecutors in Missouri, they turned their faces eastward, finding a welcome refuge in the state of Illinois. In the spring of 1839 they purchased property and began settling at Commerce on the east bank of the Mississippi River. Soon the Saints renamed their community Nauvoo, a Hebrew word meaning "beautiful." Within two years they would begin construction on yet another temple. Before this sacred structure would be completed, however, a series of events—the restoration of holy ordinances—would have far-reaching significance. This development, in turn, would be reflected in the temple's design.

Baptism for the Dead

The principles underlying salvation for the dead had already been made known. In 1836 when the Lord showed Joseph Smith the glorious character of the celestial kingdom, he also affirmed:

> All who have died without a knowledge of this gospel, who would have received it if they had been permitted to tarry, shall be heirs of the celestial kingdom of God. Also all that shall die henceforth without a knowledge of it, who would have received it with all their hearts, shall be heirs of that kingdom; for I, the Lord, will judge all men according to their works, according to the desire of their hearts. (D&C 137:7-9.)

Nevertheless, the Savior had stipulated that one must be baptized or "he cannot enter into the kingdom of God" (John 3:5). Hence the New Testament Saints were authorized to perform baptisms in behalf of those who had died without this opportunity (see 1 Corinthians 15:29).

The practice of vicarious baptisms for the dead was taught for the first time in the present dispensation on August 15, 1840, at the funeral of Seymour Brunson, a faithful member of the Nauvoo high council, who had died five days earlier.[1] The Prophet Joseph Smith noted that in the congregation there was a widow whose son had died without baptism. He read from 1 Corinthians 15:29 on baptism for the dead "and remarked that the Gospel of Jesus Christ brought glad tidings of great joy" to this widow and to all mankind. He indicated that the Saints could "now act for their friends who had departed this life, and that the plan of salvation was calculated to save all who were willing to obey the requirements of the law of God."[2] Almost immediately Church members began receiving the ordinance of baptism in the Mississippi River in behalf of deceased loved ones.

The Prophet's discourse on baptism for the dead, delivered in a conference session the following October 4, was received "with considerable interest by the vast multitude." He covered the main points of this sermon in a letter written two weeks later to the Apostles then on a mission to Great Britain. He presumed that news about the new practice "may have raised some inquiries" in their minds. The Prophet insisted that baptism for the dead "was certainly practiced by the ancient churches" and reminded the Twelve that the Apostle Paul had cited this practice as evidence for the resurrection. He indicated that in recent weeks he had given "general instructions" on the subject to the Church.

> The Saints have the privilege of being baptized for those of their relatives who are dead, whom they believe would have embraced the Gospel, if they had been privileged with hearing it, and who have received the Gospel in the

spirit, through the instrumentality of those who have been commissioned to preach to them while in prison.[3]

The Prophet Joseph Smith continued to give emphasis to this principle. Preaching at a conference on October 2, 1841, he declared:

> Suppose the case of two men, brothers, equally intelligent, learned, virtuous and lovely, walking in uprightness and in all good conscience…. One dies and is buried, having never heard the Gospel of reconciliation; to the other the message of salvation is sent, he hears and embraces it and is made the heir of eternal life. Shall the one become the partaker of glory and the other be consigned to hopeless perdition? Is there no chance for his escape? Sectarianism answers "none."

The Prophet then referred to "the wisdom and mercy of God in preparing an ordinance for the salvation of the dead." When they are baptized by proxy, "their names [are] recorded in heaven." Then, in the spirit of warning, he concluded: "Those Saints who neglect it in behalf of their deceased relatives, do it at the peril of their own salvation."[4]

With such encouragement, the Saints eagerly took advantage of the opportunity to make gospel ordinances and blessings available to their departed loved ones. By 1844, the year of the Prophet's martyrdom, some 15,722 baptisms had been performed in behalf of the dead. Typically these were for immediate family members. Of sixty-six names in one record, sixty were grandparents or even closer relatives. Members of Joseph Smith's own family, for example, received baptism in behalf of close relatives: Hyrum was baptized for his brother, Alvin. Emma received the ordinance for her father, mother, two sisters, an uncle, and an aunt. Lucy was baptized for a sister, her parents, and for all four of her grandparents. Samuel H. Smith was baptized for an uncle, while his brother Don Carlos received this ordinance in behalf of General George Washington as "friend."[5]

Elder Wilford Woodruff later reflected the enthusiastic spirit in which these early ordinances were performed:

> How did we feel when we first heard [that] the living could be baptized for the dead? We all went to work at it as fast as we had an opportunity, and were baptized for everybody we could think of, without respect to sex. I went and was baptized for all my friends, grandmothers, and aunts, as [well as for]

those of the male sex; but how was it? Why, by-and-by it was revealed, through the servants of the Lord, that females should be baptized for females, and males for males.[6]

Nauvoo Temple

This is an illustration of how the Lord unfolds his work "line upon line, precept upon precept" (2 Nephi 28:30). While these ordinances were being inaugurated, the Saints had already turned their attention to building the temple.

Temple Construction Commanded by Revelation

Early in August 1840 the First Presidency declared that "the time has now come, when it is necessary to erect a house of prayer, a house of order, a house for the worship of our God, where the ordinances can be attended

to agreeably to His divine will." To this end, a building committee was
named at the conference which convened the following October 3.[7]

A revelation received January 19, 1841, had specifically pointed out
the need for the temple. Echoing instructions given to Moses concerning
the ancient tabernacle, the Lord now commanded his Latter-day Saints to
gather precious materials from afar and build a house "for the Most High
to dwell therein. For there is not a place found on earth that he may come
to and restore again that which was lost unto you, or which he hath taken
away, even the fulness of the priesthood." (D&C 124:25-28; compare
Exodus 25:8, 22.) Specifically, the Lord declared that the ordinance of
baptism for the dead "belongeth to my house," and that he had temporarily
allowed the Saints to perform this ordinance outside of the temple "only in
the days of your poverty." He therefore commanded them to provide an
appropriate font in the temple. He would grant them "a sufficient time" to
accomplish this, during which period he would continue to accept their
baptisms performed in the river. (D&C 124:29-33.) Hence the Nauvoo
Temple, like holy sanctuaries in former dispensations, was to serve the dual
purpose of being a place of contact between God and man where also
sacred priesthood ordinances are performed. The Lord promised to show
the Prophet "all things pertaining to this house," including "the place
whereon it shall be built" (D&C 124:42). The site chosen for the temple
was on elevated ground at the east edge of the city. It commanded a striking
view of the great horseshoe bend of the Mississippi River.

At about this same time the Prophet Joseph Smith invited interested
individuals to submit designs for the proposed temple. Several were
received, but none suited him. When William Weeks, a recent convert who
was an architect and builder from New England, came in with his plans,
"Joseph Smith grabbed him, hugged him and said 'You are the man I
want.'"[8] Weeks became the general superintendent of temple construction.

The Prophet was commonly regarded as the author of the Nauvoo
Temple's design. As had been the case with the Kirtland Temple, however,
he testified that the basic plan had been given to him by revelation. On a
later occasion, for example, the architect Weeks questioned the appropri-
ateness of placing round windows on the side of the building. Joseph
Smith, however, explained that the small rooms in the temple could be illuminated with one light at the center of each of these windows, and that

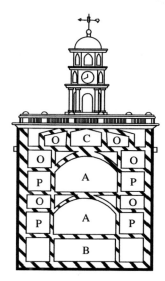

A Assembly room
B Baptistry
C Council room
O Offices
P Pillars

Nauvoo Temple Cross-Section

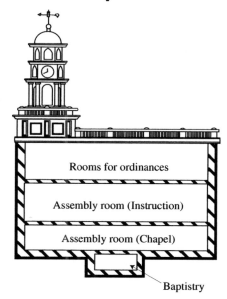

Rooms for ordinances

Assembly room (Instruction)

Assembly room (Chapel)

Baptistry

Nauvoo Temple (1845)

"when the whole building was thus illuminated, the effect would be remarkably grand." "I wish you to carry out *my* designs," the Prophet insisted. "I have seen in vision the splendid appearance of that building illuminated, and will have it built according to the pattern shown me."[9] Evidently Joseph Smith outlined the major features of the temple, and William Weeks drew up the working plans and saw that they were carried out.[10] The Nauvoo Temple followed the general plan of the earlier temple in Kirtland. The two large meeting halls (one above the other) would have arched ceilings, having space for a row of small rooms between the arch and the outside wall above each of the large rooms. The temple would also include a baptismal font in the basement, and facilities for other sacred ordinances on the attic level. Early in 1841 Joseph Smith declared that the Nauvoo Temple "is expected to be considerably larger than the one in Kirtland, and on a more magnificent scale."[11]

A stone quarry was located just north of the city, and in February of 1841 excavations for the temple's foundation began. In March the cellar was dug and foundation stones were set. By April 6 the walls were high enough for the cornerstone ceremony. Thousands gathered for this special program, which began at noon. After music by the choir and an hour-long discourse by Sidney Rigdon, the southeast cornerstone was lowered into place under the direction of the First Presidency. Joseph Smith then stated:

> This principal corner stone in representation of the First Presidency, is now duly laid in honor of the Great God; and may it there remain until the whole fabric is completed; and may the same be accomplished speedily; that the Saints may have a place to worship God, and the Son of Man have where to lay His head.

The southwest, northwest, and northeast cornerstones were then laid by the stake president, high council, and bishops respectively.[12]

During the summer and fall of 1841 the Saints eagerly pushed the temple's construction. In July William Weeks began preparing plans for a baptismal font to be located in the temple basement. On October 2 when the Prophet preached on salvation for the dead, he emphatically declared: "There shall be no more baptisms for the dead, until the ordinance can be attended to in the Lord's House; and the Church shall not hold another General Conference, until they can meet in said house. *For thus saith the Lord!*"[13]

Just five weeks later, the basement rooms were enclosed by frame walls and were covered by a temporary roof. A wooden font, carved by Elijah Fordham under Weeks's direction, measured twelve by sixteen feet. It rested on the backs of twelve oxen, four on each side and two at each end. These were patterned after "the most beautiful five-year-old steer that could be found in the country." Joseph Smith dedicated these facilities on Monday, November 8. The first baptisms were performed there two weeks later. On Sunday, November 21, a large congregation gathered at 4:00 P.M. to witness this event. Elders Brigham Young, Heber C. Kimball, and John Taylor baptized about forty persons in behalf of their dead. Elders Willard Richards, Wilford Woodruff, and George A. Smith confirmed. Hereafter the Prophet and members of the Twelve frequently officiated in the temple. On December 28, 1841, for example, Joseph Smith recorded: "I baptized Sidney Rigdon in the font, for and in behalf of his parents; also baptized Reynolds Cahoon and others."[14]

Lumber was needed for the temple and other building projects in Nauvoo. During the fall of 1841 a group of about a dozen men traveled to the pine country in Wisconsin. They established a mill site on the Black River, a tributary of the Mississippi about five hundred miles north of Nauvoo. The following spring they were joined by over fifty more workmen. For the next few years they formed the lumber into huge rafts which they then floated down the river. The first of these rafts arrived in Nauvoo on August 4, 1842. The raft covered nearly an acre and contained about 100,000 feet of sawed lumber and 192,000 square feet of hewn timber. As men dismantled the raft, teams hauled the lumber to the building site.[15] By October 30, 1842, the temple walls were four feet above the basement, and a temporary floor had been completed for the main story. On that date about three thousand gathered for the first official meeting held in the temple.[16]

Constructing such a magnificent structure required considerable sacrifice on the part of the Saints. Because they had very little capital available for such a venture, they willingly donated their labor. The conference of October 1840 which had approved the building project also voted that "every tenth day be appropriated for the building of the house."[17] Under this system of "tithing in time," each man and boy was expected to contribute every tenth working day. In addition to this voluntary system, many skilled workmen were employed full-time on the temple. Sometimes, however, these craftsmen had to work without guarantee of compensation.

Charles Lambert, for example, had been a master workman and contractor in England. When he arrived in Nauvoo as a new convert, he applied for work on the temple. He was told that there was plenty of work but no pay at the present time. Having no working clothes, he nevertheless reported for work in what he had worn as a contractor in England—a fine suit and high silk hat. He put on an apron and went to work. Brigham Young later recalled that there were those who worked on the temple who had no shoes for their feet or shirt to cover their arms.[18]

Women also played a key role. In fact, the origin of the Relief Society can be traced to the temple-building project. During the spring of 1842 Sarah M. Kimball and her seamstress, Miss Cook, discussed combining their efforts "for assisting the Temple hands." The seamstress wanted to help but had no means to contribute. "I told her I would furnish material," Sarah recalled, "if she would make some shirts for the workmen." These sisters realized that others "might wish to combine means and efforts," so they invited some neighbors "to come and consult with us on the subject of forming a Ladies' Society." These discussions led directly to the formation of the Relief Society on March 17 of that year.[19] Many sisters donated time in knitting socks or mittens and in preparing other items of clothing for the workmen. Louisa Decker remembered how her mother sold their best china dishes and a fine quilt in order to contribute her part.[20] The Relief Society sisters more than met the challenge to contribute one cent per week to purchase nails and glass for the temple. In many homes there were small cans or jars in which the spare pennies began to accumulate. Many donated far more than the amount requested.[21]

An outstanding example of those willing to sacrifice for building the temple was Joseph Toronto, a convert from Sicily, who contributed his entire life's savings. Brigham Young later remembered:

> It was difficult to get bread and other provisions for the workmen to eat. I counseled the committee who had charge of the temple fund to deal out all the flour they had, and God would give them more; and they did so; and it was but

a short time before Brother Toronto came and brought me twenty-five hundred dollars in gold…so I opened the mouth of the bag and took hold at the bottom end, and gave it a jerk towards the bishop, and strewed the gold across the room and said, now go and buy flour for the workmen on the temple and do not distrust the Lord any more; for we will have what we need.[22]

While the Saints were making such sacrifices to build the temple, the Lord was unfolding important temple-related blessings.

The Endowment and Other Blessings

The Saints had received a preliminary or partial endowment in Kirtland, and the time had now come to unfold these blessings more fully. Elder James E. Talmage described the temple endowment as a "course of instruction" that reviews key events in the history of mankind—the Creation, the fall of Adam, the Apostasy, the Restoration, and our eventual reunion with God—giving emphasis to the plan of redemption and to our living according to the high standards of the gospel.[23] These instructions would need to be given in a place of privacy because they were sacred and would make known "things which have been kept hid from before the foundation of the world" (D&C 124:41). Such a facility became available when Joseph Smith opened his store early in 1842. The second story of this twenty-five by forty-four-foot red-brick structure included the Prophet's small personal office and a large area which came to be known as the "assembly room." Here the Relief Society was organized on March 17, 1842, and the first endowments were given seven weeks later.[24]

With the assistance of five or six workmen, the Prophet divided the main room to represent the various stages in man's eternal progress. "We therefore went to work making the necessary preparations," one of the workmen later recalled, "and everything was arranged representing the interior of a temple as much as the circumstances would permit, [the Prophet] being with us dictating everything." These preparations were completed before noon on May 4, 1842, and later that same day the first endowments were given.[25]

The instructions of the endowment were unfolded as the group moved from one area to another in the main assembly room. Those receiving these blessings on this occasion included Hyrum Smith (Associate President and

Patriarch to the Church); William Law (Second Counselor in the First Presidency); Elders Brigham Young, Heber C. Kimball, and Willard Richards of the Quorum of the Twelve (who would form the new First Presidency just over five years later); Stake President William Marks; Bishops George Miller and Newel K. Whitney; and James Adams (a patriarch and branch president in Springfield, Illinois). Concerning this significant event, Joseph Smith recorded:

> I spent the day in the upper part of the store...in council with [seven brethren] instructing them in...all those plans and principles by which any one is enabled to secure the fullness of those blessings which have been prepared for the Church of the First Born, and come up and abide in the presence of the Elohim in the eternal worlds.... And the communications I made to this council were of things spiritual, and to be received only by the spiritual minded: and there was nothing made known to these men but what will be made known to all the Saints of the last days, so soon as they are prepared to receive, and a proper place is prepared to communicate them, even to the weakest of the Saints: therefore let the Saints be diligent in building the Temple.[26]

About a month after Elder Heber C. Kimball had received his endowment, he wrote of this experience to a colleague in the Twelve, Elder Parley P. Pratt, who was away doing missionary work: "We have received some pressious things through the Prophet on the preasthood that would cause you Soul to rejoice. I can not give them to you on paper fore they are not to be riten."[27]

Since the endowment had its origin in antiquity, and members of the Masonic order believe their rituals are derived from the ceremonies at Solomon's Temple, Latter-day Saints are not surprised that there may be some parallels between the two. "That there are similarities in the services of the temple and some secret organizations may be true," conceded Elder John A. Widtsoe. "These similarities, however, do not deal with basic matters but rather with the mechanism of the ritual." Elder Widtsoe explained that Church members who formerly belonged to various fraternal organizations recognize that, unlike the rituals of these organizations, the temple endowment emphasized instructions to make our eternal journey "increasing and progressive." It presents "covenants that we will so live as to make the journey an upward one."

It embodies "a warning that sometime we will be called upon to show whether we have kept our covenants," and offers "the great reward that comes to the faithful and the righteous."[28]

After giving these first endowments, the Prophet turned to Brigham Young and remarked: "Brother Brigham, this is not arranged perfectly; however we have done the best we could under the circumstances in which we are placed. I wish you to take this matter in hand: organize and systematize all these ceremonies."[29] It appears that by the time of the Prophet's martyrdom, over fifty individuals had received the blessings of the endowment, these instructions being given in the assembly room above Joseph's store or in private homes.

By means of two letters written during the first week of September 1842 the Prophet gave yet further instructions concerning work for the dead. He emphasized the importance of having a recorder present, not only to keep an accurate record, but also to assure that each ordinance is done properly. (D&C 127:6; 128:3.) The Prophet linked this keeping of proper records with the power to bind or loose on earth and have this action recognized in heaven. He indicated that in all ages any ordinance that is performed "truly and faithfully" by proper authority and is properly recorded would be recognized in heaven. (D&C 128:8-9; compare Matthew 16:18-19.) This power to "bind on earth" and in heaven was associated with the keys which Elijah had restored in 1836 just after the dedication of the Kirtland Temple. Because temple baptismal fonts symbolize the grave, the Prophet explained, they should be located "underneath where the living are wont to assemble" (D&C 128:12-13). Finally, expanding on the writings of Paul, Joseph Smith declared that "they [the fathers] without us cannot be made perfect—neither can we without our dead be made perfect," and that "their salvation is necessary and essential to our salvation." This is so because in the celestial kingdom we will be organized as God's family according to the patriarchal order. Hence he taught that there must be "a welding link of some kind or other between the fathers and the children." (D&C 128:15, 18.) Vicarious ordinances for the dead, he concluded, were the means of establishing this link.

Among the other blessings unfolded during these years was eternal marriage. During his earthly ministry the Master had stressed the sanctity of the family. "What therefore God hath joined together," he declared, "let not man put asunder" (Mark 10:9). The Apostle Paul similarly insisted: "Neither is the man without the woman, neither the woman without the man, in the Lord" (1 Corinthians 11:11). During the present dispensation a revelation had affirmed that "marriage is ordained of God" as the means of providing earthly tabernacles for the spirits which had lived before the world was made (D&C 49:15-17).

Even though the first couple was married for eternity as early as April 5, 1841, there were relatively few of these "sealings" at first. In May 1843 the Prophet instructed the Saints that in order to attain the highest degree of the celestial kingdom, one must enter "the new and everlasting covenant of marriage" (D&C 131:1-4). Two months later he recorded a revelation that, among other things, declared: "If a man marry him a wife in the world, and he marry her not by me nor by my word, and he covenant with her so long as he is in the world and she with him, their covenant and marriage are not of force when they are dead, and when they are out of the world" (D&C 132:15). After these instructions, the number of marriages for eternity increased.

In his 1841 revelation, the Lord had urged the construction of the temple so that he might restore "the fulness of the priesthood" (D&C 124:28). During the closing year of his life, the Prophet Joseph Smith made sure that the Twelve and others received the highest blessings available through temple ordinances so that the authority necessary to roll forth the Lord's work would remain on the earth. Elder Orson Hyde later recalled that Joseph Smith "conducted us through every ordinance of the holy priesthood, and when he had gone through with all the ordinances he rejoiced very much, and says, now if they kill me you have got all the keys and all the ordinances and you can confer them upon others, and the hosts of Satan will not be able to tear down the kingdom."[30]

Nearly a half-century later, President Wilford Woodruff recalled the Prophet's instructions:

> He stood upon his feet some three hours. The room was filled as with consuming fire, his face was as clear as amber, and he was clothed upon by the power of God.... "I have had sealed upon my head every key, every power, every principle of life and salvation that God has ever given to any man who

ever lived upon the face of the earth.... Now," said he addressing the Twelve, "I have sealed upon your heads every key, every power, and every principle which the Lord has sealed upon my head.... I tell you, the burden of this kingdom now rests upon your shoulders; you have got to bear it off in all the world, and if you don't do it you will be damned."[31]

Concerning this same event, Parley P. Pratt testified that the Prophet conferred "the keys of the sealing power" upon Brigham Young, indicating that this was the "last key," the "most sacred of all," and that it pertained "exclusively to the First Presidency."[32]

Impact of the Martyrdom

The martyrdom of Joseph and Hyrum Smith on June 27, 1844, caused only a temporary lull in temple construction. Even though the Saints knew they would soon be forced to leave Nauvoo and lose access to the temple, they were willing to expend approximately a million dollars to fulfill their Prophet's dream of erecting the House of the Lord. On July 2, just five days after the martyrdom, they reaffirmed their commitment to finish the temple and voted to resume work at once even though they had no money to pay the workmen. Determination to complete the temple united the people to an unprecedented degree. So many responded to calls for help that some workmen had to be assigned to other projects. The sisters pledged to continue their "penny contributions," and other donations began to come in.

Unique features of the Nauvoo Temple's design were thirty pilasters containing symbolic ornamental stones. The base of each pilaster was a large stone depicting the crescent moon. Each capital featured the sun's face. In the cornice above each pilaster was a five-pointed star. These stones reminded the Saints that there are three degrees of glory, and that faithfully receiving the ordinances of the temple is essential to attaining the highest exaltation in heaven. The temple workmen were eager to complete these pilasters before the onset of winter, and the weather during the fall of 1844 was favorable. The last of the capital stones, each weighing more than two tons, was put into place at about noon on December 6. Only two hours later, a brisk and substantial snowfall commenced. "It seems as though," the Saints believed, "the Lord held up the storms and the cold for our advantage, until the important piece of labor had been accomplished."[33]

Work on the temple resumed in the spring, and soon the walls were completed. The capstone was formally put in place on May 24, 1845. The ceremony was conducted at 5:45 A.M. in order not to attract the attention of the Saints' enemies. William Pitt's band played the "Capstone March," which he had composed for the occasion. "The last stone is now laid upon the Temple," declared Brigham Young as he tapped the capstone into its proper position, "and I pray the Almighty in the name of Jesus to defend us in this place and sustain us until the temple is finished and we have all got our endowments." The congregation then shouted "Hosanna, to God and the Lamb."[34] By August the roof was finished, the building enclosed, and work begun on the tower. The British Saints raised money to purchase a bell for the temple. Eventually this Nauvoo bell would be taken west with the pioneers and would be heard hourly from Temple Square as a time signal for Salt Lake City's radio station KSL.

The only conference to be held in the temple convened on Sunday, October 5, 1845. "I opened the services of the day by a dedicatory prayer," President Brigham Young announced, "presenting the Temple thus far completed, as a monument of the Saints' liberality, fidelity, and faith."[35]

Ordinances Received Amid Preparation for Exodus

Emboldened by the acquittal of those accused in the murder of Joseph and Hyrum Smith, a mob of some three hundred men began during September of 1845 to systematically pillage and burn outlying Mormon homes and farms. In the face of such pressure, the Saints agreed to leave Illinois the following spring. Suddenly Nauvoo became a beehive of activity as wagons were built, provisions gathered, and other preparations made for the coming westward exodus. One of the Saints' highest priorities amid these preparations was the completion of the temple. "They felt," believed Elder Wilford Woodruff, "that these ordinances would give to them a new spiritual life and that they would be better qualified in consequence as messengers of the word of God to the nations of the earth."[36] As violence increased, however, work on the temple was sometimes interrupted when craftsmen had to be recruited as guards to protect what they had already accomplished.

Specific parts of the temple were completed and dedicated piecemeal so that ordinance work could begin as soon as possible. On November 30, 1845, for example, Brigham Young and twenty others who had received their endowments from Joseph Smith gathered to dedicate the attic story for ordinance work. During the next ten days Brigham Young, Heber C. Kimball, and others were busy preparing the attic's eighty-eight by twenty-nine foot central hall for the presentation of the endowment. As had been done in the red brick store, the "council chamber" in the temple was divided by means of canvas partitions into separate areas. Saints throughout the city contributed furnishings for these rooms. Potted plants, for example, were gathered for the area representing the Garden of Eden. The room on the east had a large Gothic window and was furnished with fine carpets and wall hangings. This most beautiful area represented the celestial kingdom. When Joseph Fielding entered this part of the temple for the first time, he felt as though he had truly "gotten out of the World."[37] Flanking each side of the central hall were six rooms, each about fourteen feet square, which served as private offices for Church leaders, as places where priesthood quorums could gather for prayer, and as rooms for the ordinances connected with the endowment. Sealings were performed in some of these side rooms.

Endowments were given beginning December 10. Despite threats of arrest and other forms of harassment from their enemies, the Twelve came to the temple regularly in order to take an active lead in this service. Elder Heber C. Kimball was assigned the major responsibility, and his personal journal became the official temple record. Dozens of people participated in these blessings each day. On Christmas Day some 107 received their endowment. Workers decided to wash temple clothing at night so ordinance could go forward without interruption. By the end of the month over a thousand Saints had received their endowment blessings.

As the year 1846 dawned, pressure on the Saints to leave Illinois mounted. There were rumors that even federal troops might be used against them. Hence Church leaders decided to commence the exodus early in February rather than waiting until spring. This decision increased the Saints' eagerness to receive temple blessings before leaving Nauvoo, so the level of temple activity during January was even greater than during the previous month. On January 12 Brigham Young recorded: "Such has been the anxiety manifested by the saints to receive the ordinances [of the Temple], and such the anxiety on our part to administer to them, that I have given myself up entirely to the work of the Lord in the Temple night and day, not taking more than four hours sleep, upon an average, per day, and going home but once a week."

Others of the Twelve were "in constant attendance," but had to leave the temple from time to time "to rest and recruit their health."[38] The daily total of endowments exceeded two hundred for the first time on January 21. During this same month other temple ordinances were made available for the first time: Living individuals were sealed to a deceased spouse beginning on the ninth. Children were sealed to their parents for the first time on January 25.

February 4 had been selected as the day on which the exodus would begin. As this date drew closer, the pace in the temple became even more intense. On February 3 Brigham Young recorded:

> Notwithstanding that I had announced that we would not attend to the administration of the ordinances, the House of the Lord was thronged all day, the anxiety being so great to receive, as if the brethren would have us stay here and continue the endowments until our way would be hedged up and our enemies would intercept us. But I informed the brethren that this was not wise, and that we should build more Temples, and have further opportunities to receive the blessings of the Lord, as soon as the saints were prepared to receive them. In this Temple we have been abundantly rewarded, if we receive no more. I also informed the brethren that I was going to get my wagons started and be off. I walked some distance from the Temple supposing the crowd would disperse, but on returning I found the house filled to overflowing.
>
> Looking upon the multitude and knowing their anxiety, as they were thirsting and hungering for the word, we continued at work diligently in the House of the Lord.[39]

Nearly three hundred persons received their endowment on that day alone. Daily entries in the *History of the Church* indicate that a total of over 4,400 endowments were given during January and the first seven days of February. Hence during the eight weeks prior to the exodus, approximately

5,500 were endowed, fulfilling the Prophet Joseph Smith's compelling desire to make these blessings available to the Saints in Nauvoo. Erastus Snow testified: "The Spirit, Power, and Wisdom of God reigned continually in the Temple and all felt satisfied that during the two months we occupied it in the endowments of the Saints, we were amply paid for all our labors in building it."[40]

During the hectic time just before and following the exodus, some of the Saints ate, tended babies, or slept in the unused small rooms on the mezzanines above the two main halls. Some people even used the unfinished second-floor auditorium for recreational purposes. Concerned about such irregularities, Elder Heber C. Kimball insisted that only persons with official invitations be admitted to the temple. In this way he was able to restore proper order. This may be the origin of issuing "recommends" to those judged by local Church leaders to be worthy of temple attendance.[41]

The Temple Dedication and Abandonment

By the end of April, two months after most of the Saints had left Nauvoo, the temple was ready for dedication. Fearing a possible disruption by the mob, Elder Orson Hyde, who had been left in Nauvoo to direct the completion and dedication of the temple, and Elder Wilford Woodruff, who had just returned from a mission to England, scheduled a private dedicatory service for the evening of April 30. Elder Woodruff described the service in his journal:

> In the evening of this day I repaired to the Temple with Elder Orson Hyde and about twenty other elders of Israel. There we…dedicated the Temple of the Lord…. Notwithstanding the predictions of false prophets and the threat of mobs that the building should never be completed nor dedicated, their words had fallen to the ground. The Temple was now finished and dedicated to Him.

Elder Hyde offered the dedicatory prayer at the public service on the following day.[42]

After the Saints' departure from Nauvoo, various groups used the temple as a place for meetings and entertainments, etc. When the Icarians,

Bronze replica of the Nauvoo Temple

a French communal group, settled in Nauvoo, they hoped to purchase the temple for their own use. In the early hours of October 9, 1848, however, fire broke out in the temple and quickly engulfed the entire structure. In a few hours was destroyed what the Saints had labored and sacrificed for several years to build. The prevailing opinion was that the fire had been set by those who wanted to remove the temple as a tangible link that might tempt the Mormons to return. A tornado in 1850 leveled part of the temple walls and weakened the rest. Gradually they crumbled, and by the mid-1850s nothing was left standing.

As part of its twentieth-century interest in historic sites, in 1937 the Church began reacquiring the Nauvoo Temple property. Nauvoo Restoration, Inc., was formed in 1962 and took charge of archaeological excavations at the temple site. Soon the outline of the temple's foundation was discovered, and it was eventually marked by a line of stones in the grass of the nicely-landscaped plot. In 1977 a nine-foot-tall bronze replica of the temple was placed at the site.[43] Here modern visitors can contemplate the faith of those nineteenth-century Saints who willingly made their million-dollar sacrifice.

Chapter Four

Temples in the Tops of the Mountains

When the Latter-day Saints left Nauvoo and headed toward the Rockies, they were forced to leave their nearly completed temple behind. Their interest in temple service did not diminish, however. If anything, it became stronger as they were deprived of the opportunity to receive these blessings. At Winter Quarters, for example, President Brigham Young declared that when the Saints should reach their resting place in the mountains, his intention was to labor hard to build another temple. This matter was constantly on the pioneers' minds during their trek across the plains.[1]

Within four days of President Young's arrival in the Salt Lake Valley, he designated the site for the future temple. On July 28, 1847, he and a few others were walking across the area that one day would be Temple Square. He stopped between the two forks of City Creek, struck the ground with his cane, and declared: "Here will be the Temple of our God." Wilford Woodruff placed a stake in the ground to mark the spot which would become the center of the future building. Many years later President Woodruff would call the construction of the temple on the designated site "a monument to President Young's foresight and prophetic accuracy."[2]

During the pioneers' early years in the Salt Lake Valley, the endowment was given in a variety of places. In the fall of 1849, Elder Addison Pratt, who had served as a missionary for several years in the South Pacific, was appointed to a second mission in that same area. Before his departure he received his endowment on Ensign Peak, just north of the center of Salt Lake City.[3] This action was consistent with the Prophet Joseph Smith's carrier instructions that under certain circumstances these sacred blessings could be received on mountain tops, as had been the case with Moses.[4]

Cornerstones Laid for a Temple in the Desert

As early as December 23, 1847, an official circular letter of the Twelve had invited the Saints to gather, bringing precious metals and other materials "for the exaltation of the living and the dead," for the time had come to build the Lord's house "in the tops of the mountains."[5] Soon afterwards, Brigham Young named Truman O. Angell as temple architect, a post he would hold until his death in 1887. His having worked as a joiner on both the Kirtland and Nauvoo Temples provided useful background for his new assignment. He would have an able assistant, William Ward, who received his architectural training in England and was skilled in stone construction. (Angell's experience was primarily with wooden structures.) A skilled draftsman, Ward prepared the drawings for the Salt Lake Temple under Angell's direction.[6]

To aid with this and other building projects in the valley, Church authorities in January 1851 established the Department of Public Works with Daniel H. Wells, a military and civic leader and future member of the First Presidency, as superintendent. Soon carpenter, paint, stone-cutting, and blacksmith shops were set up in the northeast corner of the temple block where they could get power by means of a water wheel in City Creek. The Public Works provided an immediate job for newly arrived immigrants and also channeled their skills into building the community. During the 1850s as many as five hundred were employed on various Public Works projects.[7]

Meeting on the Bowery on Temple Square in April 1851, the general conference accepted by acclamation the resolution "to build a Temple to the name of the Lord our God" and appointed Daniel H. Wells as building superintendent.[8] Because of a lack of materials and of manpower—fewer than five thousand Saints lived in the immediate area of the projected temple—construction could not commence immediately. In 1852 the Public Works put men to work building a fourteen-foot wall of sandstone and adobe around the temple block. This project not only provided security for the construction site but also created worthwhile employment for men who otherwise would have been idle.

The general conference of October 1852 considered which material would be best for building the temple. Some favored sandstone from nearby Red Butte Canyon. Brother Brigham, perhaps tongue-in-cheek, suggested adobe, because harder rock had already reached its zenith of perfection and was hence now subject to the processes of decay.[9] Heber C. Kimball, Brigham Young's first counselor, submitted the following question to the conference: "Shall we have the Temple built of stone from Red Butte, adobes, rock, or the best stone the mountains afford?" The congregation unanimously voted "that we build a Temple of the best materials that can be obtained in the mountains of North America, and that the Presidency dictate where the stone and other materials shall be obtained."

Elder James E. Talmage later concluded that this significant decision reflected the faith and determination of the Saints: "The Temple they were about to rear should be in every particular the best the people could produce. This modern House of the Lord was to be no temporary structure, nor of small proportions, nor of poor material, nor of mean or inadequate design." The Saints knew that the temple would not be finished for many years. By that time "the few would have grown to a multitude of souls. The Temple was to be worthy of the great future."[10] In the mid-1850s when deposits of granite were discovered in Little Cottonwood Canyon twenty miles southeast of Salt Lake City, President Young determined that the temple should be built of this material.

The Salt Lake Temple site was dedicated on February 14, 1853. Standing in a small buggy, President Brigham Young addressed the crowd of several thousand who had gathered for the occasion. The band played "Auld Lang Syne," and then Heber C. Kimball offered the dedicatory prayer. Because the ground was frozen, it had to be broken with a pick. President Young then declared the ground officially broken for the temple.[11]

During the next several weeks excavation for the temple proceeded. Cornerstones were to be laid on April 6, 1853, the twenty-third anniversary of the Church's organization. Large stones, measuring approximately two by three by five feet, had been placed in convenient positions ahead of time. They were of "firestone" brought from nearby Red Butte Canyon. This was a beautiful spring day in the valley as general conference convened in the old adobe tabernacle on the southwest corner of the temple block.

Accompanied by military honor guards and the music of three bands, a procession headed by Church leaders marched to the spot where the First Presidency and the patriarch laid the southeast cornerstone. President Brigham Young then spoke, explaining that the temple had to be built in order that the Lord "may have a place where he can lay his head, and not only spend a night or a day, but find a place of peace."[12] The southwest cornerstone was next laid by the Presiding Bishopric representing the lesser priesthood. The presidency of the high priests, the stake presidency, and the high council then placed the northwest cornerstone. Finally the northeast cornerstone was laid by the Twelve and representatives of the seventies and the elders. The laying of each stone was accompanied by special music, speeches and a prayer. On this occasion Elder Parley P. Pratt perceived "by the power of the Spirit" that Joseph Smith and others "hovered above us."[13] These proceedings lasted from 10:00 A.M. through 2:00 P.M., at which time President Brigham Young blessed the assembled congregation "in the name of Jesus Christ of Nazareth, and pray my Father in heaven to encircle you in the arms of His love and mercy, and protect us until we have finished this Temple, received the fullness of our endowments therein, and built many more."[14]

After a one-hour break, the conference resumed in the Old Tabernacle. Concerning the future temple, President Young declared:

> I scarcely ever say much about revelations, or visions, but suffice it to say, five years ago last July [1847] I was here, and saw in the Spirit the Temple not ten feet from where we have laid the Chief Corner Stone. I have not inquired what kind of a Temple we should build. Why? Because it was represented before me. I have never looked upon that ground, but the vision of it was there. I see it as plainly as if it was in reality before me. Wait until it is done. I will say, however, that it will have six towers, to begin with, instead of one. Now do not any of you apostatize because it will have six towers, and Joseph

only built one. It is easier for us to build sixteen, than it was for him to build one.The time will come when there will be one in the centre of Temples we shall build, and on the top, groves and fish ponds. But we shall not see them here, at present.[15]

Some temples built in the twentieth century would represent a fulfillment of President Young's prophecy.

The great temple would not be completed for forty years. In the meantime the Saints would need to have access to temple blessings, so temporary facilities would need to be provided.

The Endowment House—A Temporary Temple

Beginning in February 1851 the endowment was again given on a regular basis. These blessings were received in a variety of places. Some temple ordinances during this time were administered in Brigham Young's office, for example. By 1852 endowments were being given in the Council House, located on the southwest corner of what are now South Temple and Main streets. This two-story structure measured

Council House, 1869

Endowment House

forty-five feet square. The outer walls of the first story were of red sandstone, while those above were adobe. The building was surmounted by a square tower. There were two offices and a large hall on each floor. One of these large rooms was divided by white canvas screens into sections…much as had been done in the upper room of the Nauvoo Temple. During the years 1851, 1852, and 1854 over two thousand received their endowment here. (None were recorded in 1853.) Because the Council House also was the site for a variety of ecclesiastical and governmental gatherings and the *Deseret News* was even printed there, there was a need for a separate building where endowment blessings could be given without interruption.[16]

Construction on the "new endowment rooms" or "Endowment House," as the structure soon came to be called, got under way during the summer of 1854. The building's architect, Truman O. Angell, referred to it as a "temple pro tem," reflecting how the Saints regarded this new structure. Located in the northwest corner of the temple block, the Endowment House was a two-story adobe structure which measured forty-four by thirty-four feet. Construction was relatively simple and so progressed rapidly. The building was completed by the spring of the following year.

The Endowment House was dedicated May 5, 1855. President Brigham Young declared that "the house was clean and named it 'The House of the Lord'" and explained that "the spirit of the Lord would be in it, for no one would be permitted to go into it to pollute it." Over the years this prophetic statement would be confirmed by repeated spiritual experiences in the Endowment House. The dedicatory prayer was offered by Heber C. Kimball, who would preside over the work in this holy house. The first endowments and sealings were performed that same day.[17]

For the next three decades the Endowment House would be an influence for good in the lives of thousands of Latter-day Saints. In 1856, the year after the building opened, an addition provided a baptismal font, which was dedicated on October 2. Here the Saints renewed their covenants as they prepared to enter important new phases of their lives. From 600 to over 3,000 received the endowment each year, between 25 and 30 receiving these blessings on a typical day. Outgoing missionaries received instructions from Church leaders and were set apart here. The Endowment House also provided the setting for as many as 2,500 eternal marriages annually. President Heber C. Kimball continued to have general supervision of this work until his death in 1868. Elder Wilford Woodruff was also heavily involved, spending from thirty to sixty days each year helping to administer the sacred ordinances in the Endowment House.

Work Continues on Salt Lake Temple

Meanwhile the Saints maintained their interest in constructing the temple. In the spring of 1856 President Young sent architect Angell on a special mission. "You shall have power and means to go from place to place, from country to country, and view various specimens of architecture," the President blessed him. "You will be quick to comprehend the architectural designs of men in various ages." President Young instructed him to make sketches of important architectural works in order to become better qualified to continue his work on the temple and other buildings.[18] It is possible, for example, that Angell got his idea for the four corner stairways with their supporting central column from the Nelson Monument at Trafalgar Square in London.

On July 24, 1857, as the Latter-day Saints were celebrating the tenth anniversary of their entrance into Salt Lake Valley, they received the disturbing word that a potentially hostile United States army was approaching Utah. Not knowing the army's intentions, the Saints were concerned that the temple foundation might be in danger. On August 13 President Young placed some important records in the temple foundation. He directed that dirt be hauled in to fill the excavation and cover the foundation walls. When the army arrived the following year, Temple Square looked like a freshly plowed field, and there was no visible evidence of the temple's construction. As it turned out, the army marched through without harming any property and set up its camp some forty miles to the south near Utah Lake. By 1860 Church leaders concluded that the temple was safe and directed that the work of reexcavation get under way. With the outbreak of the American Civil War in 1861 the army was needed elsewhere, and it departed from Utah in December of that year.

At this time President Young examined the newly uncovered foundation and became aware that it was defective. He and his associates concluded that its small stones could not carry the massive weight of the temple. On January 1, 1862, he announced that the inadequate foundation would be removed and replaced by one made entirely of granite. The footings would be sixteen feet thick. "I want this Temple to stand through the Millennium," he declared a few months later, "and I want it so built that it will be acceptable to the Lord."[19] The work of rebuilding the foundation moved slowly, and the walls did not reach ground level until the end of the construction season in 1867, fourteen years after the cornerstones had been laid.

Renewed Emphasis on Vicarious Service

While the Saints were struggling to get established in the Rocky Mountains, Church-sponsored activities were limited. Emphasis in temple work was on providing needed ordinances for the living, and work for the dead virtually ceased following the exodus from Nauvoo. Even with the opening of the Endowment House in 1855 this pattern did not change. Official records indicate that only thirty-three deceased couples were sealed vicariously during the pre-Endowment House period, and no such ordinances at all were performed during the following decade. Similarly, there is a record of only one baptism for the dead in 1855 and of only two in 1857, and of no others during the Saints' first two decades in Utah.

In the mid-1860s, however, ordinance work for the dead resumed. Sealings of six deceased couples were recorded in 1865, and two baptisms for the dead the following year. In 1869, over four hundred deceased couples were sealed, and over five thousand vicarious baptisms were recorded. Available records do not state why these ordinances resumed at this particular time, but several factors may have been involved: By this time the Saints who had participated in baptisms for the dead at Nauvoo were growing older. They, together with more recent immigrants, undoubtedly voiced their anxiety to have further opportunity to vicariously provide the saving ordinances for their departed loved ones. On the other hand, the Saints understood that endowments for the dead could be performed only in a temple, and may have supposed that this restriction applied to other vicarious ordinances as well.

Most looked forward to returning to Jackson County, Missouri, and anticipated that they would have the privilege of building the great temple there in the not-too-distant future. In 1862, for example, Brigham Young felt the Saints would be going back within a few years, and wanted "to get the [Salt Lake] Temple most done before we go." Nevertheless, he believed that no other temple would be completed before the one in Jackson County.[20] Some may have thought that the American Civil War would open the way for the Saints' return. When the war ended in 1865 without having wrought the expected changes in Missouri, however, attention shifted to the possibility of performing vicarious ordinances in Utah.

By this time the pioneers were more securely established and were in a position to take on additional religious activities. It was in 1867, for instance, that President Brigham Young directed that steps be taken to establish Relief Society and Sunday Schools in all branches of the Church for the first time. Whatever the contributing factors may have been, by the later 1860s vicarious ordinances were being performed in increasing numbers under the direction of inspired leaders. For example, Elder Wilford Woodruff recorded in his journal that during 1870 he had personally witnessed 4,400 baptisms for the dead performed by Elders Joseph F. Smith and Samuel H.B. Smith.[21] In 1872 President Brigham Young declared: "We are now baptizing for the dead, and we are sealing for the dead, and if we had a temple prepared, we should be giving endowments for the dead—for our fathers, mothers, grandfathers, grandmothers, uncles, aunts, relatives, friends and old associates." He testified that the Lord was "stirring up the hearts" of many people to search out their pedigrees "and it will continue and run on from father to father, father to father, until they get the genealogy of their forefathers as far as they possibly can."[22]

Nevertheless, "there are some of the sealing ordinances that cannot be administered in the house that we are now using," President Young explained in 1863. "We can only administer in it some of the first ordinances of the Priesthood pertaining to the endowment. There are more advanced ordinances that cannot be administered there."[23] He later explained that ordinances designed "to connect the chain of the Holy Priesthood from Father Adam until now, by sealing children to their parents, being sealed for our forefathers, etc., they cannot be done without a Temple.... Neither will children be sealed to their living parents in any other place than a Temple." In 1865 he therefore urged couples to be endowed before their marriage and to be sealed by proper authority, otherwise their children could not be theirs as "heirs to the priesthood." President Young also specified that "no one can receive endowments for another, until a Temple is prepared in which to administer them."[24]

An 1876 circular letter from the First Presidency and the Twelve acknowledged these restrictions but challenged the Saints to overcome them: "We feel led to say to the Latter-day Saints throughout these mountains: Let us arise and build Temples unto our God at such places as He shall designate, into which we and our children can enter and receive those blessings that He has in store for us." The Presidency now called for the construction of two temples in addition to those already under way in Salt Lake City and St. George, and called on ward bishops to provide donated labor for this task.[25]

The St. George Temple

The first Latter-day Saint colonists sent to "Utah's Dixie" in 1861 went to raise needed cotton and also to provide a stopping place along the trail connecting southern California and the central areas of colonization surrounding Salt Lake City. After ten years of struggle to gain a foothold in the desert, St. George's population had reached only twelve hundred. At a council meeting with local leaders on January 31, 1871, President Brigham Young proposed that a temple be built in the city. This announcement was received with "Glory! Hallelujah!" from Elder Erastus Snow of the Twelve, who had presided in Dixie. These feelings were shared by all present.[26]

The construction of this temple had been prophesied as early as 1855, six years before the town of St. George was even founded. While he was in the community of Harmony, about forty miles northwest of the future temple site, President Heber C. Kimball declared that "a wagon road would be made from Harmony over the Black Ridge; and a temple would be built in the vicinity of the Rio Virgin."[27] At that time the construction of such a road and temple seemed highly unlikely.

With such a small population in the area during the early 1870s, many wondered why a temple was to be built in St. George. President John Taylor later pointed out that "it was found that our Temple in Salt Lake City would take such a long time to build, it was thought best" to erect another one in southern Utah. In the warmer climate, construction could proceed the year around. Furthermore, President Taylor continued, "there was a people living here who were more worthy than any others.... God inspired President Young to build a Temple here because of the fidelity and self-abnegation of the people."[28]

Brigham Young directed local Church leaders to consider possible sites where the temple might be built. Two hilltop locations were proposed. Nevertheless, the group could not agree on which to recommend. A young man who was present described later what had happened: when President Young arrived, he "somewhat impatiently chided them, and at the same time asked them to get into their wagons, or whatever else they had, and with him find a location." He had them drive to the lowest part of the valley, a swamp infested with marsh grass and cattails.

"But, Brother Brigham," protested the men, "this land is boggy. After a storm, and for several months of the year, no one can drive across the land without horses and wagons sinking way down. There is no place to build a foundation." President Young countered, "We will make a foundation."

Later on, while the brethren were plowing and scraping where the foundation was to be, a horse's leg broke through the ground into a spring of water. The brethren then wanted to move the foundation line twelve feet to the south, so that the spring of water would be on the outside of the temple.

"Not so," insisted Brigham Young. "We will wall it up and leave it here for some future use. But we cannot move the foundation. This spot was dedicated by the Nephites. They could not build [the temple], but we can and will build it for them."[29] According to one popular tradition, Moroni, the last survivor of the Nephites, dedicated the site for this temple.[30]

Because of the sparseness of the population and the lack of funds, many wondered how the temple could be built. "We do not need capital," President Young responded. "We have raw material; we have labor: we have skill. We are better able to build a temple than the Saints were in Nauvoo." All tithing collected south of Beaver was to be used for the St. George Temple.[31]

Ground was broken November 9, 1871. Music was provided by a Swiss brass band from nearby Santa Clara. President George A. Smith offered the prayer dedicating the site. "If the brethren undertake to do this work with one heart and mind," President Brigham Young promised, "we shall be blessed exceedingly, and prospered of the Lord in our earthly substance."

Placing his spade in the ground, President Young declared: "I now commence by moving this dirt in the name of Israel's God." All present responded with "Amen." Erastus Snow earnestly prayed "that our beloved President, Brigham, might live to officiate at [the temple's] dedication." The people "gave a hearty Amen." After the congregation sang "The Spirit of God," President Young stood on a chair and led them in the Hosanna Shout. That very afternoon, plows and scrapers began excavating for the foundation.[32]

As the excavation progressed, workmen discovered that the site was filled with water and mud. To provide a firm foundation for the temple, hundreds of tons of rock had to be pounded into the ground. Not any rock would do. Black volcanic rock which would not decay in the moisture had to be brought by wagon from a ridge west of the settlement. To pound this rock into place, a primitive pile driver was improvised. A small brass cannon, which the Mormon Battalion had acquired at Sutter's Mill, was filled with lead. A heavy framework about thirty feet high was constructed, and the thousand-pound weight was hoisted by means of horse power, and then allowed to fall. So great was its momentum that the weight often bounced three times before coming to rest.[33]

During the six years of construction, the whole community demonstrated a spirit of cooperation and dedication. Men took wagons some eighty miles to Mount Trumbull in Arizona to obtain timber of sufficient size. Often eight days of travel across the hot desert were required to bring as few as two huge logs back to St. George.

Local able-bodied men were expected to donate one day in ten as tithing labor, following the pattern which had been established in Nauvoo. Eighteen-year-old John Stucki walked five miles from the Swiss colony in order to work in the stone quarry; he then gave half of his pay back to the temple fund. Also, men from the northern settlements were called on forty-day missions to help with the construction.[34]

On Wednesday, April 1, 1874, President Brigham Young and other general and local Church leaders gathered to place a metal box in the temple's southeast cornerstone. The box contained copies of the standard works, other books, and newspapers of the time. Also placed in the box was a silver plaque listing key events in Church and St. George history and the names of the General Authorities then serving. President Young explained that these items were selected "in token of our faith, to be here preserved until the Savior comes; and then to be subject to His will and pleasure, together with the Temple, for the use of the living and the dead."[35]

The baptismal font and oxen, constructed in Salt Lake City, were a personal gift of President Brigham Young. The font was shaped in sections and assembled in the partially completed St. George Temple. It was dedicated August 11, 1875, and beginning that same day was used for baptisms initiating people into the United Order. When Elder Orson Hyde visited the temple and saw the font in place, "he came out weeping with joy. He thanked God that he had lived to see another font in place in a temple of the Lord."[36]

The main walls of the temple were of red sandstone, quarried just north of town. These were covered with plaster to give the temple its familiar white appearance. Visiting the temple just before its dedication, Wilford Woodruff was impressed with the structure that was "as white snow as inside and out and is a beautiful contrast with the red appearance of the surrounding country."[37] The temple's whiteness distinguished it from other buildings in the area and symbolized its holy purposes.

The southern Utah Saints were eager to see the temple completed and to have the opportunity of performing sacred ordinances therein. On Christmas Day of 1876, for example, "forty women were sewing carpets and all the men were at work" to get the temple ready for dedication.[38]

The Saints gathered at the temple on New Year's Day of 1877 in order to dedicate the portions of the building sufficiently completed at that time, In the baptistery, Elder Wilford Woodruff reminded the congregation what a privilege it was once again to be able to enter a temple built by the Lord's command and especially dedicated to him. After prayer was offered there, the group moved to the main assembly room on the ground floor, where Erastus Snow offered a dedicatory prayer.

St. George Temple

President Brigham Young was determined to attend the services even though he was so ill that he had to be carried about in a large chair by four men. He had not expected to speak, but during the service he received enough strength that he was able to walk to the pulpit and address the congregation with great power:

> Now we have a Temple which will all be finished within a few days.... We enjoy privileges that are enjoyed by no one else on the face of the earth. Suppose we were awake to this thing, namely the salvation of the human family, this house would be crowded, as we hope it will be, from Monday morning until Saturday night.... What do you suppose the fathers would say if they should speak from the dead? Would they say, "We have lain here thousands of years, here in this prison house, waiting for this dispensation to come?"...When I think upon this subject, I want the tongues of seven thunders to wake up the people. Can the fathers be saved without us? No. Can we be saved without them? No.

One who was present recalled that as President Young spoke, he "brought his cane down very hard on the pulpit. He said, 'If I mar the pulpit some of these good workmen can fix it up again.' He did mar the pulpit, but the people did not fix it up again. They left it for a mark to be carried through the years."[39]

The First Endowments for the Dead

Baptisms for the dead commenced in the St. George Temple on January 9, 1877, with Elder Wilford Woodruff personally baptizing and confirming the first 141. President Brigham Young also assisted in the laying on of hands.[40] Two days later, for the first time in this dispensation, the endowment was also given in behalf of the dead. Not long before, President Young had told some workers in the St. George Temple that he had just learned by revelation "that it takes as full and complete a set of ordinances for the dead as for the living."[41]

The introduction of endowments for the dead focused greater attention on these sacred instructions. Up to this time, these teachings had been communicated from one person to another only in oral form. President Young, however, as the lone survivor of the original group receiving the endowment from Joseph Smith in 1842, was concerned that this ordinance be preserved in a perfect form. He therefore spent much time during the early months of 1877 giving instructions on the important subject. On January 14, he specifically assigned Elders Wilford Woodruff and Brigham Young Jr. to write these ceremonies from beginning to end. During the next several weeks these two Apostles met with President Young, who reviewed what they had written and made corrections as necessary. By March 21 the project was completed, and the approved endowment ceremonies were then taught to the temple workers.[42]

While directing the unfolding of vicarious service at St. George, Elder Wilford Woodruff became increasingly concerned about the redemption of his own deceased relatives. Not having any family members in St. George, he worried about how this could be accomplished. On February 23 he made this a special matter of prayer. "The Lord told me," he recalled, "to call upon the Saints in St. George and let them officiate for me in that temple and it should be acceptable unto him."[43] "I saw an Eff[ectual] door open to me for the redemption of my dead. And...I felt like shouting Glory Hallalulah [sic] to God and the Lamb."

On March 1, Elder Woodruff's seventieth birthday, some 154 sisters came to the temple to act as proxies for his female relatives. "I feel thankful to you my sisters for this manifestation of kindness," he told them as they gathered at the beginning of the endowment session, "for you might have searched the world over and you could not have found a present as dear to me as this. What is gold or silver in comparison to the redemption of our dead? Nothing."[44] One sister later recalled that when she heard Elder Woodruff needed help "we prayed that we might be chosen, and our joy was great when we received our notice that we were to be numbered with the proxies of this first company." She and others returned to the temple again and again to officiate for those on the Woodruff list.[45]

In the midst of these developments, the Church's annual general conference was held in the now completed St. George Temple. In connection with this conference the temple was officially dedicated on April 6, the dedicatory prayer being offered by Daniel H. Wells, a counselor to Brigham Young in the First Presidency. Many traveled long distances to be present. They had to bring their own provisions because there were only limited accommodations along the way or in St. George.

A singular event occurred not long before Elder Woodruff ended his duties as the first president of the St. George Temple. He later described what happened:

> The spirits of the dead gathered around me, wanting to know why we did not redeem them. Said they, "You have had the use of the Endowment House for a number of years, and yet nothing has ever been done for us. We laid the foundation of the government you now enjoy...and were faithful to God." These were the signers of the Declaration of Independence, and they waited on me for two days and two nights. I thought it very singular, that notwithstanding so much work had been done...nothing had been done for them.... Heretofore our minds were reaching after our more immediate friends and relatives.[46]

Elder Woodruff went into the temple baptismal font on August 21, 1877, and was baptized by John D. T. McAllister for one hundred prominent men of the seventeenth and eighteenth centuries, including the signers of the Declaration of Independence and other noted individuals such as Benjamin Franklin, Daniel Webster, Henry Clay, John Wesley, Benito Juarez, and Christopher Columbus. Elder Woodruff then baptized Brother McAllister for all the deceased presidents of the United States except three (whose ordinances have been performed by relatives in the Church more recently). Sister Lucy Bigelow Young was then baptized for seventy prominent women, including Martha Washington and Elizabeth Barrett Browning.

"I felt thankful that we had the privilege and the power to administer for the worthy dead esspecially [sic] for the signers of the declaration of Independence," Elder Woodruff recorded in his journal, "that inasmuch as they had laid the foundation of our Government that we Could do as much for them as they had done for us."[47]

While these events were taking place in St. George, steps were being taken which would lead to the construction of yet two other temples in Utah.

Chapter Five

A New Generation of Temples

The St. George Temple had followed the basic pattern of the earlier Kirtland and Nauvoo Temples in the arrangement of its major rooms. The inauguration of endowments for the dead, however, created a greater need for temple facilities specifically adapted to the presentation of this sacred ordinance. The decade and a half following the dedication of the St. George Temple witnessed a dramatic acceleration in temple construction. Not just one, but three of these sacred edifices—the Salt Lake, Logan, and Manti temples—were under construction at the same time.

Inspired Variations in Temple Design

Speaking at the time that the St. George Temple was being completed, several Church leaders indicated that the design of future temples would meet these new needs. In 1879 Elder Orson Pratt pointed out that the Church by then had tabernacles and other buildings for the Saints' regular meetings. Therefore temples would be dedicated especially for more "sacred and holy purposes," for ordinances associated with "the Priesthood of the Most High God." Elder Pratt insisted that the Lord is "not confined" to a single pattern in temple building any more than he is in the creation of worlds, "but he will construct his temples in a great variety of ways."[1] "The Lord begins little by little," Elder Pratt had explained two years previously, "he does not reveal everything all at once." There were no rooms for ordinances in the Kirtland Temple. When baptisms for the dead were restored, a font was provided in the Nauvoo Temple. Endowments for the dead, not known in the first two temples, were now being performed at St. George. Therefore "by and by," Elder Pratt concluded, "we will have Temples, with a great many things contained in them which we now have not."[2]

That there would be variations in temple design had been made known to President Brigham Young in St. George. "Oh Lord," he had prayed, "show unto thy servants if we shall build all temples after the same pattern." Men do not build their homes the same when their families are large as when they are small, came the inspired response. "So shall the growth of the knowledge of the principles of the gospel among my people cause diversity in the pattern of temples."[3] Years earlier at the time ground was broken for the Salt Lake Temple, President Young had taught that the order of priesthood ordinances is made known by revelation, and therefore we should know what facilities must be included in our temple.[4]

In his landmark work, *The House of the Lord,* Elder James E. Talmage pointed out that "while the general purpose of temples is the same in all times, the special suitability of these edifices is determined by the needs of the dispensation to which they severally belong. There is a definite sequence of development in the dealings of God with man." Therefore, "we may affirm that divine revelation of temple plans is required for each distinctive period of the Priesthood's administration." Consequently, Elder Talmage concluded, the temple buildings themselves are a tangible record of God's unfolding revelations to his people concerning temple work.[5]

The pattern of separate ordinance rooms was first seen in the Endowment House, dedicated in 1855. After receiving preliminary ordinances and instructions, one would pass successively through the garden, world, and terrestrial rooms. All were located on the ground floor, and each was one step higher than the preceding room. One would then ascend a stairway to the second floor where the celestial room and sealing rooms were found.

This new concept in temple design would be reflected in the Logan,

Manti, and Salt Lake temples, completed during the last two decades of the nineteenth century. The basic architectural concept for these new temples was worked out by Truman O. Angell under the personal direction of the Prophet Brigham Young. Both the Manti and Logan temples would have similar dimensions, be built in the castellated style with local stone, and have two towers. By the later 1870s, however, Angell was in poor health, so the task of completing the design for these buildings was turned over to his two capable assistants. William H. Folsom, who had helped to design the Salt Lake Tabernacle, became architect for the Manti Temple, while Truman O. Angell Jr. received the assignment to complete the plans for the temple in Logan.[6]

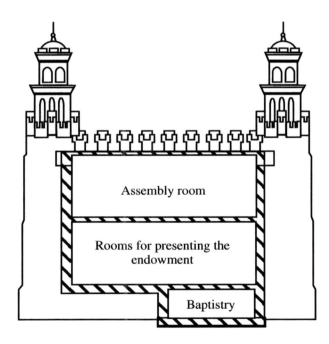

Logan (1884) and Manti (1888) Temples

Even though the Logan and Manti Temples were completed under the direction of John Taylor, their architects acknowledged that the concept for their design had originated with Brigham Young. Both men wrote to President John Taylor during the same month, May 1878, referring to the instructions they had received from his predecessor: "it was not required that temples should [always] be alike, neither in their interior or exterior design and construction," but they should be arranged for the "convenience of performing the labors therein."[7] Six years later in his dedicatory prayer for the Logan Temple, President John Taylor would acknowledge Brigham Young as the one who had "contemplated and designed" that structure.[8]

Two 1877 descriptions of the Manti Temple seem to be a transition from the earlier concept of temples with two large assembly rooms, one above the other. According to these descriptions, the Manti Temple would have three main floors: The "main rooms," measuring 80 by 104 feet, would occupy the first and third floors, while the "middle chambers" would be located on the second floor.[9] As it turned out, the Logan and Manti temples retained only the large hall on the upper floor, while the entire lower part of the building was devoted to rooms designed for presenting sacred ordinances. Hence, these were the first temples to include creation, garden, world, terrestrial, and celestial rooms. The construction of these temples was a major focus of the Church during the later 1870s and the 1880s.

A Temple in Cache Valley

Speaking at Wellsville on July 4, 1857, John Thirkill, a convert from England, prophesied that a temple would be built on the east bench.[10] The settlement of Logan at that location would not begin until two years later. Then, in 1863, President Brigham Young and a number of other General Authorities visited Cache Valley. Preaching at the bowery in Logan on August 22, Elder Wilford Woodruff was impressed to direct his remarks particularly to the youth: "You will have the privilege of going into the tower of a glorious temple built unto the name of the most high God, east of us upon the Logan Bench." President Young then testified that what Elder Woodruff had said was revelation.[11]

Ground was broken May 18, 1877, by President Brigham Young and a large group of other general and local Church leaders. Four inches of snow had fallen during the previous night, and the day was brisk yet sunny. Someone in the congregation placed his coat on the ground so that Elder Orson Pratt would not have to kneel in the mud and snow as he offered the prayer dedicating the site.[12] Following the prayer, President Young reminded the Saints that the temple would be constructed by volunteer labor and that "wages are entirely out of the question." Nevertheless, the temple can be built "without any burden to ourselves," he insisted, "if our hearts are in the work, and we will be blessed abundantly in doing so. We will be better off in our temporal affairs when it is completed than when we commenced." Speaking on this same occasion, Elder John Taylor quoted Jacob's affirmation that "this is none other but the house of God, and this is the gate of heaven" (Genesis 28:17). "That is not simply a metaphorical expression, but a reality," Elder Taylor insisted, "for it is in [temples] that the most sacred ordinances of God are to be performed, which are associated with the interest and happiness of the human family, living and dead."[13]

Construction got under way immediately. Only two feet of dirt had to be excavated in order to reach bedrock. By September the seven-foot-wide foundations were in place, and the temple's cornerstones were laid on the seventeenth of that month, just over three weeks following President Young's death. The southeast or chief cornerstone was laid by the Twelve, who were then the presiding quorum in the Church. The other cornerstones were laid at the southwest by Presiding Bishop Edward Hunter, who represented the Lesser Priesthood; at the northwest by the high priests; and at the northeast by the seventies and elders.

Elder Wilford Woodruff testified that a host of departed spirits were "witnessing these proceedings [even] more intently and anxiously" than the ten thousand Saints who were physically present, "for they well know in their prison homes that their salvation depends upon these things."[14]

Charles O. Card was named superintendent of construction, and during the next several years over two hundred men were almost constantly engaged in building the temple. Many were volunteers from the various towns in the area, each coming when assigned to donate his skill as a mason, carpenter, plasterer, or in some other way to help build the house of the Lord. For example, each Monday morning Julius Smith left his large family at their small farm near Brigham City and hiked over the mountain about twenty miles to Logan. Although he was a slender man just over five feet tall, he worked all week carrying heavy loads of mortar or plaster up ladders to the workmen. After finishing his work on Saturdays, he walked back home in order to spend Sundays with his family.[15]

Of the more than $600,000 contributed for the Logan Temple, only a relatively small amount, $93,000, was donated in cash. The remainder came in a variety of forms: $30,000 in merchandise, $30,000 in livestock, $71,000 in produce, and $3,000 in wagons and teams. The equivalent of $380,000 was donated in the form of labor (using the prevailing wage rate of $1.50 per man per day). Over 60 percent came from the Saints within the Logan Temple district.[16] Those who worked on the temple received food, clothing, livestock, or other items donated by the wards and stakes in the area. In Bear Lake Valley, for example, all the eggs laid on Sundays were donated for the temple. Some Saints even donated some of their hair to strengthen the plaster in at least two of the sacred rooms. Children of the Cache Stake contributed $2,300 toward the temple by means of a Sunday School "nickel fund." One day a young boy attempted to climb the scaffolding to have a close look at the temple, but was stopped by a guard. Permission was granted when he explained that he "had paid his nickel to the temple" and therefore felt he had a right to see it.[17]

The Saints established their own quarries, sawmills, mechanical shops, and other facilities in order to supply as many materials as they could for the temple without having to use their scarce finances to purchase goods elsewhere. The temple's construction had a far-reaching impact on the development of the whole area. "One can hardly distinguish the building of the...temple from the general building of the community," historians have concluded. "The network of temple industries not only supplied the temple itself but provided material for the construction of homes, barns, and shops." Skills learned by those working on the temple subsequently aided the construction of other important buildings in the area.[18]

Even the heavy snows of Cache Valley winters did not halt work on the temple. More volunteer labor was available at this time of the year, so stone, lumber, and other supplies were made ready for the coming building season. After the roof was completed in 1881, work on the temple's interior could move forward throughout the year. In about 1882 the temple's dark gray limestone exterior was painted white. This outside paint scheme was maintained until about the turn of the century, after which the temple's stone was allowed to weather back to its original color.

The supply of commercially produced carpeting in Utah Territory was not adequate to meet the temple's needs. Just two months before the dedication, the sisters in the temple district received the overwhelming assignment to produce the needed floor coverings. They worked energetically collecting rags, tearing them into strips, matching colors, and then stitching together the carpets. By the time ordinance work began,

Logan Temple

the women had produced over two thousand square yards of finely
woven rag carpeting.[19]

The Logan Temple Dedicated

Dedication was set for May 17, 1884, and was planned to coincide
with the conference of the Cache Stake. This weekend would mark the
seventh anniversary of ground-breaking for the temple. The railroad
offered special excursion rates, so large crowds were anticipated for the
events in Logan. The Saints opened their homes, and local Church leaders
arranged to feed the crowds; as a result none of the visitors had to pay
anything for meals or lodging. Because not all could be accommodated
inside the temple during the dedicatory services, bishops were instructed
to issue tickets only to those who were worthy to be admitted into the
Lord's house.[20] These tickets were personally countersigned by President
John Taylor. This was the first time invitations of this kind were used at
a temple dedication.

The temple's large east doors were opened promptly at ten o'clock
Saturday morning, May 17. The approximately fifteen hundred Saints
bearing tickets to this first dedicatory session climbed the winding
corner stairways to the large upper assembly room. The first speaker
was President George Q. Cannon of the First Presidency. "Heaven itself
and our co-workers of the past are delighted with the accomplishment
of this temple," he declared. "We are the representatives of the ages....
How boundless should be our gratitude that we are permitted to officiate in the ordinances that will save those who have gone before us."
Elder Wilford Woodruff also testified that "the spirits of Elias, Elijah
and other holy men of old are hovering over us and are ready to aid us
in any way that is possible." He declared that Joseph Smith, Brigham
Young, and the Savior were especially interested in the dedication of
this temple, and that "if the veil were taken from our eyes we would
behold their faces.... God and the heavens are with us today and the
Lord is pleased with our labors."[21]

At the conclusion of this dedicatory service, those in attendance were
permitted to see other parts of the temple. Led in a procession by

Presidents Taylor and Cannon, who were followed by other Church officials, they walked quietly two by two through the various rooms in the building. As they exited the building, they were greeted by the music of brass bands from Logan and Tooele (the latter having traveled about one hundred miles to be present for this occasion).

A session of stake conference convened Saturday afternoon in the Logan Tabernacle, about two blocks from the temple. Speaking in this service Elder Franklin D. Richards of the Quorum of the Twelve referred to the importance of the occasion: "The dedication of the Temple this morning awakens anew in our souls a heavenly, family feeling." Our interest extends beyond this earth to those who are in the spirit world, he explained, and "inspires a feeling that we are part of them and that they are part of us." On such occasions by the power of faith we view "that portion of the family of God with whom we have before associated, and with whom we expect hereafter to be associated."[22]

To accommodate others who wished to attend, additional dedicatory sessions were scheduled for Sunday and Monday, and about 3,500 more tickets were issued. At one of the three dedicatory sessions, President John Taylor and Charles O. Card stood at the top of the stairs as the throngs were surging into the assembly room. President Taylor noticed a woman whom he did not know, but instructed Brother Card, "Don't let that woman come into the assembly, she is not worthy." When asked for an explanation, President Taylor replied: "I know not but the Spirit of God said, 'She is not worthy.'" Brother Card therefore told the woman she would have to leave. She offered no resistance. When questioned about the matter, she admitted that she had not been able to get a recommend from her bishop, but had purchased one for a dollar from a man on the street.[23]

President John Taylor had also been guided by inspiration in the selection of the first president for the Logan Temple. Several prominent men were under consideration, but because of some prejudiced reports about Marriner W. Merrill, he was not included among the candidates. However, as President Taylor earnestly prayed for guidance, "a voice seemed to say that the man for the post was Bishop Merrill of Richmond." Because of the reports he had received, the president questioned this impression, so he prayed on. "Then there came the distinct and unmistakable impression of a voice, 'Bishop Merrill of Richmond.'" That settled the matter, and Merrill was chosen as temple president. Just five years later he also was called as a member of the Quorum of the Twelve, and he continued to serve in both positions until his death in 1906.[24]

At the time of the dedication, President Taylor gave instructions concerning the selection of workers for the temple. With the exception of about six who would need to be employed on a permanent basis, men and women should be chosen "who can leave their farms for a season and supply their own necessities for living and doing their work without being dependent on the Temple for their sustenance." These workers should be prepared to stay "as long as shall be needed," from six months to three years. They were to serve much on the same basis as missionaries to the living. President Taylor instructed that this pattern was also to be implemented at St. George and in all other temples.[25] Two years earlier a group of nine key individuals had been asked to spend several months in St. George working in the temple in order to learn essential procedures. While on this assignment these individuals were supported by their home wards.

The first ordinances were performed two days after the dedication, under the personal supervision of the General Authorities who were present. Before leaving Logan, President Taylor instructed that the following be placed in the official temple records:

> The Lord is well pleased and has accepted this House, and our labors in its Dedication, also the labors of the people in its building and beautifying.... I state this as the Word of the Lord. And the Lord will continue to reveal unto us every principle that shall be necessary for our guidance in the future in all matters pertaining to our labors both spiritually and temporally.[26]

Site Selected for the Manti Temple

Although construction on the Manti Temple did not commence until the later 1870s, the idea of a temple in the Sanpete Valley began much earlier. Manti, founded in 1849, was the fourth settlement established by the pioneers in the Rocky Mountains—only Salt Lake City, Ogden, and

Provo preceded it. When the residents of Manti laid out a fifty-nine-acre fort in 1854, they identified a central block as the site for a future temple. At about this same time President Heber C. Kimball prophesied that the temple would be built on the hill above Manti. "And more than that," he continued, "the rock will be quarried from that hill to build it with, and some of the stone from that quarry will be taken to help complete the Salt Lake Temple."

President Kimball's prophecy would be fulfilled completely, as stone from Manti was used for decorative tablets at the east and west ends of the Salt Lake Temple.[27]

As early as December 4, 1873 at a conference in Ephraim, President Brigham Young announced that the temple in Sanpete Valley would be built soon; while in the area he made some preliminary investigations of possible sites and available materials. By this time, Ephraim, located seven miles north of Manti, had become the principal settlement in the valley. Hence a controversy arose over where the temple should be built. People in Manti advocated a site in or just above town, while the residents of Ephraim believed the temple should be located in their community. This matter was decided at another conference in Ephraim on June 25, 1875, when President Young declared that the temple would be built at the "Manti stone quarry."[28]

This was where the first settlers had lived in "dugouts" on the side of the rattlesnake-infested hill during the winter of 1849-1850. A large stone from this same quarry had been Utah Territory's contribution to the Washington Monument at the nation's capital. Carved by William Ward, the slab bore a beehive, the "all-seeing eye," and the name "Deseret." The rock at Manti, known as oolite, is of a warm cream color.

Initially Joseph A. Young was appointed to design the temple, but, following his death only a few months later, William H. Folsom received the assignment as temple architect and superintendent of construction. His work was to be supervised by a committee composed of three members of the Twelve—Elders Wilford Woodruff, Orson Hyde, and Erastus Snow.

On his way back to Salt Lake City from the St. George Temple dedication, President Brigham Young stopped in Manti to dedicate the temple site there. He arrived April 24, 1877, and on that same afternoon he personally supervised the work of William Folsom and Truman O. Angell Jr.

as they surveyed the site and set stakes. During a stake conference meeting the following morning, Brigham Young unexpectedly stood up and left. He asked Warren S. Snow to go with him to the temple hill. Snow recalled that they proceeded to the southeast corner of where the temple would stand. "Here is the spot where the Prophet Moroni stood and dedicated this piece of land for a Temple site," President Young affirmed, "and that is the reason why the location is made here, and we can't move it from this spot; and if you and I are the only persons that come here at high noon today, we will dedicate this ground." [29] Apparently the matter of the temple's location had not been fully resolved among local residents even yet. Nevertheless, several hundred were present at the appointed hour.

When President Brigham Young dedicated the site for the Manti Temple, he exhorted the people to labor on the temple with "clean hands and pure hearts" so that they might be worthy to receive blessings in the temple and to officiate in behalf of their dead. He explained that the women could assist by giving encouragement to their husbands and sons and by making clothing for those working on the temple. He instructed bishops in the area to have men and their teams come and prepare the site for construction. He hoped that from fifty to one hundred would respond, and explained that they could be rotated as often as necessary. "Now, Bishops," President Young concluded, "if any person should inquire what wages is to be paid for work done on the temple, let the answer be, 'Not one dime.' And when the temple is completed, we will work in God's holy house without inquiring what we are going to get, or who is going to pay us, but we will trust in the Lord for our reward, and he will not forget us." [30]

Construction Begins

Only five days later, some one hundred men with their teams from Manti and surrounding communities reported to the temple site at 8:00 A.M. After kneeling in prayer, they commenced the work of excavation. Work on the hillside was discouragingly slow. Explosions shattered the stillness of the rural valley as men worked to provide a level building site for the temple. In the last blast on June 27, 1878, for example, 875 pounds of powder threw out over 4,600 cubic yards of rock and debris. By the end of the year rough retaining walls were completed, and material removed from the hill had been graded to form four terraces nearly a quarter-mile long. A level plot, about sixty feet above the road at the base of the hill, was now ready for temple construction to begin in the spring.

Cornerstones were laid on April 14, 1879. A steady rain fell during most of the morning on the appointed day, but the sun broke through as about four thousand Saints gathered for the 11:30 service. As the Stars and Stripes fluttered overhead, the southeast cornerstone with its zinc box containing historical memorabilia was laid by William Folsom under the personal supervision of President John Taylor of the Quorum of the Twelve, who also spoke. The Presiding Bishop, representing the Aaronic priesthood, laid the southwest cornerstone. The presidency of the high priests and seventies laid the northwest and northeast cornerstones respectively. The two-hour service featured other talks by General Authorities as well as music provided by the Manti choir and by a band from Nephi. As the last Saints left the hill, the rains began to fall again.[31]

Many people became involved in raising funds for the temple. A dramatic company put on two performances, donating half of their proceeds. Two brethren were appointed to travel from settlement to settlement soliciting funds. Beaver, over a hundred miles from Manti, contributed $1,500. Only a small fraction, however, less than 4 percent, of the donations came in the form of cash. Most contributions were commodities including beef, chickens, wheat, flour, quilts, shoes, socks, overalls, and other items of clothing. Children gleaned wheat from which their mothers made bread for the workmen. A young father gave his only cow even though his small children needed the milk; soon afterwards, however, a bachelor neighbor offered to provide from his own cow all the milk the little family needed. The Greenwood United Order provided a wagonload of butter. Such supplies were distributed to the workmen through the local bishop's "tithing office."

Almost all the materials needed for the temple were donated or produced locally. A few items, however, had to be shipped in from the East. Nails were particularly scarce; twenty pounds of nails cost sixty dollars. (At this time one hundred pounds of flour sold for only two dollars.) Glass was sent from New York to California by ship, and then had to be carried carefully by wagon across the desert.[32]

Stake President Canute Petersen became the assistant superintendent of construction with the specific assignment to promote and coordinate the donation of material and labor. Under the direction of his wife, Sarah, women of the Relief Society made cheese and donated "temple eggs"; many were convinced that their hens laid twice as many eggs on Sunday for the temple as on any other day of the week. As had been done for the Logan Temple, these women wove hundreds of yards of carpet.[33]

Construction on the temple progressed slowly because most of the work had to be done by hand. Lumber from the surrounding mountains was delivered to the site during the winter, when the normally muddy roads were frozen and hence in the best condition and when the men were free from farm work. Craftsmen shaping stones for the walls used hammers and chisels and took particular pride in their work. Once when master mason Edward Parry noticed a slightly cracked stone about to be placed in the wall, the workman said that the little crack would make no difference and, being on the inside, would never be seen. Parry, however, insisted that the flaw would be known by three people—"you, me, and the Lord." The stone was replaced.[34] By April 1882 the walls reached the height of fifty feet.

A concern for excellence also motivated those who accomplished the intricate wood carving in the temple. "When I see the Terrestrial Room," a woodworker later remarked, "a feeling of deep reverence comes over me as I imagine myself attempting the pieces of wood work there. These men were inspired with a higher cause."[35] The unique spiral stairways in the two west corner towers are an outstanding example of pioneer craftsmanship. Unlike most spiral staircases, which wind around a central support column, those in Manti are open in the center. Even though the temple's floors are not all the same distance apart, each story is reached by one complete revolution of the stairway. The difficult curved panels and perfectly executed curved banisters of imported black walnut are a marvel of woodworking.[36]

Temple workmen believed they had divine assistance and protection while building the temple. Joseph Taylor, who kept a record of the hours each man worked, made his rounds in the same sequence day after day. On one occasion, however, he felt prompted to visit the stone quarry earlier than usual; just after he had called the workmen to come out and check in with him, an overhanging ledge caved in. Had Taylor arrived at his accustomed time, the men in the quarry undoubtedly would have been crushed by the falling rock.[37]

The temple was nearing completion when President John Taylor died in the summer of 1887. That fall President Wilford Woodruff, his successor, advised Church members that the Manti Temple was ready for its interior furnishings and invited the Saints to make their last donations toward the completion of this temple. Contributions poured in from many locations in Utah and Idaho and from such far-flung places as England, Germany, Switzerland, and the Sandwich Islands, Hundreds of Saints responded, most donations ranging from twenty-five cents to five dollars.

Manti Temple

Private and Public Dedications

The public dedication of the Manti Temple was scheduled to begin on Monday, May 21, 1888. However, because of the bitter anti-Mormon persecution then raging, primarily over the issue of plural marriage, most of the General Authorities were forced to remain in secluded "retirement" on the "underground." Hence a private dedicatory service was scheduled a few days earlier. President Wilford Woodruff left Salt Lake City Sunday night and traveled by private railroad car to Nephi. There he remained in seclusion until the following night, when he journeyed by carriage across the mountain to Manti, arriving at 1:00 A.M. on Tuesday. He remained in the temple the next few days conferring with local officials and naming Daniel H. Wells, formerly a counselor to Brigham Young, to be the temple's first president. In the presence of only a few General Authorities and other invited guests, President Woodruff offered the dedicatory prayer at noon on Thursday, May 17.

Before leaving the temple on Friday, President Woodruff "consecrated upon the Altar [the] seers Stone that Joseph Smith found by revelation [and which was] carried by him through life."[38]

On Saturday and Sunday the roads leading to Manti were clogged with teams and wagons bringing people to the public dedication. Early Monday morning the Saints began to gather on the hill east of the temple, from which they would be admitted into the building, "and by 9:30 the grounds were black with people." The doors were opened at 10:00 and the service began at 11:00. Elder Lorenzo Snow presided. He reminded the congregation that the dedicatory prayer for the Kirtland Temple had been given by revelation. "So the prayer we are now about to offer up," he testified, "was written and inspired by holy men of God in our day." The prayer referred to existing difficulties and petitioned: "As thou hast in the past overruled the violence of mobs and the cruelty of the wicked for the glory of thy name and the salvation of thy people, we ask thee, Righteous Father, to so control this present persecution that thy purposes may be accomplished in the redemption of thy Zion."[39]

Following the prayer, the choir sang the "Dedication Hymn," the words having been composed by Charles Walker especially for the occasion:

Righteous God th'eternal Father
  Lend Thine ear, accept our praise,
While we dedicate this Temple
  Reared to Thee in latter days.
Let Thy blessings rest upon it,
  Hallow now this sacred shrine,
Fill its courts with joy and gladness,
  Holy Father, it is Thine.

Rays of sunshine pierce the prison,
  Jesus lighten up the gloom,
Millions hail the joyful tidings,
  Vict'ry o'er death, hell and tomb.
Oh what rapture fills the captive!
  Christ hath crushed the serpent's head,
And another House erected,
  Links the living with the dead.

Oh how anxious souls are waiting,
  Eager watching for the day,
When kind friends on earth will save them,
  In God's own appointed way.
Let no loved one's spirit linger,
  Loose the bands, we have the keys;
Christ hath wrought for all a ransom,
  And will grant them sweet release.[40]

Once again the solemn shout of Hosannas accompanied the presentation of yet another temple to the Lord.

Several members of the Twelve addressed the congregation, expressing gratitude for the plan of salvation and for sacred temple ordinances that extend its blessings to the millions who died without the opportunity of accepting the gospel on earth. "The erecting of [a] Temple," Elder Franklin D. Richards declared, "was a matter of as much interest and concern to those who had passed behind the veil as to the living." Ever since the site for the Manti Temple had been selected "they had watched with anxiety for its completion."[41] This service continued until 3:00 P.M.

Similar services convened on the following two days, with from 1,500 to 1,700 in attendance. In each the dedicatory prayer and Hosanna Shout were repeated, and other members of the Twelve addressed the congregation. Following each session, those in attendance were given the privilege of walking two by two through the various rooms of the temple, as had been done at Logan. In the evening of the first day, children too young to attend one of the regular dedicatory services were invited to tour the temple.

Remarkable spiritual experiences accompanied these memorable dedicatory services. The Church's *Millennial Star* reported:

> On the 21st of May. before the opening exercises commenced, Brother A.C. Smyth, the chorister, seated himself at the organ, and rendered a piece of sacred music, a selection from Mendelssohn, at the conclusion of which, persons sitting near the centre of the hall. and also on the stand at the west end, heard most heavenly voices and singing—it sounded to them most angelic, and appeared to be behind and above them, and they turned their heads in the direction of the sound, wondering if there was another choir in some other part of the Temple.

There was no other choir. Then, several of the Saints beheld departed Church leaders during the services. Typical of several accounts published in the same article in the *Millennial Star* were these:

> On the 22nd of May, when Brother John W. Taylor was speaking, a bright halo surrounded him, and in that halo the personages of Presidents Brigham Young, John Taylor, and a third personage, whom she believed to be the Prophet Joseph, were seen by Sister Emma G. Bull, of Salt Lake City; also the personage of Brother Jedediah M. Grant was seen by her standing by his son, Brother Heber J. Grant, looking towards him while he was speaking; they were surrounded by a bright halo.... On the 23rd...I was sitting at the foot of the east stand, taking notes of the services; I looked up while Brother Heber J. Grant was speaking, and saw a bright halo surrounding him, which swayed to and fro as he moved his body. I laid down my pencil and gazed steadily at him for a few moments.[42]

In summarizing its account, the *Star* affirmed: "The Saints enjoyed a spiritual feast extending over the three days and many shed tears of joy while listening to the testimonies and admonitions of the servants of God. There can be no question but that God has accepted the Manti Temple at the hands of His Saints."[43]

"When we dedicated the Temple at Manti," Elder Franklin D. Richards of the Quorum of the Twelve recalled a few years later, "there were many brethren and sisters that saw the presence of spiritual beings, which could only be discerned by the eyes of the inner man. The prophets Joseph, Hyrum, Brigham, and various other Apostles that have gone, were seen; and not only so, but the ears of many of the faithful were touched, and they heard the music of the heavenly choir that was there."[44]

Yet another spiritual manifestation occurred the day following the temple's dedication. That night when a pounding rain hit the building, custodian Peter Alstrom ran to close a window. "Opening the door of the sealing room he was surprised to see, standing above the altar, a personage clothed in white robes, a brilliant light surrounding him and filling the whole room." Upon hearing about this, temple president Daniel H. Wells replied, "that there are angels in this place we can have no doubt, but it is not given to every one to see them."[45]

While these remarkable experiences were transpiring in Manti, the Saints in the Salt Lake area were eagerly anticipating the completion of the great temple there.

Chapter Six

The Salt Lake Temple Completed

Even though the construction and dedication of the temples at St. George, Logan, and Manti attracted a great deal of attention and placed substantial demands on the people's energies and resources, the Saints never lost sight of the objective of erecting a great temple at Church headquarters in Salt Lake City. Even during the years when the army was in Utah and the Salt Lake Temple's foundation was covered with dirt, draftsmen in the architect's office were busy planning the exact size and shape for each of the thousands of stones that would be needed for the temple.

Construction Accelerates

As construction resumed, an immediate need was to obtain granite from the mountains southeast of the city. Generally, it was not necessary to quarry the rock from the mountainsides because huge granite boulders were strewn thickly along the canyon floor. Using hammers, chisels, and sometimes explosives, the workmen split these boulders into the specified sizes and shapes. The work moved slowly because there were only a few stone cutters with sufficient skill. These men worked grueling ten-hour days beginning at 7:00 A.M., but they took time for prayer and for spiritual discussions in the evenings. As the work expanded, a village of small cottages sprang up in a beautiful grove of trees near the canyon's mouth.

Transporting the granite some twenty miles from the quarry to Temple Square posed a major challenge. From four to six oxen toiling to pull a heavy wagon hauling only a single monstrous stone, or perhaps two medium ones, was a common sight on the streets of Salt Lake City in the 1860s. Some of the individual stones for the temple weighed as much as three tons. Special low-slung wagons were designed to facilitate loading and unloading. The journey from the quarry took three to four days. As a result, progress on the temple seemed to be painfully slow. As late as 1867 the walls were still below ground level. Construction on a canal began, but the necessity of crossing uneven terrain and several canyon streams proved to be an insurmountable barrier. Hence this project was never completed. A further slowdown occurred in 1868 when workmen were diverted from the temple to help finish the transcontinental railroad. Nevertheless the coming of the railroad ultimately would expedite temple construction in a significant way.

The transcontinental rail line was completed through Ogden in 1869, and the following year a branch line reached Salt Lake City. During the early 1870s tracks of the Utah Southern (later part of the Union Pacific) pushed southward toward Utah Valley. Rather than following a direct route, they were swung to the southeast in order to pass closer to the temple quarry. In 1873 a spur was constructed from the main line at Sandy Station to the quarry a few miles to the east. A connection was also made downtown with streetcar tracks from which a rail spur was constructed through the south gate into the temple block. Because these tracks were light weight, the loaded rail cars had to be pulled by horses the final four blocks along South Temple Street.

A short time later the tracks along South Temple were replaced with a heavier rail, and steam locomotives took the place of the horses. At the time of President Brigham Young's death in 1877 the temple walls were still only twenty feet high, just above the level of the first floor. Thus most of the temple's construction was yet to be accomplished, even though twenty-four

Salt Lake Temple Under Construction

the forty years' building period had already passed. During the next few years, however, with the problems of transportation resolved, the pace would accelerate considerably.

Derricks were constructed in each of the temple's four corners to lift the heavy stones into place. Unfortunately there was only one steam hoisting engine available. It powered the derrick in one corner to lay five courses, or levels, of rock before moving on to the next corner. With the completion of the Logan temple in 1884 a second engine became available, so construction moved more quickly. The structure was very solid, because the builders recalled that President Young had expressed the desire that this temple would stand through the Millennium. Even at their tops, the walls were six feet thick, and the granite blocks were individually and skillfully shaped to fit snugly together. Nearly a century later Elder Mark E. Petersen attested to the soundness of the temple's construction. He was in the temple when a rather severe earthquake hit, damaging several buildings around the Salt Lake Valley. "As I sat there in that temple I could feel the sway of the quake and that whole building groaned." Afterwards, he recalled, the engineers "could not find one semblance of damage" anywhere in the temple.[1]

Many people contributed to the temple's construction either directly or indirectly. Under the concept of "labor tithing," able-bodied men were asked to donate one day in ten to working on the temple. Wards in the area were assigned in rotation to provide workmen a week at a time. The women assisted by washing and mending clothing for the workmen and by teaching the children of those working on the temple. President Heber C. Kimball had admonished the sisters to give up costly jewelry and fancy hair ornaments in order to donate to the temple fund.[2] Priesthood quorums as well as individuals with means hired mechanics to work on the temple. During the 1880s each ward was expected to maintain one workman in the quarry. "As a boy," President Heber J. Grant recalled many years later, "I paid twenty-five-cents regularly to help in the erection of the Salt Lake Temple. Subsequently, as my wages became more, I increased my contribution."[3]

James B. Wilson was typical of the many who contributed to the temple's construction. As a school teacher his monthly salary was meager, so he had almost no cash to pay his tithing. "I finally decided to give the Church one of the two oxen I had in spite of the fact that it would break a wonderful team." Shortly afterwards he happened to pass by the temple block. "I noticed two fine oxen working on a drag which moved the giant blocks about. I was so interested in them that I moved closer for a better view and discovered one of them as my favorite ox, fattened and in perfect condition. I then fully appreciated the significance of tithing. I was building the temple with my ox."[4]

The temple's exterior walls were nearing completion in the mid-1880s when the architects proposed significant changes for the interior. With his responsibilities for the Logan Temple finished in 1884, Truman O. Angell Jr. turned his attention to assisting his elderly father in completing drawings for the Salt Lake Temple. Early the following year he proposed that rather than having two large assembly rooms with elliptical ceilings, as had been the case in Nauvoo, the Salt Lake Temple should follow the pattern that Presidents Young and Taylor had already approved for Logan and Manti. There would be only one assembly room, on the upper floor, and it would have balconies under the elliptical windows along each side. The temple's main floor would contain spacious rooms for presenting the endowment, while an intermediate floor would provide smaller council rooms for the use of various priesthood groups. This plan would accommodate three hundred persons in the endowment sessions, more than twice the number that could be served in the basement under the original arrangement.

Truman O. Angell Sr. however, urged President Taylor to finish the temple according to the original plans. No final decision was made prior to President Taylor's death in July of 1887. Although the general features of the younger Angell's proposal were eventually adopted, none of his plans were followed exactly. The final plans for the temple appear to have been drawn under President Wilford Woodruff's direction by Joseph Don Carlos Young, who became Church architect in 1890—just three years before the temple's completion.[5] It is evident, therefore, that most of the work on the temple's interior must have been accomplished during these last few years of construction.

The Impact of Revived Persecution

Before his death in 1868, Heber C. Kimball had prophesied that "when [the Salt Lake Temple's] walls reached the square the powers of evil would rage and the Saints would suffer persecution."[6] This point was reached in 1885, when the main walls of the temple, excluding the towers, were completed.

Three years earlier Congress had enacted the Edmunds Anti-Bigamy law, which defined "polygamist cohabitation" as a crime, punishable by stiff fines and prison sentences. Thus the stage was set for the anti-Mormon crusade that raged during the mid-1880s. Dozens of Church members, including many general and local leaders, were imprisoned "for conscience' sake." Others found it necessary to withdraw into "retirement" or to go "on the underground." Between 1885 and 1887 general conferences were held at locations away from Salt Lake City, and members of the First Presidency did not appear in public for several years.

There were fears that government officials might attempt to confiscate property held by the Church, even including the temples. To avert this, President John Taylor directed the formation of the independent nonprofit Logan, Manti, and St. George temple associations to hold the titles of these sacred buildings and related properties. Similarly, the Salt Lake Literary and Scientific Association received title to property facing the temple block, including the Council House and Deseret Museum.[7] These unique arrangements would continue into the early years of the twentieth century.

The Logan Temple Association served another function as well. In his 1884 dedicatory prayer President John Taylor had petitioned that, consistent with instructions in the Doctrine and Covenants (88:76-80, 117-119), the Logan Temple "may be indeed a house of learning under Thy guidance, direction and inspiration."[8] In that same year President Taylor suggested that Church leaders in Logan follow the pattern set by the Prophet Joseph Smith in Kirtland and make the temple a "house of learning" as well as a "house of God." Therefore the association not only received title to the temple but also sponsored monthly lectures in such subjects as theology, civil government, languages, history, natural science, and economics. There was no charge, but only those holding temple recommends could attend. An average of about one hundred persons attended each of these lectures, which convened in the temple recorder's room on the first Saturday afternoon of the month.[9]

Following passage of the yet harsher Edmund-Tucker Law in 1887, government officials seized the partially completed Salt Lake Temple even though the law specifically exempted houses of worship from such action. This stopped work on the building only temporarily. The Church appealed the seizure but was required to pay one dollar per month for the use of the property. This amount was minimal, but the requirement was intended to be humiliating. The Saints' enemies boasted that the Mormons would never be allowed to finish the temple, but that the "gentiles" would complete the building for their own purposes. Eventually, however, the Church's efforts were successful, and by October 1891 the title to Temple Square was regained.[10] These events underscored the difficult circumstances through which the Church and its members had passed.

The Capstone Celebration

During the dark days of persecution, completing the Salt Lake Temple was one bright objective around which the Saints could and did rally. They took courage as they saw the great temple nearing completion despite tremendous difficulties. Finally the decision was made to lay the uppermost stone on the temple in connection with the sixty-second annual general conference in 1892. "As the sixth of April drew near," one observer recorded, "the joy which swept over the hearts of the Saints was visible.... It was to them a day of triumph for which they had patiently toiled, many of them the greater part of a lifetime."[11]

On Wednesday morning, April 6, the Saints congregated in the Tabernacle for the concluding conference session. President Wilford Woodruff urged the speedy completion of the temple, declaring that "this is the most important work that we have upon our hands."[12] At eleven-thirty the meeting closed, and the congregation, which had been seated by quorums, moved out onto the grounds. As the band played "The Capstone March," they gathered south of the temple. An estimated forty thousand people crowded into Temple Square, while an additional ten thousand filled the surrounding streets or watched from windows and the roofs of adjacent buildings. This was the largest group of Saints to be met in one place so far in the history of the Church. With the flag waving overhead, general and stake authorities took their places on an eight-foot-high stand constructed for the occasion.

Promptly at high noon President Woodruff stepped to the podium, raised "both hands to heaven," and proclaimed in a loud voice: "Hearken all ye House of Israel and All Ye Nations of the Earth, we will now lay the top stone of the Temple of our God!" The official capstone was the upper half of the round ball atop the east center spire. It had been hollowed out to accommodate selected books and other historical mementos. President Woodruff pressed a button on the stand, and an electrically operated device lowered the capstone slowly and securely. As the stone descended into place, Elder Lorenzo Snow led the "Hosanna Shout," thousands of white handkerchiefs waving in unison. From high up on the temple, architect Joseph Don Carlos Young called out: "The capstone is duly laid!" With great emotion the fifty thousand assembled Saints joined in singing "The Spirit of God Like a Fire Is Burning." Following this service, the multitude lingered, not wanting to give up the spirit of the occasion.[13] Later that after-noon the statue of the angel Moroni was hoisted to its position on top of the capstone. The twelve-and-one-half-foot-tall figure of hammered copper

The Capstone Shout

had been prepared in Salem, Ohio, from a model by Utah sculptor C. E. Dallin. Unveiled at ceremonies at 3:00 P.M., its gold-leaf surface gleamed in the sun. The statue was of a heavenly herald sounding his trumpet, representing the latter-day fulfillment of John's prophecy of an angel bringing "the everlasting gospel to preach unto them that dwell on the earth, and to every nation, and kindred, and tongue, and people" (Revelation 14:6).

Symbolism of the Temple's Exterior

With the statue of the angel Moroni in place, the Salt Lake Temple appeared, at least from the outside, to be virtually completed. Its architecture was a blend of the castellated style with the Romanesque or "Round Gothic." Several unique features of the temple's exterior were apparent. As had been the case in ancient times, the physical arrangement was calculated to teach important lessons. The intent of the temple's design, one architectural historian has observed, was "to aid man in his quest to gain entrance back into the presence of God from whence he came."[14]

William Ward, who had a key role in drafting the plans for the temple, testified that the basic concept of the building's design had not come from the architects. Writing in the *Deseret News* in 1892, just a few days after the capstone had been laid, he recalled:

> Brigham Young drew upon a slate in the architects office a sketch, and said to Truman O. Angell: "there will be three towers on the east, representing the President and his two counselors; also three similar towers on the west representing the Presiding Bishop and his two counselors; the towers on the east, the Melchizedek Priesthood, those on the west the Aaronic Priesthood. The centre towers will be higher than those on the sides, and the west towers a little lower than those on the east end. The body of the building will be between these."[15]

As was the case with the Nauvoo Temple, special ornamental stones were an important feature of the Salt Lake Temple's exterior. An "earth stone" formed the base of each of the temple's fifty buttresses. These were the largest stones in the temple, weighing over six thousand pounds and having on their face a representation of the globe four feet in diameter. These stones depicted various parts of the world, serving as a reminder, architect Angell explained, that the gospel message had to go to all the earth.[16] Each buttress had a "moon stone" about half-way up, and a "sun stone" near its top. These, together with the numerous "star stones," recall the three degrees of glory described by Paul and explained in latter-day revelation. (See 1 Corinthians 15:40-42 and D&C section 76.)

An interesting feature of the temple's moon stones is often overlooked. Proceeding from right to left, they successively represent the moon's new, first-quarter, full, and third-quarter phases. Since the fifty buttresses cannot be divided evenly by these four phases, at some point the cycle must inevitably be interrupted. This break occurs on the north wall. If the date of January 1 is assigned to the new moon immediately after this break, dates can also be assigned to each of the succeeding phases. The right buttress on the face of the temple's main east center tower would represent April 6. Gilded letters on this same tower identify April 6 as the date of the Church's organization and of the temple's dedication.[17]

The buttresses of the east center tower also include "cloud stones" showing rays of sunlight penetrating through the clouds. These are representations of the gospel light piercing the dark clouds of superstition and error (see Isaiah 60:2-3). On the same tower the keystone at the top of the lower large window depicts clasped hands. These are reminders of the power that comes from brotherly love and fellowship, and of the unity that must exist among those who would build Zion (see Galatians 2:9, Moses 7:18, and D&C 88:133). The keystone above the upper window depicts God's "all-seeing eye" which watches over both the righteous and the wicked (see Proverbs 15:3).[18]

Conspicuous above the windows on the west central tower is a representation of the Big Dipper, oriented in such a way that the two "pointer stars" at the end of the dipper point toward the north star. Architect Truman O. Angell Sr. explained that the message of this feature is that those who are lost may "find themselves" and "find their way" with the aid of the priesthood.[19] In more recent years, as Elder Harold B. Lee was introducing family home evening and other priesthood-centered programs, he referred to Angell's statement and likened it to the increasingly important role being given to the priesthood.[20]

The Final Years of Construction

At the capstone-laying ceremonies on April 6, 1892, Elder Francis M. Lyman of the Quorum of the Twelve issued a challenge to the vast multitude of Saints assembled for the occasion. He spoke to them of President Wilford Woodruff's desire to live long enough to dedicate the temple. He proposed a resolution that those present pledge to provide the funds necessary to complete the building so that it might be dedicated just one year later—the fortieth anniversary of the cornerstone laying. This proposition was adopted unanimously. Elder Lyman wanted to head the list of contributors, so he donated a thousand dollars on the spot.[21]

Fund-raising efforts received increased emphasis. The first Sunday in May was designated as a special fast day to thank God for his blessings and to ask for his help in completing the temple. (At this time the regular fast

day was on the first Thursday of each month; the change to Sunday would
not come until 1896.) The money collected on this special fast day went to
the temple fund. By October $175,000 was still needed to complete the
building, exclusive of furnishings. At this time a special meeting of priesthood leaders convened in the upper assembly room of the nearly completed
temple. When the need for funds was explained, those present pledged
some $50,000 within a few minutes.[22]

When the goal of completing the temple within one year was set,
most believed that the remaining work would take at least three more
years. In fact, as late as March 1893 many still wondered if the temple
could be finished by the following month. Nevertheless, those working
on the temple made a special effort to complete the project on time. One
of the workmen wrote in his diary: "Although sick, I felt strongly
impressed to go and do my very best." He also recalled a personal visit
by President Wilford Woodruff:

> President Woodruff called all of the workmen together. He said he had
> been told that some of the workmen had stated that it would be impos-
> sible to have the temple completed by April 6th. He said when he looked
> at this body of men he didn't believe a word of it. "Some of you may be
> sick and weak" (I thought he was talking to me) he continued, "Some of
> you may give out at night, but you will be here in the morning if you are
> faithful. You are not here by accident. You were ordained in the Eternal
> World to perform this work. Brethren I will be here April 6th to dedicate
> this building."[23]

After the placing of the capstone, visitors to Salt Lake City were
given the opportunity of touring the temple. Unfortunately, many did
not show proper appreciation for this privilege or respect for the temple.
Some broke off pieces of woodwork or defaced the walls by carving initials and scribbling graffiti. As the construction proceeded at an
increasingly feverish pace, the privilege of visiting the temple was soon
withdrawn.[24]

The temple was completed and ready for dedication by noon on April
5, 1893, just a few hours ahead of the deadline. Between three and five
o'clock that afternoon the temple was opened for the visit of prominent
non-Latter-day Saints of the area. Some six hundred responded to the
invitation, including clergymen, business and professional men, federal

Salt Lake Temple

officials, and their families. They were permitted to pass through every room in the temple from the basement to the roof and to examine any portion of the interior they desired. Qualified guides escorted them and answered their questions. Many expressed appreciation to the Church for this hospitable gesture.[25]

The Temple Dedicated

At last the long-anticipated day was at hand—the dedication of the great temple at Salt Lake City following a forty-year period of construction. Of those who had participated in the 1853 cornerstone-laying ceremonies, only a few were still living—one member of the high priests quorum presidency, and three members of the Twelve: Wilford Woodruff, Lorenzo Snow, and Franklin D. Richards. The temple's original architect, Truman O. Angell Sr. had died in 1887. The supervising architect at the time of dedication, Joseph Don Carlos Young, had been born in 1855, two years after construction had begun.[26] During this period, more than a generation had passed away.

In March of 1893 the First Presidency called on the Latter-day Saints to prepare for the temple's dedication by repenting of their sins, keeping all of God's commandments, and seeking forgiveness from one another. "None can for a moment doubt the extreme importance of every member of the congregation being at peace with all his or her brethren and sisters, and at peace with God."[27] At the sixty-third annual general conference, which convened in the Tabernacle on Tuesday and Wednesday, April 4 and 5, President Woodruff once again spoke of the need for spiritual preparation: "I have a desire in my heart that every one of you, the night before you go into the Temple, before retiring to rest, will go by your-selves in secret prayer...pray that your sins may not only be forgiven, but that you may all have the Spirit of God and the testimony of the Lord Jesus Christ; that the Spirit of God may be with those who assemble in that Temple."[28] Thus the dedication was to be a time for personal in-trospection and reformation.

Only worthy members holding a "recommend" signed by their local Church leaders were admitted. The Saints entered the temple through the southwest door, descended to the basement, and then walked through the various rooms on each floor before reaching the main upper assembly room. This room could accommodate about 2,250 persons in each dedica-tory session.

The first session, Thursday morning April 6, was for general and stake leaders and their families. The venerable President Wilford Woodruff, fol-lowed by the other General Authorities, led the group into the temple for this first session. This scene was compared to Joshua's leading the children of Israel into the promised land.[29]

The temple's dedication was a spiritual highlight for those who attended. The thirty-one dedicatory sessions, featuring music by special choirs and talks by the General Authorities, all were regarded as part of the Church's annual general conference. In each, the dedicatory prayer was followed by the unique "Hosanna Shout," led by Elder Lorenzo Snow. As the choirs sang the "Hosanna Anthem," composed by Evan Stephens espe-cially for this occasion, the congregation joined at the appropriate point with the traditional singing of "The Spirit of God." One Saint who had come from Arizona for the dedication was impressed when the vast congregation "spontaneously" arose as the choir began singing "The Spirit of God," the "melody seemingly enhanced by a heavenly choir." He noted that many commented on the Hosanna Shout being "commingled with the voices of angels."[30]

The temple's dedication was obviously an eagerly anticipated highlight in the life of President Wilford Woodruff, who regarded it as the fulfillment of prophetic dreams: "Near 50 years ago while in the city of Boston I had a vision of going with the Saints to the Rocky Mountains, building a Temple, and I dedicated it." Furthermore, "two nights in succession before John Taylor's death, President Young gave me the keys of the Temple and told me to go and dedicate it, which I did."[31]

Following the first day's sessions, President Woodruff recorded in his journal: "The spirit and Power of God rested upon us. The spirit of Prophecy and Revelation was upon us and the Hearts of the Saints were melted and many things were unfolded to us."[32] On the following day President Woodruff told the congregation of a remarkable experience he had had during the night:

> If the veil could be taken from our eyes and we could see into the spirit world, we would see that Joseph Smith, Brigham Young and John Taylor had gathered together every spirit that ever dwelt in the flesh in this Church since its organization. We would also see the faithful apostles and elders of the Nephites who dwelt in the flesh in the days of Jesus Christ. In that assembly we would also see Isaiah and every prophet and apostle that ever prophesied of the great work of God. In the midst of these spirits we would see the Son of God, the Savior who presides and guides and controls the preparing of the kingdom of God on the earth and in heaven.
>
> From that body of spirits, when we shout "Hosanna to God and the Lamb!" there is a mighty shout goes up of "Glory to God in the Highest!" that the God of Israel has permitted his people to finish this Temple and prepared it for the great work that lies before the Latter-day Saints....
>
> The spirits on the other side rejoice far more than we do, because they know more of what lies before in the great work of God in this last dispensation than we do.[33]

President George Q. Cannon explained why those in the spirit world would be unusually interested in the dedication of this particular temple.

Because the Saints in the Salt Lake area come from many nations, he said, "we represent a vast number of the families of the earth," and each individual is actually "the representative of thousands of souls."[34]

Morning and afternoon dedicatory sessions continued through April 24 (with one evening session on April 7). A total of approximately seventy thousand attended. Two special "Sunday School services," April 21 and 22, were designed for those too young to attend the regular sessions. About twelve thousand children and their teachers attended these meetings. One of those present on Saturday the twenty-second was seven-year-old LeGrand Richards, a future Apostle. He was impressed that his grandfather, Franklin D. Richards, was among those leaders on the stand.[35]

A young couple from Provo, Benjamin and Emma Bennett, would likely never forget the temple dedication. As the Friday evening session of April 7 continued, Emma went into labor. She was rushed into an adjoining room and shortly afterwards gave birth to a son. For the next week mother and child were cared for in a home near Temple Square. Then, on Saturday evening, April 15, the little family returned to the temple. In the same room where the baby was born, he was blessed by President Joseph F. Smith and given the name Joseph Temple Bennett.[36]

On Wednesday, April 19, no regular dedicatory sessions were held, but the General Authorities, stake presidents, and other specially invited brethren gathered for a testimony meeting. The morning session lasted three hours, and the afternoon five. "There was a very heavenly spirit throughout," Elder B.H. Roberts wrote in his journal, "and many were melted to tears." The following afternoon, this same group of 115 men gathered in the celestial room and united in prayer. Following this experience, the group partook of the sacrament. They then reminisced about Joseph Smith and the early decades of the latter-day work. Of the 115 present, only 36 had witnessed the cornerstone laying for the Salt Lake Temple forty years before; 33 had known the Prophet Joseph Smith, and only 10 had attended meetings in the Kirtland Temple.[37]

The nearly three weeks of inspirational meetings had an impact for good on the Saints. "I believe this Temple Dedication will prove to have a reformatory character among the people," remarked Elder Anthon H. Lund. "The many thousands of Saints will leave these sacred premises with resolves to serve God better than in the past."[38] Elder B. H. Roberts confided that he had been moved with a desire to reform and humble himself.[39] Speaking at the special meeting of priesthood leaders on April 19, President Wilford Woodruff declared: "Heaven has accepted this people and God has forgiven their sins…if they sin no more." He testified that he had felt the influence of the Holy Ghost more powerfully during the dedicatory services than at any other time in his life excepting the occasion when the Prophet Joseph gave his final charge to the Twelve.[40] Elder Roberts described the dedication as "a Pentecostal time for me" and added: "The dedication of this Temple has not been attended with many visions or the appearance of angels: but the spirit of the Lord has been near—the Holy Ghost, and that is greater than the angels!"[41]

The Great Temple Enters Service

Elder Lorenzo Snow, nearly eighty years of age and at the time serving as president of the Quorum of the Twelve, was named to be the first president of the Salt Lake Temple. He was provided with an apartment in the temple where he could live and personally supervise its sacred activities.

The first ordinances were performed in the Salt Lake Temple on May 23, 1893. Its opening resulted in a more than 50 percent increase in the number of endowments performed for the dead each year. Almost immediately the temple faced a problem of overcrowding. Temple authorities instructed: "Overcrowding should be especially avoided when work of a sacred character is being performed; otherwise the solemnity which ought always to be attached to it is liable to be depreciated. Conditions in the temple should never contribute to 'physical discomfort' or 'mental perturbation.'" To solve the problem, each stake in the area was assigned certain days when its members were invited to attend the temple.[42] This practice of assigning "stake temple days" would become common during the twentieth century.

Because of its location at church headquarters, the Salt Lake Temple included some features not found in other temples. Between the endowment rooms and the main assembly room is an intermediate floor with a series of rooms for the use of various priesthood quorums. Especially important is the Council Room for the First Presidency and the Twelve. In the

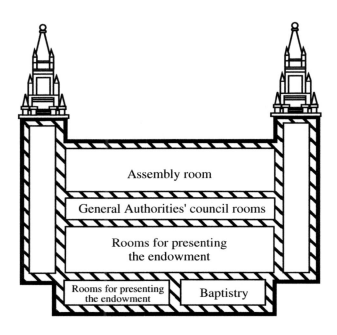

Salt Lake Temple (1893)

front of the room are seats for members of the First Presidency. Facing them in a semi-circle are the chairs occupied by members of the Twelve. Elder Spencer W. Kimball later described the spirit of the key weekly meetings held in this sacred place:

> When in a Thursday temple meeting, after prayer and fasting, important decisions are made, new missions and new stakes are created, new patterns and policies initiated, the news is taken for granted and possibly thought of as mere human calculations. But to those who sit in the intimate circles and hear the prayers of the prophet and the testimony of [this] man of God; to those who see the astuteness of his deliberations and the sagacity of his decisions and pronouncements, to them he is verily a prophet. To hear him conclude important new developments with such solemn expressions as "the Lord is pleased"; "that move is right"; "our Heavenly Father has spoken," is to know positively.[43]

Another and even more sacred place is located adjacent to the celestial room, "the inner room or Holy of Holies of the Temple." Elder James E. Talmage suggested that the Holy of Holies corresponds to the most sacred areas of the ancient tabernacle and temple.[44]

Elder Boyd K. Packer wrote: "Hidden away in the central part of the temple is the Holy of Holies where the President of the Church may retire when burdened down with heavy decisions to seek an interview with Him whose Church it is. The prophet holds the keys, the spiritual keys and the very literal key to this one door in that sacred edifice."[45]

A remarkable experience five years after the temple's dedication confirmed that the Lord truly regarded this as his house. President Wilford Woodruff had instructed that following his death the First Presidency should be reorganized immediately rather than after waiting two or three years as had been done in the past. Elder Lorenzo Snow, the senior Apostle, who would become the next President of the Church, went immediately to the Salt Lake Temple upon learning of President Woodruff's death. He went to the sacred altar in the Holy of Holies, where he poured out his heart to the Lord: "I have not sought this responsibility but if it be Thy will, I now present myself before Thee for Thy guidance and instruction. I ask that Thou show me what Thou wouldst have me do." After finishing his prayer he expected that there might be some special manifestation from the Lord. He waited and waited but there was no reply, no voice, no manifestation.[46]

Disappointed, he left the sacred room, and walked through the celestial room out into the large hallway. Here he received a glorious manifestation, which he later described to his granddaughter. She wrote:

> One evening while I was visiting grandpa Snow in his room in the Salt Lake Temple, I remained until the door keepers had gone and the night-watchmen had not yet come in, so grandpa said he would take me to the main front entrance and let me out that way. He got his bunch of keys from his dresser. After we left his room and while we were still in the large corridor leading into the celestial room, I was walking several steps ahead of grandpa when he stopped me and said: "Wait a moment, Allie, I want to tell you something. It was right here that the Lord Jesus Christ appeared to me at the time of the death of President Woodruff. He instructed me to go right ahead and reorganize the First Presidency of the Church at once and not wait as had been done after the death of the previous presidents, and that I was to succeed President Woodruff."

Then grandpa came a step nearer and held out his left hand and said: "He stood right here, about three feet above the floor. It looked as though He stood on a plate of solid gold."

Grandpa told me what a glorious personage the Savior is and described His hands, feet, countenance and beautiful white robes, all of which were of such a glory of whiteness and brightness that he could hardly gaze upon Him.

Then he came another step nearer and put his right hand on my head and said: "Now granddaughter, I want you to remember that this is the testimony of your grandfather, that he told you with his own lips that he actually saw the Savior, here in the Temple, and talked with Him face to face."[47]

The Salt Lake Temple would continue to occupy an important place as the Church moved into the twentieth century.

Chapter Seven

Temples in a New Century

A new era in temple building opened with the dawning of the twentieth century. The six temples dedicated in the nineteenth century had been built in the same city or at least in the same state as Church headquarters. The first two decades of the new century, on the other hand, witnessed the construction of temples in Hawaii and Alberta. The far-flung locations of these temples reflected the geographical expansion of the Latter-day Saints, which would continue to be an important feature of Church history.

President Joseph F. Smith early recognized the need for temples in more scattered locations. Speaking at the first general conference after the beginning of the twentieth century (at which time he was a counselor to President Lorenzo Snow), he stated: "I foresee the necessity arising for other temples or other places consecrated to the Lord for the performance of the ordinances of God's house, so that the people may have the benefit of the House of the Lord without having to travel hundreds of miles for that purpose."[1]

Joseph F. Smith became the first to visit the continent of Europe while serving as President of the Church. During his 1906 visit to Europe, he made an important prophetic statement. At a conference in Bern,

Switzerland, he stretched out his hands and declared, "The time will come when this land [Europe] will be dotted with temples, where you can go and redeem your dead." He also explained that "temples would be built in diverse countries of the world."[2] The first Latter-day Saint temple in Europe would be dedicated nearly a half century later in the very city where President Smith had made his prophecy. Although President Joseph F. Smith did not live to see temples built in Europe, he did inaugurate the construction of the first two of these sacred edifices away from the traditional centers of Mormon colonization in Utah.

A Temple in Canada

The first temple outside of the United States was erected in Alberta, Canada. In 1887 a group of Latter-day Saint pioneers, most from the Logan, Utah, area, established a settlement on Lee's Creek in southwestern Alberta. Eventually this community would be named Cardston in honor of its first leader, Charles O. Card. One of the early settlers, Jonathan Layne, addressed a meeting of the Saints about two weeks after their arrival in Canada: "While speaking the spirit of prophecy rested upon me, and under its influence I predicted...that Temples would yet be built in the land. I could see it as plain as if it already was here."[3]

Just over a year later, on October 8, 1888, Elders Francis M. Lyman and John W. Taylor of the Council of the Twelve were in Cardston. President Card gave the visitors a tour of the area by carriage and took them to a low hill just west of town. As the group stood in a semicircle looking down on the town site, Elder Taylor offered a prayer dedicating that land as a place of habitation for the Saints. He paused, and then made this prophetic statement: "I now speak by the power of prophecy and say that upon this very spot shall be erected a Temple to the name of Israel's God and nations shall come from far and near and praise His high and holy name."[4] Another person in the group, evidently moved by the same spirit, then remarked that some of those present would live to work in the temple.[5] The following year while on a visit to Alberta, President Wilford Woodruff once again spoke of the time when a temple would be erected in Canada.[6]

At the priesthood session of general conference in October 1912, President Joseph F. Smith announced that the idea of building a temple in

Canada had been under consideration "for some time." He now proposed to move forward with this project "in some city in Alberta...as soon as arrangements can be perfected." This proposition was approved unanimously. President Edward J. Wood of the Alberta Stake, present in the meeting, was surprised and excited when he heard the announcement. The Saints in the neighboring towns of Cardston and Raymond, headquarters of the Alberta and Taylor Stakes respectively, each thought their community should be the sight for the proposed temple.[7]

Later, President Joseph F. Smith sent Presiding Bishop Charles W. Nibley to Canada to recommend the best possible sites for a temple. He brought back photographs of four locations. President Smith thoughtfully studied the pictures and, pointing to one of them, said, "I feel strongly impressed that this is the one." He had selected the same site Elder Taylor had dedicated years earlier.[8]

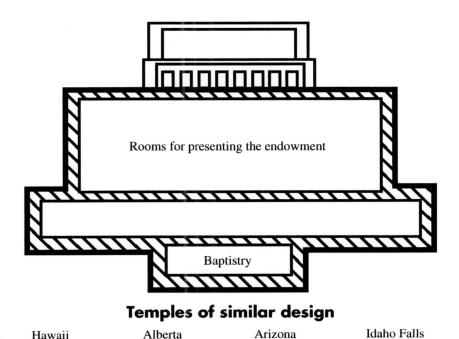

Temples of similar design

Hawaii	Alberta	Arizona	Idaho Falls
(1919)	(1923)	(1927)	(1945)

The First Presidency decided that the new generation of twentieth century temples would depart from traditional designs in at least two important respects: they would not be adorned with towers; and they would be smaller, not including a large assembly room on the upper floor. (See temple profiles in chapter 10.) Hence, these temples would not be multi-purpose buildings but would be designed almost exclusively for giving sacred ordinances. In determining the architecture for these temples, "the Presidency decided to seek the advice of the most talented men available." They therefore invited prominent Latter-day Saint architects of the day to participate in an anonymous competition for the Alberta Temple's design. Seven firms submitted proposals. These were placed on public display before the final selection was made. The First Presidency passed over designs which looked to the pinnacled buildings of the past for their inspiration and chose instead a "daringly modern design" for the new temple.[9]

Architect Hyrum Pope was impressed that a Latter-day Saint temple should not be just a copy of a Gothic cathedral or classic temple but "an edifice which should express in its architecture all the boldness and all the truth for which the Gospel stands." He felt that because the gospel dates from before the foundation of the earth, temple architecture "should be ancient as well as modern. It should express all the power which we associate with God."[10] Because we live in the last dispensation, which represents a "final consummation of the work of the Lord," President Anthony W. Ivins concurred, "the past and the present and the future have undoubtedly been brought together in these modern temples as they have never been brought together before."[11]

In earlier temples the large upper assembly room had essentially determined the basic shape of the whole building. With this facility omitted, the Alberta Temple's architects had greater flexibility in arranging the various elements of the structure. The four endowment lecture rooms were placed in wings projecting outward from the celestial room, which was located in an elevated position at the center of the temple. In each of the buildings four corners were smaller diagonal wings containing stairs. Hence the basic floor plan was in the form of a Maltese cross 118 feet square.

President Joseph F. Smith dedicated the site on July 27, 1913, and ground was broken the following November 9. Daniel K. Greene, a resident of the area, repeatedly telephoned to ask when he might help to build the temple. He was given the honor of plowing the first furrow marking the beginning of excavation for the temple.

By 1915 construction progressed to the point that the cornerstone could be laid. Some 2,000 Saints gathered for this occasion on September 19, including 250 who had come by special train from other areas of Alberta. They formally marched from the nearby tabernacle to the southeast corner of the temple. Stake President Edward J. Wood, who also served as chairman of the temple building committee, led the congregation in "an acclamation of praise and blessing." While waving white handkerchiefs overhead, the throng repeated in unison: "God bless the Temple! God bless the Church!...God bless Canada! God bless the British Empire!" After the group joined in singing the Canadian national anthem, Elder David O. McKay of the Quorum of the Twelve officially moved the

Alberta Temple

cornerstone into its place. The commemorative box contained the usual memorabilia plus a lock of hair from the Prophet Joseph Smith. Weather for the occasion was far from ideal. "It rained and it hailed, and it stormed," President Wood recalled, "but it did not discourage us...Brother McKay expected everybody to run to the Tabernacle. But no. We stood it out, and we had a good time."[12]

Within two years the temple's exterior of light gray British Columbia granite was finished. The courtyard in front of the building featured a sculptured frieze by Torlief Knaphus depicting the Savior's promise of "living water" or eternal life to the woman at Jacob's well (John 4:5-15). A poem by Elder Orson F. Whitney appeared on a bronze tablet near the temple's main entrance:

> Hearts must be pure to come within
>   these walls,
> Where spreads a feast unknown to
>   festive halls.
> Freely partake, for freely God hath
>   given,
> And taste the holy joys that tell of
>   heaven.
> Here learn of him who triumphed o'er
>   the grave,
> And unto men the keys, the Kingdom,
>   gave:
> Joined here by powers that past and
>   present bind,
> The living and the dead perfection
>   find.

On September 23, 1917, the capstone was laid by Heber S. Allen, president of the neighboring Taylor Stake.

The Alberta Temple's main rooms were richly paneled with hardwoods from many parts of the world. In the endowment lecture rooms, skilled craftsmen blended the distinctive grains of golden oak from eastern North America with the varied hues of different walnut woods from South

America. The celestial room was finished chiefly in African mahogany with delicate inlays of ebony, rose maple, and tulip woods. Adjacent to this room were three particularly beautiful sealing rooms. Colors in the room designated for the living sealings were bright, while those in the room intended for vicarious sealings in behalf of the dead were more somber.[13]

By the summer of 1921 construction was virtually complete, but another two years were required to furnish the temple and have it ready for use. During this period, some fifty thousand visitors were escorted through the temple and grounds.[14]

The Alberta Temple Dedication

A special train brought almost all the high officials of the Church to Cardston for the Alberta Temple's dedication. This was the first time that such a large number of General Authorities had ever gathered outside of the United States. There were eleven dedicatory sessions, beginning Sunday morning, August 26, 1923, and continuing through Wednesday afternoon. Approximately 600 persons could be accommodated in the temple's various rooms and corridors; those not seated in the celestial room listened to the services by means of recently developed loud-speaking equipment. President Heber J. Grant, who had succeeded Joseph F. Smith in 1918, spoke in each service. Other speakers included general as well as local Church leaders. President Edward J. Wood declared that he knew that early Latter-day Saint pioneers to Canada, including Charles O. Card, were rejoicing "on the other side" that the temple was at last dedicated. David A. Smith, first counselor in the Presiding Bishopric, confided that for some time he had longed for the opportunity of once again counseling with his father, the late President Joseph F. Smith. "Yesterday," he testified, "I walked with him in these halls, [and] by his side I stood while offering up the sacred shout of Hosanna."[15]

President Grant stated that he felt "the same sweet, peaceful, Godlike, and inspiring" influence which he had experienced at the dedications of the Logan and Manti Temples. He rejoiced that "there was a rich outpouring of the spirit of the Lord during all of the eleven sessions." He announced that the total cost of the Alberta Temple, including furnishings and grounds, was $781,479.90.[16] The first endowments in the new temple were given

Wednesday evening, August 29, under the personal supervision of Elder George F. Richards, the member of the Twelve assigned to supervise temple work Churchwide.

Edward J. Wood became the temple's first president. His twenty-five year ministry was characterized by remarkable healings and numerous instances of spiritual discernment. Once, when about to seal a family, he heard a voice insisting "I am her child"; a careful check revealed that a daughter who died in infancy had been omitted.[17]

Within a few years, "automobile caravans" to the Alberta Temple became eagerly anticipated annual events among the Saints of the Northwestern States Mission. When William R. Sloan became mission president, he discovered that less than 10 percent of the members had their temple blessings. He was impressed with the need "to convert these good people" to the importance of temple ordinances. Under his direction, 193 Saints from the Portland area, most of whom had never been to the temple before, made the sixteen-hundred-mile round trip to Cardston in July of 1927. The group conducted outdoor "street meetings" in several towns en route and attracted much favorable publicity. "The spirit of temple work began to manifest itself upon the return of these good Saints" to their various branches, reported President Sloan. "Nothing has ever been experienced in this mission," he noted, "that has been such a potent factor in building up the faith of our Saints."[18] These "caravans" became forerunners of the "temple excursions" which would become so important in the lives of an increasing number of Latter-day Saints not living near a temple.

The Hawaii Temple

While the Alberta Temple was under construction, a site for a second and similar temple was chosen in Hawaii. Progress on this latter structure was so rapid that it was dedicated four years before the temple in Canada.

In 1865 Church leaders had purchased the Laie plantation on the island of Oahu to become the gathering place for the Hawaiian Saints.

President George Q. Cannon, one of the original missionaries and a member of the First Presidency, returned to the islands for the mission's fiftieth anniversary celebration. Speaking at Laie on December 23, 1900, he declared that if the people "would be faithful enough...the time would come when some would be given the power to seal husband and wife for time and eternity." A week later he repeated these thoughts at Honolulu. The Saints regarded this as a prophecy that a temple would one day be built in Hawaii.[19]

President Samuel E. Woolley of the Hawaiian Mission regularly encouraged the Saints to prepare for the time when a temple would be in their midst. Speaking at a mission conference on April 3, 1915, he asked: "Have we searched out our genealogies? Are we prepared for a temple to be built?...who knows but what the Lord wants to build a temple in this land? I tell you that...the time will come, in my judgement, that a temple will be built here."[20]

Joseph F. Smith, yet another early missionary to the Islands, who by 1915 was President of the Church, was once again in Hawaii on official business. Following a meeting in his honor in Laie, June 1, 1915, he invited Elder Reed Smoot and Presiding Bishop Charles W. Nibley to join him for an evening walk into the nearby tropical grounds. "I never saw a more beautiful night in all my life," Elder Smoot later recalled. While they were strolling, President Smith unexpectedly confided, "I feel impressed to dedicate this ground for the erection of a Temple to God, for a place where the peoples of the Pacific Isles can come and do their temple work....I think now is the time to dedicate the ground." Elder Smoot continued, "I have heard President Smith pray hundreds of times...but never in all my life did I hear such a prayer. The very ground seemed to be sacred, and he seemed as if he were talking face to face with the Father. I cannot and never will forget it if I live a thousand years."[21]

At the general conference in October President Smith announced the site's dedication and plans to build a temple in Hawaii: "Away down in the Pacific Ocean," he explained, "are various groups of islands, from the Sandwich Islands down to Tahiti, Samoa, Tonga, and New Zealand. On them are thousands of good people...of the blood of Israel. When you carry the gospel to them they receive it with open hearts. They need the same privileges...that we enjoy," President Smith insisted, "but these are out of their power. They are poor, and they can't gather means to come up here to be endowed, and sealed for time and eternity, for their living and their dead and be baptized for their dead." The conference congregation unanimously approved the proposition to build a temple for these people.[22]

The natural setting for the new temple was unusually beautiful. The temple at Laie would stand on top of a gentle rise covered with luxuriant ferns, trees, and other semi-tropical vegetation, about a half-mile from the shores of the Pacific. In the area were sugar cane plantations and pineapple fields.

Because Church leaders were pleased with the general arrangement of the Alberta Temple, they directed the same architects to prepare a slightly smaller but similar design for the Hawaii Temple. The resulting plan took the form of a Grecian cross seventy-eight feet square, with the flat roof of the central portion rising to a height of fifty feet. Many people, however, questioned the departure of these temples from the basic pattern of those built in the previous century. In 1916 President Samuel E. Woolley of the Hawaiian Mission was invited to give a talk in which he would respond to these criticisms. Seeking inspiration, he opened a book at random and found President Brigham Young's 1853 prophecy about the time when temples would have one central tower with greenery and fishponds on the roof. He was impressed that the Hawaiian Temple, with provisions for flowerboxes and ponds on top of the building, fulfilled President Young's description. Writing in the *Improvement Era* later that year, Elder John A. Widtsoe presented these circumstances as evidence of Brigham Young's prophetic calling. The architects, however, "asserted that they knew nothing of President Young's prophecy until several years after they had planned the Canadian and Hawaiian Temples."[23]

Raising funds for the temple posed a challenge to the scattered Saints in Hawaii. Nevertheless they responded with faith and determination. In the little village of Laie, the Primary of 100 children raised over one thousand dollars. A group of Relief Society women went into the hills to gather bamboo, which they made into fans, mats, and other craft items offered for sale at bazaars. Concerts presented by the Polynesian Saints were also popular fund-raisers. Even though the people were making a substantial sacrifice for the temple, President Woolley reported that during this same period tithe paying increased by 30 percent throughout the Hawaiian Mission.[24]

The lack of many building materials in the islands posed a formidable challenge. The builders determined that local volcanic rock and coral could be crushed to make good concrete. Reinforced with steel, the temple became "a monolith of artificial stone" having a creamy white surface.[25] Those associated with building the temple were convinced that they had divine assistance. At one point, construction came to a standstill because of the lack of lumber, which was not abundant in the islands. Contractor Ralph Woolley prayed for divine assistance. Two days later, after a particularly severe storm, the people of Laie spotted a freighter stranded on a nearby coral reef. This was a strange sight because ships of that size did not normally sail along that side of the island. To lighten his vessel, the captain offered to give his entire cargo—of lumber—if the people would unload it. Young men from the community swam out to the ship,

Hawaii Temple

threw the lumber overboard, and lugged it up to the Temple site. Work on the temple resumed.[26]

Recognizing the possibilities of the cement surface, the architects asked the First Presidency for permission to adorn the upper portion of the temple with sculptures. President Joseph F. Smith approved, and he commissioned J. Leo and Avard Fairbanks to do the work. In the resulting friezes, 123 nearly life-size figures depict God's dealings with man in four great dispensations from the time of Adam to the present. The figures lean slightly outward in order to present a better appearance when viewed from the ground. The panel on the west presents the history of Israel during the Old Testament period. The story of the Book of Mormon is represented in the north frieze, including the departure of Hagoth and others, believed to be among the ancestors of the Polynesians. The panel to the south depicts the New Testament dispensation followed by the Apostasy. The sculptures on the temple's east front represent the latter-day restoration of the gospel with its saving principles.[27]

Inside, the temple's chapel featured small reproductions of these friezes. The oak benches in the chapel and the temple's main rooms seated about fifty persons. These rooms were finished with Hawaiian koa wood, noted for the beauty of its grain and color. Amid a profusion of tropical flowers and vegetation on the temple grounds, one statue depicted a Hawaiian mother and child, while another portrayed Lehi blessing his family. A series of cement-lined pools led to the temple's entrance. The total cost of the temple and grounds was $215,000.

Dedication of the Hawaii Temple

Hundreds were able to visit the temple before its dedication on Thanksgiving Day, November 27, 1919. Several hundred Saints from Honolulu and from other islands came to Laie for the dedication. Dressed in their light-weight and brightly colored clothing, they were a picturesque sight as they arrived by special train.

The five dedicatory sessions, beginning on Thursday and continuing through Sunday, were conducted in the celestial room. Curtains in three small adjoining sealing rooms and in the terrestrial room were pushed aside so that up to three hundred people could witness the proceedings. President

Heber J. Grant keenly regretted that President Joseph F. Smith, who had died just one year before and who had such a deep love for the Hawaiian people, was not able to preside at this eagerly anticipated temple dedication. Speakers typically opened their remarks with an "Aloha" and received a warm "Aloha" from the congregation in response.[28]

In the Thursday afternoon session, a twelve-voice choir sang "A Temple in Hawaii," with words by Ruth May Fox of the General Young Women's Board and music by Orson Clarke, a former missionary. David Kailimai, one of the few Hawaiian Saints who had already received his temple endowment, offered the closing prayer. A number of years earlier he and his family had sacrificed their life savings in order to travel with a group of returning missionaries to Utah, where they received their temple blessings.[29]

There were special meetings in addition to the regular dedicatory sessions. Some 235 children were present in the temple Sunday morning; most were Hawaiian, and the girls looked quite angelic in their white dresses. President Grant personally led the group in singing "Who's on the Lord's Side, Who?" and then asked the children who actually was on the Lord's side. All hands were raised. The mission president also conducted public conference meetings during these same days at hours when no dedicatory sessions were scheduled.[30]

Speaking at the dedication, Elder Stephen L Richards declared that "the temple is something more than a beautiful building. It is a monument to the great truths of the gospel, and stands for all that is best and holiest in life. While it is a house for salvation of the dead," he insisted, "it should never be forgotten that it is a house for the living and intended to stimulate us to higher things."[31]

In his dedicatory prayer President Grant expressed appreciation that "tens of thousands of the descendants of Lehi, in this favored land, have come to a knowledge of the Gospel." He petitioned the Lord to aid the peoples of the Pacific "to secure the genealogies of their forefathers, so that they may come into this holy house and become saviors unto their ancestors."[32]

Some of those who were present for the temple's dedication had roots going back to the beginnings of the Church in Hawaii. Sister Manaoheakamalu, who had cared for Joseph F. Smith during his first mission to Hawaii and was now a very old lady, had to be carried into the temple. She returned a week later to receive her endowment. While in the temple she heard the voice of President Joseph F. Smith greeting her with "Aloha" and "this caused her to weep for joy." She passed away only a short time later.[33]

For generations the Polynesian peoples had kept oral genealogies. During the early years of the twentieth century, Mr. Abraham Fornander, a Hawaiian historian, convinced the people to write down these legends. He translated them and found that some of the genealogies extended back to the time of Christ. The results of his work were published in six large volumes.

"For twenty years," commented Susa Young Gates, "this Hawaiian genealogist and antiquarian has been at work on the preparation of these volumes; and now, with the completion...of the Hawaiian Temple, comes the publication of this master work for the people of that land. Surely God moves in a mysterious way, his wonders to perform.[34]

Faithful Polynesian Saints from Samoa, Tonga, Tahiti, New Zealand, and other South Pacific island groups brought a special spirit as they sacrificed to come to the Hawaiian Temple. Castle Murphy, who served many years as temple president, recalled days when he was "voice weary" from performing so many sealing ordinances. Nevertheless he felt spiritually lifted up from rendering this service for these wonderful people. Often he noticed "the coverlets of the altars, where those sacred ordinances were performed, dampened by the tears of gratitude, which flowed from the eyes of those who knelt so humbly there."[35] Truly the Alberta and Hawaii temples were sources of spiritual strength to the Saints in these far-flung areas.

Chapter Eight

Continued Expansion

During the second quarter of the twentieth century, roughly the period between the ends of World Wars I and II, the pattern of extending temple building into new areas continued. Not only were the Hawaii and Alberta temples dedicated, but others were constructed in Arizona and Idaho. Two sites for future temples were also purchased in California. This expansion would come despite problems created by depression and war.

The Arizona Temple

From the beginning of the Saints' settlements in Arizona during the 1870s, they had eagerly looked forward to the time when a temple would be erected there. As early as 1908 the presidency of the Maricopa Stake in Mesa discussed with the General Authorities the possibility of an Arizona temple. Then, in 1912, the First Presidency met with the leaders of the several Arizona stakes and of the California Mission. Although each stake president had believed that his area offered the best location, most now agreed that the proposed temple should be built in Mesa. No final decision was made at this time, and the outbreak of World War I caused plans for the temple to be shelved for the duration.[1]

With the close of hostilities in 1918, plans for building the temple were revived. At the general conference in October of the following year, President Heber J. Grant formally announced that the Church would soon build a temple in Arizona. Fund raising efforts had already begun, and by 1921 $110,000 had been contributed. This represented the largest per capita contribution to a temple to that date. Even members of other churches in the area donated $6,000. Throughout the Church, September 12 of 1920 was designated "Arizona Temple Day" and an additional $112,000 came in.[2]

Meanwhile, President Grant with other General Authorities and representatives of the Church's building program personally traveled to Mesa in order to select the temple site. On February 1, 1920, the visitors from Church headquarters and the presidency of the Maricopa Stake selected a twenty-acre tract on what was then the east edge of Mesa. The location was ideal because the "Apache Trail," the local segment of the southern transcontinental highway, ran along the property's north boundary. Hence thousands of tourists each season would pass by the temple.

On November 28, 1921, President Grant once again was in Mesa. In the presence of over three thousand people, he formally dedicated the site. The outline of the future building was marked with branches from date palms. A large group of children, accompanied by an orchestra, sang "Jesus Wants Me for a Sunbeam," "Shine On," and "I Want to See the Temple" as they marched around the temple's perimeter strewing flowers.[3]

Experience with the Alberta temple strongly influenced the planning of the temple in Arizona. The First Presidency invited three designated architectural firms to submit proposals. The winning design was submitted by Don Carlos Young Jr, and Ramm Hansen, who had recently designed the Utah state capitol building. They described the temple as an American adaptation of classical architecture. The exterior would be covered with glistening cream-colored terra cotta tiles. The temple itself rises above a surrounding one-story annex, and the whole structure is situated on a raised platform. Hence the design is reminiscent of the terraced courts of ancient temples. The temple's interior was arranged around a central grand staircase. As one enters the temple, the stairs, with the celestial room at their top, can be seen straight ahead. Before reaching the top, the individual must interrupt his upward progress in order to receive instructions and accept the sacred covenants associated with the temple endowment. Only then is he prepared to reach the ultimate goal of celestial exaltation represented by the beautiful room at the head of the stairs. Hence this staircase is a fitting symbolic representation of mankind's upward progression back into the presence of God.

The first ground was broken for the new temple on April 25, 1922, when excavation began for the basement. Arthur Price of the Church's building department arrived the following January to take personal charge as construction architect. He immediately began stockpiling materials needed for the project. The right kinds of sand, gravel, and cement were carefully selected, and tests were thoroughly conducted to determine the optimum mixture to produce flawless concrete which could withstand the ravages of time. On November 12, 1923, the cornerstone was laid under the direction of Elder Richard R. Lyman of the Quorum of the Twelve. The metal box contained items of interest related to the Church in Arizona and to the temple's construction. By February of the following year, the reinforced concrete outer structure was completed.

During the last two years of construction, the First Presidency authorized volunteer guides to conduct visitors through the building and grounds. A local journalist acknowledged that the Church could reasonably have excluded all visitors from the construction site and expressed his appreciation of this demonstration of generous hospitality. An estimated two hundred thousand visited the temple during this extended open-house period.[4]

A unique feature of the temple's exterior were the friezes in the parapet at each corner of the building. Based on sketches by A. D. Wright of Salt Lake City, the sculptures were modeled by Torlief Knaphus reflecting scenes he had personally observed in various parts of the world. These sculptures depict the fulfillment of Isaiah's prophecy that in the latter days the Lord would "set up an ensign for the nations" and gather "the remnant of his people" from "the four corners of the earth" and from "the islands of the sea" (Isaiah 11:11-12). The friezes on the north represent the gathering from the Old World, while those on the south depict the gathering of the Lord's people in America and in the Pacific islands. The gathering of the Jews is not shown because they will gather in the Eastern Hemisphere rather than in America.[5]

Paintings flanking the grand stairway serve as a reminder that this temple was intended to provide a place where the Lamanites of the Southwest and of Mexico could come to receive sacred ordinances. These paintings were the work of Lee Greene Richards of Salt Lake City. The painting on the north wall shows Joseph and Hyrum Smith preaching to a group of Indian chiefs, presenting them with the Book of Mormon, which contains the record of their fathers. The painting on the south presents a beautiful scene in which an Indian is being baptized by a missionary elder.

While the temple itself was being completed, attention also focused on providing beautiful grounds which would create the proper setting for the Lord's house. Tall Italian cypress trees bordered the area. Palms of many varieties provided shade. Trees from diverse parts of the world were planted. A cactus garden featured the palo verde, the Arizona state

Arizona Temple

tree. Unique citrus trees with lemons or grapefruit the size of volleyballs created interest. The warm climate allowed brilliant flowers to bloom through much of the year.

Dedicatory events commenced Sunday, October 23, 1927. From five to ten thousand gathered for a special sunrise service. A combined choir from the Los Angeles and Hollywood Stakes in California stood on the roof of the temple's annex as they sang "The Vision," a cantata by Evan Stephens, bearing testimony of the latter-day restoration of Christ's gospel. These proceedings, as well as those of the dedicatory services, were broadcast by radio locally as well as in Utah.[6]

During the next four days ten dedicatory services were held so that all who were interested and qualified could attend. An evening meeting was held for children ages six through fourteen. Many Lamanites attended on Monday afternoon when a session was designated especially for them. Dozens of wagons and buggies brought Maricopa and Papago Indians to the temple. Spanish-speaking Saints came from near and far by automobile or pickup truck.[7] President Heber J. Grant pronounced the dedicatory prayer in all ten sessions. Among other things, he petitioned the Lord to bless the Lamanites "that they may not perish as a people, but that from this time forth they may increase in numbers and in strength and influence, that all the great and glorious promises made concerning the descendants of Lehi may be fulfilled in them...and that many of them may have the privilege of entering this holy house and receiving ordinances for themselves and their departed ancestors." "The time was very near at hand," President Grant remarked, "when this people would be redeemed and fulfill all the promises made to them in the Book of Mormon."[8]

No time was wasted in getting the temple into operation. The last dedicatory service took place Wednesday morning, October 26, and the first baptisms for the dead commenced that same afternoon. Endowments and sealings were inaugurated the following day.

An unusual spiritual experience confirmed that Lamanites in the spirit world had a special interest in the Arizona Temple. While a group was waiting in the creation room for an endowment session to begin, one individual happened to glance up toward the front of the room "and there stood a Lamanite, a splendid specimen of manhood clothed only with a loin cloth.

He seemed to be looking over the congregation and the room in general."
A local Church leader commented that perhaps the Lamanite had been
"sent ahead to look over the building and see how he would like [it] and the
services that were being performed."[9]

During the first quarter-century of its operation, more than 40 percent
of those attending the Arizona Temple came from outside of that state. As
had been the case with the Alberta Temple, many of these people came in
groups, typically in chartered buses. These "temple excursions" provided
good fellowship and were memorable spiritual experiences in the lives of
those taking part. In 1938 one group of ninety-one adults and twenty-eight
children from the Pasadena area left Los Angeles Friday night in two chartered railroad cars. In each coach the Saints conducted a testimony meeting
from 9 to 10:30 P.M. Early on Saturday morning they arrived in Mesa,
where they were met by a group of a dozen Saints who provided an
automobile shuttle service to the temple. After participating in two endowment sessions, they conducted yet another testimony meeting, this time
in the temple, before leaving Saturday evening for home.[10] Such excursions
made a lasting and positive impression on the young people who went to
perform baptisms for the dead.

Temples Renovated and Remodeled

While new temples were being built, others underwent important ren-
ovation or remodeling. Two of these projects were caused by disastrous
fires. After the Logan Temple closed on December 4, 1917, fire broke out
in some electrical wiring and quickly engulfed the southeast stairway. Art
windows and paintings were destroyed, and there was extensive smoke and
water damage in adjacent parts of the building. At a cost of forty thousand
dollars the stairway was rebuilt and other repairs were made so that the
temple could reopen within three months.[11] Another fire, in November
1928, destroyed the St. George Temple annex, although records and furnishings were saved.

For over a year, in 1937 and 1938, the St. George Temple was closed
for extensive remodeling. When originally built, this structure, like the
Kirtland and Nauvoo Temples, consisted primarily of two large assembly
halls, one above the other, each having sets of pulpits at both ends. The

lower of these rooms was divided by means of temporary "screens" for presenting the endowment instructions. During the remodeling, this hall was permanently partitioned to create five spacious endowment rooms. The project, including other improvements, cost more than $105,000. An elevator was installed; only one timber had to be removed to make way for the shaft. The temple's exterior was completely resurfaced, and landscaping of the grounds was made more beautiful. Six cottages were built across the street for the use of Latter-day Saints coming long distances to attend the temple.

Temple Sites in California

During the years following World War I, many Church members moved to California, seeking improved economic opportunities. These Saints were eager to have a temple in their midst, and frequently cited an 1847 letter in which the Twelve declared that "in the process of time the shores of the Pacific may yet be overlooked from the temple of the Lord."[12]

In 1921 Harry Culver, a Los Angeles area real estate developer, offered to give the Church a six-acre site plus a contribution of $50,000 if the Church would build a $500,000 temple there. In December of that year President Heber J. Grant and other General Authorities went to Los Angeles to inspect this property, located in Ocean Heights between Culver City and the sea. At first Church leaders were favorably impressed with this offer, but they eventually declined it because of financial considerations relative to completing the temples in Alberta and Arizona.[13]

Nevertheless, as Church membership continued to mushroom in southern California, interest in erecting a temple there remained high. President Heber J. Grant, who frequently visited that area, personally participated in the search for a temple site in Los Angeles. He spent a month there early in 1937 for that purpose. On March 6 the Church announced the purchase of a twenty-four-acre tract on Santa Monica Boulevard in West Los Angeles from the motion picture actor Harold Lloyd for $175,000; the plan was to erect a temple costing about $350,000.[14] President Grant enthusiastically told President J. Reuben Clark that "we have the best site in the entire country"; he personally planned to contribute at least $2,500.[15]

Apparently the people in southern California were anxious to get started immediately with the erection of their temple. Less than two weeks after the announcement that land had been purchased, the First Presidency wrote: "In the past the Lord has sometimes delayed the beginning of the work of building a temple and has carried on its construction for years...that people might come to an adequate appreciation of the spiritually high purpose toward which their efforts were directed." For example, he showed wisdom "in prolonging the experience and sacrifice of the people" in connection with building the Salt Lake Temple. The date when a temple is completed is less important than "the spirit with which the building is erected and the righteousness which it shall bring into the hearts of the people.... The building of a temple is a matter...to be carried on with the greatest dignity, [and] a spirit of reverence and even with sanctification."[16] Nevertheless, enthusiasm for the temple project continued high.

The First Presidency assigned a group of architects headed by Edward O. Anderson to design the temple under the general supervision of Church architect Arthur Price. They visited the site, tested the strength of the subsoil, and evaluated the earthquake potential. Eventually preliminary plans were completed for a temple that would accommodate companies of two hundred persons. Before planning could proceed further, World War II brought the project to a halt.

During the 1930s there was also interest in obtaining a temple site in northern California. Here again, the Saints looked back to a prophetic statement concerning a temple in their area. During the summer of 1924 George Albert Smith the Apostle was in San Francisco attending regional Boy Scout meetings. On that occasion he met with W. Aird Macdonald, who was president of the Church's small branch across the bay in Oakland. They met at the Fairmont Hotel high atop San Francisco's Nob Hill. Macdonald later recalled:

> From the Fairmont terrace we had a wonderful panorama of the great San Francisco Bay, nestling at our feet. The setting sun seemed to set the whole eastern shore afire, until the Oakland hills were ablaze with golden light. As we admired the beauty and majesty of the scene, President Smith suddenly grew silent, ceased talking, and for several minutes gazed intently toward the East Bay hills.

"Brother Macdonald, I can almost see in vision a white temple of the Lord high upon those hills," he exclaimed rapturously, "an ensign to all the world travelers as they sail through the Golden Gate into this wonderful harbor." Then he studied the vista for a few moments as if to make sure of the scene before him. "Yes, sir, a great white temple of the Lord," he confided with calm assurance, "will grace those hills, a glorious ensign to the nations, to welcome our Father's children as they visit this great city."[17]

In 1934 the Church's second stake in the San Francisco Bay area was organized in Oakland, the San Francisco Stake having been formed seven years earlier. At about this time a committee headed by Eugene Hilton was formed to locate a site in the area envisioned by Elder Smith. Hilton later recalled that the Chamber of Commerce and city officials eagerly cooperated. As the relative merits of several sites were weighed, "one particular spot always seemed to impress us as 'the one.'" Even though this site was definitely not for sale, two other sites offered free of charge were turned down. Just after World War II had started, however, the owners of the choice site found that their plans for developing it were blocked because necessary building materials were now restricted. They therefore offered the land to the Church group for eighteen thousand dollars. Hilton, who by this time had become stake president, declared: "It is an answer to our prayers."[18] After inspections by President David O. McKay and others, the First Presidency decided to purchase the site. The deal was consummated on January 28, 1943, and the purchase was announced at the following April general conference.

The erection of both California temples would not come until the period of international growth in Church membership and accelerated temple building during the 1950s and 1960s under the leadership of President David O. McKay.

A Temple in Idaho

In the midst of these efforts to secure temple sites in California, plans were also under way to construct a temple in Idaho. Leaders in various stakes urged that the temple be built in their respective communities. Ezra Taft Benson, a young counselor in the Boise Stake presidency, argued particularly eloquently that a temple should be built in the state capital.[19] Eventually, however, the General Authorities decided to construct the temple in Idaho Falls, where there was a greater concentration of Church members. The Chamber of Commerce, recognizing the boost to the economy which a temple might bring, donated to the Church an impressive five-acre tract on the banks of the Snake River just north of the LDS hospital. When the hospital had been built in the early 1920s, Church leaders had an oversized boiler installed, anticipating possible future expansion. Public announcement of plans to construct a temple in Idaho Falls came in March 1937, the same month the Los Angeles Temple site was purchased.

Latter-day Saints in the area regarded the erection of the Idaho Falls Temple as a fulfillment of prophecy. In 1884 when that part of Idaho was first being settled, Elders Wilford Woodruff and Heber J. Grant, representing the First Presidency, visited the discouraged Saints who were struggling to establish a foothold in that windswept treeless prairie. Standing in a wagon, Elder Woodruff sought to encourage the small group: "Be not discouraged; be not disheartened, because God's blessing is upon this land." He promised them that the time would come when the valley would be fruitful and would be dotted with gardens, fine homes, schools, and meetinghouses. "Yes," he continued, "as I look into the future of this great valley I can see temples—I can see beautiful temples erected to the name of the Living God where holy labors may be carried on in his name through generations to come."[20]

The board of architects headed by Edward O. Anderson was assigned to draw plans for the Idaho Falls Temple as well as for the Los Angeles Temple. These men found it best for each to prepare his own sketch. The group chose the concept prepared by John Fetzer Sr. He affirmed that after praying for guidance, "he saw in vision an ancient Nephite temple which he used as the basis for his design."[21] He prepared the floor plans, incorporating elements from the Alberta and Arizona temples. His son Henry assisted with the elevations, drawing ideas from modern skyscrapers.[22] The resulting design featured contrasting lights and shadows, and was characterized by "simplicity" and "proportion." The architect explained that the temple, "pointing skyward...seems to tell of eternal values."[23]

By April 1939 the preliminary plans were ready. The structure was to be of reinforced concrete faced with gleaming white cast stone. The main building, measuring 95 by 131 feet, would be two stories high and would be surmounted by a tower rising 124 feet above the ground level. The baptismal font in the basement. Offices, a chapel, a cafeteria, and dressing rooms would be on the main floor, while the ordinance rooms accommodating companies of 150 persons would be located on the second floor.

Ground was broken December 19, 1939, but actual construction on the Idaho Falls Temple did not get under way until the following year. Many who worked on the temple were nonmembers, but agreed to abide by Church standards while on the site. During the fall of 1940 excavation was made through the sand that covered the site to the solid lava rock beneath, which provided an ideal foundation. Within a short time the foundation walls and the basement were completed.

President David O. McKay, counselor in the First Presidency, laid the temple's cornerstone on October 19, 1940. Six-year-old John Groberg (who would become a General Authority over three decades later) received the assignment to hold President McKay's hat during the ceremony. In preparation for the occasion, the community had sponsored a general beautification project. Many merchants closed their stores during the program so their employees could join the thousands who attended the ceremonies. A trumpet quartet, who had disappeared without telling anybody where they had gone, played "An Angel from on High" from the roof of the nearby hospital when their number was announced. President McKay used this occasion to formally dedicate the temple site.[24]

The pre-cast concrete facing for the temple's exterior was produced by a cement products company operated by the Buehner family of Salt Lake City. They regarded this contract as a fulfillment of a blessing given to their father years before. Carl F. Buehner had immigrated from Stuttgart, Germany, in 1901, and started the cement business in his backyard. A few years later, his patriarchal blessing promised that "he and his sons would help erect temples of this Church."[25] The Buehners would also provide the exterior stone for the Los Angeles Temple and for a large addition to the Alberta Temple. Furthermore, the oxen for baptismal fonts of the Swiss, New Zealand, London, and Idaho Falls temples were sculpted in their shop.

Most major construction on the Idaho Falls Temple was completed during 1941, the stainless steel capstone being placed atop the tower on August 19, only ten months after the cornerstone had been laid. This represented a record in the history of temple construction. Fortunately, steel and other strategic materials had been stockpiled before World War II restrictions made them unavailable. Marble from France, Italy, and Sweden crossed the Atlantic just before hostilities made such shipments unsafe. When exterior scaffolding was taken down in September 1941 the temple appeared to be finished, and it was expected to open by the end of the following year.[26] Nevertheless, wartime shortages delayed equipping and furnishing the interior, so the temple would not be dedicated until after the war ended in 1945.

Idaho Falls Temple

The Impact of War

The coming of World War II had a dampening impact on temple activity. An increasing number of Church members, both men and women, entered the armed forces or went to work in defense industries. Gasoline and tire rationing increasingly restricted travel. As a result, the annual number of endowments for the dead fell from a level of about 500,000 just before the war to less than half that number—240,000—in 1943. The Genealogical Society's library reported a similar drop in patronage during the war years. The war not only postponed construction of the Los Angeles Temple and paved the way for purchasing a temple site in Oakland, but it had a particularly direct impact on the Idaho Falls Temple.

Although the Idaho Falls Temple had appeared from the outside to be finished when the United States became involved in World War II, much work still remained to be completed in the building's interior. Many workmen left to join the armed forces. Aluminum and other strategic materials needed to equip and furnish the temple became increasingly scarce. Other problems would also contribute to these delays. The concrete walls did not provide sufficient insulation, so the resulting condensation damaged the mural fabrics. The First Presidency named Edward O. Anderson to take charge of remedying this problem and to take steps to soften the appearance of the temple's interior. President J. Reuben Clark, for example, recommended that lighting effects in the celestial room ceiling should "typify the Spirit and its presence."[27]

As World War II drew to its close in 1945, work on the Idaho Falls Temple was also completed. The total cost, including furnishings and preparation of the grounds, was approximately one million dollars. Although wartime shortages made travel difficult, some 45,000 attended an open house September 15-20. A crew of twenty-five Relief Society volunteers worked late into the night to clean the building following each day's tours.

The temple's dedication attracted interest throughout the area and was a time of recommitment and rededication for the Saints. President Heber J. Grant, who had directed the erection of the temple, had died only four months prior to its dedication. Consequently it fell to his successor,

President George Albert Smith, to direct the eight dedicatory services held September 23-25, 1945. President Smith spoke briefly at each of the dedicatory sessions. He commended the people for having built such a beautiful temple and stressed the importance of their preparing themselves to enter the house of the Lord. He urged bishops to protect the temple by carefully interviewing those whom they recommended as worthy to enter the temple. In his dedicatory prayer President Smith expressed gratitude for the cessation of war and for the coming of peace. He prayed that the peoples of the world might be inclined to live the gospel of Jesus Christ, thereby making the peace permanent.[28] The dedication of the Idaho Falls Temple just one month following the surrender of Japan was a particularly visible harbinger of the postwar resurgence in temple activity.

Chapter Nine

Postwar Progress

The close of World War II signaled a resurgence in temple activity. The dedication of the Idaho Falls Temple in 1945, just one month after the war closed, was but the first in a series of significant developments. As gasoline rationing was lifted, more Latter-day Saints were able to travel to the temples to participate in sacred ordinances. Hence the number of endowments for the dead increased by one-third between 1946 and 1949. Furthermore, as the numbers in military service were cut back and the need for employment in defense industries waned, Church members had more time to devote to temple worship and related genealogical research.

As construction materials once again became available, Church leaders were able to turn their attention to upgrading existing temples and building new ones. Postwar renovations enhanced the beauty and efficiency of two of the nineteenth century temples in Utah. During 1947 the old plaster was sandblasted from the St. George Temple's exterior, and a new coat of gleaming white stucco was applied. The Logan Temple was closed for nearly a year during 1949 and 1950 for major improvements. This project, costing $200,000, included enlarging office, kitchen, and laundry areas in the temple annex; improving heating, air conditioning, and lighting; and installing elevators.

The Church grew at an unprecedented rate during the postwar years, and this expansion was reflected in temple building. This period brought the construction of the largest temple in Church history and the erection of the first "overseas" temples. Thus the blessings of the house of the Lord became available to an ever-broader group of Latter-day Saints.

Temple Blessings in Spanish

An important precedent was set in 1945 at the Arizona Temple when ordinances were presented for the first time in a language other than English. President Lorin F. Jones of the Spanish-American Mission regarded this as the literal fulfillment of a prophetic promise he received when he was set apart as mission president two years before. President George Albert Smith, then president of the Council of the Twelve Apostles, declared: "You will see marvelous things transpire as affecting the Lamanite people.... These will be history-making events in the Church."[1]

Even though most members of his mission spoke some English, they did not, President Jones believed, understand the full meaning of the temple ceremony in that language. He felt that the Church should enable these Saints to receive the temple ordinances in their own tongue. After touring the mission in 1943, Elder Joseph Fielding Smith of the Council of the Twelve concurred: "I see no reason why the English language should monopolize the temple session." Following the First Presidency's approval of Elder Smith's recommendation, the exacting task of translating the temple ceremonies into Spanish got under way. Working in the Salt Lake Temple, Elder Antoine R. Ivins of the first Council of the Seventy, who spoke fluent Spanish, and Eduardo Balderas, a translator for the Church, carried out this assignment during the next year. "The opportunity of translating the sacred ordinances within the confines of the Salt Lake Temple," Brother Balderas recalled, "was, of course, a wonderful privilege and blessing." He testified that the "influence of the Holy Spirit...guided them in their challenging but enjoyable labors."[2]

The Spanish-speaking Saints were also making their own preparations. Some members living in the United States made trips into Mexico to trace their family genealogies. The mission office in El Paso became a clearing house for records being submitted for temple ordinances. President Jones's wife, Ivie, spent countless hours teaching classes in genealogy and helping the members to get their records in order.

The long-anticipated event came in November 1945. Most of the Saints had to make substantial economic sacrifice, some even giving up jobs, in order to attend the Arizona Temple. Nevertheless about two hundred gathered, coming from as far away as Mexico City. Efforts were made to keep the costs down. Food was provided by the local Maricopa Stake. Housing was to be in the large Mezona recreational hall, which was divided by temporary curtains into three sections—men's sleeping area on one side, women's on the other, and the main central area for meetings. Members who were planning to attend were not concerned with their personal comfort. A branch president in Mexico reported: "We talked this matter over with our members, and they said to tell you not to worry about it. They will be happy to sleep on the floor, just so they get to Mesa."[3] This, however, would not be necessary. As late as a week before the Saints were due to arrive, sufficient bedding for such a large group had not been located. At that point a Church member stationed at a nearby army base offered the use of two hundred cots and blankets. "Don't thank me," he insisted, "thank the Lord. He is the one who prompted me to offer them, for I didn't even know you needed them."

A special "Lamanite Conference" convened on Sunday, November 4, a warm sunny day. The Spanish-American Branch chapel in Mesa was filled to overflowing during the three conference sessions. President David O. McKay of the First Presidency, Elder Antoine R. Ivins of the First Council of the Seventy, Relief Society general president Belle S. Spafford, and other auxiliary representatives were in attendance. Their presence meant a great deal to the Spanish-speaking members, most of whom had never met a member of the First Presidency or a General Relief Society president before. President McKay expressed appreciation for being present for an "outstanding event in Church history." He pointed out that other Lamanite groups had enjoyed the temple ceremonies in Hawaii, but always in English.

All day Monday was spent checking recommends and obtaining temple clothing. The history-making Spanish temple sessions began on Tuesday, November 6, 1945. Sixty-nine received their own endowments and twenty-four couples were sealed for eternity. A total of 798 ordinances for the living and the dead were performed during the next three days.[4]

President Jones regarded the all-Lamanite conference and Spanish temple sessions as the outstanding spiritual event in the mission during the year. Those who had attended could now appreciate the Church as being more than just the small group with which they met each Sunday, often in a poorly furnished room.[5] Ricardo Duran from a small branch in Northern New Mexico, for example, declared: "I came from a place where there are only two families who are members of the Church. I see that here in [Mesa] there are many members of the Church.... Perhaps we are the most blest people of all the world with the exception of those who lived during Christ's ministry.... We must now show our appreciation by doing the work for those who were not so fortunate as we."[6] Elder Alma Sonne, who toured the Spanish-American Mission shortly afterward, found that everywhere he went the Saints spoke enthusiastically of their experience in Mesa. "It has given purpose and significance to the lives of those who were able to attend."[7]

The Spanish temple sessions and associated conference became eagerly anticipated annual events. "Hasta Mesa" ("See you in Mesa") could often be heard as members from different branches parted. Hector Trevino of Monterrey, Mexico, likened these annual excursions to the ancient Jewish custom of returning to the temple in Jerusalem each year at Passover in order to perform religious ceremonies and to renew covenants with the Lord.[8]

Those coming to Mesa frequently demonstrated great faith as they made the sacrifices required for the trip. One man from Mexico came with his family two years in succession even though his employer did not give him permission to leave and told him he need not return. In each instance he was able to find a different and better-paying job. An older sister in Mexico City earned her living selling fruit. Having no refrigerator, she bought from the wholesaler each morning only enough fruit for that day's sales. From her meager income she set aside her tithing and a little for her Mesa fund. After several years she believed she had enough to make the trip. She took her small bag of coins to the mission office. The mission secretary found that the faithful sister did not have quite enough, but, rather than disappointing her, made up the difference himself.[9] Another group from the interior of Mexico was coming in two old buses. When one of the buses broke down, the group doubled up in the other. Then, in the middle of the desert, a radiator hose burst. Without needed supplies, repairs could not be made, and the group appeared to be stranded in that desolate spot. Nevertheless, the group prayed that the way might be provided for them to continue. To escape the heat in the disabled bus, most of the group climbed out. By the side of the road they found a piece of discarded hose—just what they needed. When repairs had been made, they poured drinking water from their canteens into the radiator and were soon on their way once again.[10]

In 1956 a group of ninety-five Saints from Guatemala and El Salvador traveled over three thousand miles by bus to attend the temple. Much of their journey was over dusty, unpaved roads. At dusk on the sixth day they reached Mesa. The buses drove around the beautifully illuminated temple. No sight could have been more welcome to these travel-weary Saints. "They spontaneously burst into singing 'We Thank Thee O God for a Prophet.'…Tears of joy and thanksgiving filled the eyes of those who had traveled so far to enter the Arizona Temple." During the trip, so great was the feeling of brotherhood that one of the bus drivers expressed a desire to have the missionaries teach him upon his return home.[11]

By the early 1960s so many wished to come to the temple that more than one excursion had to be scheduled each year. Arrangements were made for patriarchs who could speak Spanish to be available to give blessings. Eduardo Balderas and Lorin F. Jones were among the first to provide this gratefully received service. Eventually dormitories were built near the temple to more adequately house the growing number of visitors.

Giving endowments at Mesa in a language other than English had a worldwide impact. Just one month after dedicating the Swiss Temple, the first temple in which English would not be the predominant language, President McKay told the annual Lamanite Conference in Mesa: "It was because of your faithfulness and diligence that we felt impressed to give to other people the opportunity for receiving these [temple] blessings. You are serving as an example to the members of the Church in Europe; their eyes are upon you."[12]

The Los Angeles Temple

Active planning for a temple in Los Angeles resumed under President George Albert Smith's leadership. On January 17, 1949, President Smith announced at a meeting of Southern California Church leaders that the time had arrived to build the temple. Conferring with civic leaders in Los Angeles, the President expressed his desire that the temple should be a "contribution to the architecture and culture of the community."[13] California Church leaders were convinced that over a decade earlier President Heber J. Grant was inspired in selecting the Santa Monica Boulevard site: "It is the highest point in elevation between Los Angeles and the ocean." Furthermore, the freeway network, planned after the site was purchased, would provide excellent transportation.[14]

Latter-day Saint population in southern California had grown substantially during and immediately following World War II. President Smith was therefore concerned that the projected temple be large enough to accommodate the increased membership. In January 1949 he appointed Edward O. Anderson, who had been a member of the pre-war board of temple architects, to be the sole architect for the new temple. The President instructed him to enlarge the design to accommodate from two hundred to three hundred persons per company, the same capacity as the Salt Lake Temple, and to add a large priesthood assembly room on the upper floor, the first of only two such facilities to be built in the twentieth century.[15]

Anderson prayed for the same inspiration that had guided earlier temple architects, so that his design "might express in appearance" and facilitate "the spiritual work" to be carried on in the temple. A staff of twenty-eight specialists assisted with the preparation of the sixty-three large pages of plans. Architect Anderson and his associates worked closely with the First Presidency, from whom they received constant inspiration and direction. He later testified that whenever a problem arose in designing the building, "the answers or individuals we needed were forthcoming."[16]

By December 1950, the General Authorities had approved the enlarged design for the Los Angeles Temple. It reflected Mayan architecture and featured plantings on the roof, around the large reflecting pool, and inside the building.[17] The temple would be 364 feet long and 241 feet wide, and would be surmounted by a tower more than 257 feet high. The building's six levels would include about four and one-half acres of floor space, making this the largest temple the Church had ever built.

During the same time, Preston D. Richards, a Los Angeles attorney, worked at no expense to the Church in contacting the planning, safety, engineering, and many other government bureaus to obtain permits necessary for the temple's construction. Zoning was also needed to prevent any undesirable businesses or industries from locating nearby. The purposes of the temple were explained to the Los Angeles Building Department. "When these men realized the importance of the temple and reviewed the record of Latter-day Saints living in California," they were pleased to "help in every way to obtain the necessary permits."[18] The final approval was received from the city council early in 1951.

Groundbreaking for the new temple was delayed by the death of President George Albert Smith and the sustaining of a new First Presidency in April. Under the direction of President David O. McKay the long-anticipated event finally took place on September 22, 1951. In the presence of 250 invited guests, he turned the first spade of earth, declaring that the Los Angeles Temple would be "reared to the glory of God and to the salvation of his people." As other leaders took their turns, the earth proved to be too hard; and President McKay had to "soften it up" for them with his shovel, much to the delight of those present. After the groundbreaking, the President officially dedicated the temple site.[19]

Following careful planning by southern California Church leaders, President McKay personally launched the fund-raising campaign as he met with 1,200 ward and stake leaders. He challenged them to raise one million of the projected four million dollars the temple would cost. He counseled them to have the "young people, even the children in the 'cradle roll' [nursery], contribute to the temple fund, for this is their temple, where they will be led by pure love to take their marriage vows."[20] The Saints responded generously, raising over $1,648,000. When one deacon pledged $150, his bishop thought he had put the decimal in the wrong place. Within two years, however, the young man had paid the full amount from his paper route and lawn cutting earnings.[21]

Those responsible for building the temple felt the need for divine assistance. Hence, at the beginning of each day the workmen gathered to offer prayer. Among them were men who had never prayed before in their lives. As construction progressed, some of these men were so touched by these devotionals that they eventually requested the privilege of leading the prayer themselves.[22]

The temple was constructed of reinforced concrete specifically engineered to withstand southern California's earthquakes. The huge building was faced with some 2,500 separate perfectly matched crushed-stone panels. They covered over 126,000 square feet, more than the area of three football fields. The panels were etched with acid in such a way that the stone crystals in them sparkled in the light. Once again the Buehner brothers received the contract to provide the stone, which they regarded as a further fulfillment of their father's patriarchal blessing. Carl W. Buehner reported that when the specific material was chosen for the temple's exterior, "there was just enough to make the stone for this building and the Bureau of Information [Visitors' Center]—no more, no less."[23]

The temple's cornerstone was laid December 11, 1953. A party of sixty-seven, including more than twenty General Authorities, arrived from Salt Lake City aboard Union Pacific's "Los Angeles Limited." They were met at the downtown depot by local Saints in sixteen cars to take them directly to the temple site about twelve miles away, escorted by two motorcycle policemen. The lead officer was Albert J. Aardema, who happened to be bishop of a local Latter-day Saint ward.[24]

Some 10,000 people, the largest gathering of Latter-day Saints in California to that date, filled the grounds east of the partially completed temple. President David O. McKay conducted the ceremony; his first counselor, Stephen L Richards, gave the main address; and J. Reuben Clark Jr., second counselor, placed the metal box, which had been contributed by the Kennecott Copper Co. The Los Angeles County Board of Supervisors presented a formal resolution congratulating the Church, whose members were "well known and highly respected" citizens in the community.[25]

Meanwhile, a fifteen and one-half foot figure of the angel Moroni had been sculpted by Millard F. Malin and then cast in aluminum in New York. In October 1954 the one-ton statue was hoisted to the roof, coated with twenty-three carat gold, and then placed on the tower. According to the architectural plan, the angel faced the front of the temple. David O. McKay frequently visited the temple, "observing with an avid interest each phase of the work."[26] On one of these trips, not long before the dedication, "President McKay noticed that the Angel Moroni faced southeast as does the temple." He told Edward O. Anderson and recently appointed temple president Benjamin L. Bowring "that it was not correct in that position. He said that the angel must face east. He asked Brother Anderson to have it adjusted so that it would face due east."[27] Most, but not all, Latter-day Saint temples face east. This may be symbolic of watching for the Lord's Second Coming, which has been compared to the dawning in the east of a new day (Matthew 24:27).

The figure on the tower became a source of interest. One neighbor indicated, perhaps tongue-in-cheek, that she "certainly never would be interested [in learning more about the Church] until the angel faced her home."

Los Angeles Temple

Then one morning she awoke to discover that the statue had been turned and "was looking directly at her place." Another neighbor reported that she had always felt uneasy when her husband was away on business, but since the angel on the spire was watching over her home, "she had a sense of security that she had never felt before."[28] Yet another neighbor told the director of the temple visitors' center that each morning she looked out of her window and saw "St. Moroni blessing the people" and felt sure he was blessing her as well.[29] As the temple neared completion, the thirteen-acre grounds were beautifully landscaped. Trees and other plants came from all over the world, including olives, pines, palms, and the Chinese Ginkgo. Teenage Latter-day Saint girls from the area contributed roses for a beautiful, quiet garden.[30]

The temple's large ordinance rooms featured beautiful murals. Joseph Gibby, a Los Angeles artist and technical illustrator, received the assignment to paint for the baptistry a mural depicting the Savior's baptism. As this work neared completion, the artist experienced a problem, so he went to visit with President David O. McKay. "I cannot paint the Savior's face to my satisfaction. I need to know his complexion and coloring." Without hesitation the prophet described the Savior's features for the artist.[31]

Nearly 700,000 persons visited the temple during the fifty-one-day open house. A local television station carried an hourlong program featuring the new landmark. The viewers gained an impression of the building's size as the television camera slowly moved the nearly three-hundred-foot length of the upper assembly room, all the time focusing on the Southern California Mormon Choir at one end as they sang "Battle Hymn of the Republic." The temple was dedicated in eight sessions March 11-14, 1956, by President David O. McKay. For the first time, closed-circuit television carried proceedings from the assembly room to other areas in the temple. Referring to such marvels of modern communication, President McKay commented: "How easy it must be in the spirit world to tune in on an occasion of this kind."[32]

The First "Overseas Temple"

President David O. McKay played a key role in the internationalization of the Church. This began with his worldwide tour of missions in 1921 and, according to a recent biographer, "culminated with his initiatives in constructing temples abroad." He stressed that "Zion" is not confined to any particular geographical location, but is "a condition of heart and mind" which can be found in any part of the world.[33]

The notion of temples being built overseas was not new. President Joseph F. Smith's 1906 prophecy had spoken specifically of temples in Europe and other lands. Then when speaking at the Alberta Temple dedication in 1923, President Heber J. Grant had made a similar prophecy: "I have no doubt in my mind that Temples of the Lord will be erected in Europe, none whatever. How soon that will come I do not know. It will not come until the spirit of peace has increased among the people of Europe."[34]

Just after the close of World War II, Elder Ezra Taft Benson was assigned to supervise the distribution of welfare supplies and to reopen missions in Europe. He invited Frederick W. Babbel, who had served a mission to Germany just before the war, to be his companion and personal secretary. On their first visit to Berlin, a German sister came up to Brother Babbel and reminded him that in 1937 he had challenged the Saints in her branch "to lead the Church in preparing their genealogical records." She then read to him from her little black notebook a prophetic promise he had made on that occasion: "If we proved our sincerity and faith, given ten years of peace in which to work, the Lord would bless us with a Temple in Europe where we might receive our own sealings and endowments."[35] World War II ended in Europe in 1945, and the first temple on that continent would be dedicated just ten years later.

At their meeting in the Salt Lake Temple on April 17, 1952, the First Presidency and the Quorum of the Twelve made the historic decision to build temples in Europe. In June of that year President David O. McKay was in Europe to personally supervise selection of the sites. Switzerland was chosen because of its relative peace, central location, and multi-lingual population. Kneeling in prayer with mission leaders at the headquarters in Basel, President McKay was impressed to locate the temple at Bern, Switzerland's capital.[36] At a news conference in Glasgow as he was about to end his eight weeks in Europe, President McKay announced that negotiations were under way for a temple site in Switzerland. Upon arriving home he further stated that the Swiss Temple would be but the first of several temples to be built in Europe, explaining that "the Church could bring temples to these people by building smaller edifices for this purpose and more of them."[37]

Despite several months of negotiations with the owners of the site President McKay had approved, no definite agreement could be reached. "Finally, during a sleepless night in October" the Swiss Mission president, Samuel E. Bringhurst, recalled, "the thought occurred that perhaps there was a reason for the delay, and that we should pray for a decision, and leave the matter with the Lord." He therefore asked all the missionaries to fast with him. The following day he was notified that the property was no longer for sale. "This answer so quickly, while a little disappointing, was a wonderful testimony to all of us."[38] The mission president reported these developments to President McKay, who replied: "As I read your letter stating that all effort had failed and a negative decision had been rendered, I was not surprised, but at first disappointed; however, strangely enough, my disappointment soon disappeared and was replaced by an assurance that the Lord will overrule all transactions for the best good of his Church, not only in Switzerland but throughout Europe."[39]

Meanwhile, President Bringhurst and his real estate agent found another site in the Bern area. "As we walked over it," President Bringhurst testified, "all doubt seemed to leave and we felt certain we were on the site the Lord wished for the first European temple.... At this time we learned why the Lord did not allow us to purchase the first site." The construction of a new highway preempted the key section of the original site.[40] The new property included twice the area of the former one and, on November 20, 1952, was purchased for half the cost.

While these negotiations were moving forward, the process of planning the new temple had already begun. Edward O. Anderson, who was still supervising construction of the Los Angeles Temple, received the assignment to plan the new structure. Designing a temple to be used by members speaking several languages presented a complex problem. He worked closely with President David O. McKay, who explained that "you cannot carry the Salt Lake Temple...which took forty years to build, over to Switzerland.... You cannot present the entire plan of going from room to room. Some modification had to be made." President McKay later testified that "when the revelation came" to make temples accessible to the Saints abroad, he was also told how to make the same ceremonies and covenants available "to the Saints on the outskirts of Zion;" the "divine requirements of that revelation" had been followed.[41]

"When President McKay told me that the Church was going to build this new type of temple in Switzerland," architect Anderson recalled, "his description of it fixed a picture so firmly in my mind that I could draw it." Later, as the process of designing progressed and some changes in the original plan were suggested, President McKay countered, "Brother Anderson, this is not the temple that you and I saw together." "Of course," the architect acknowledged, "the changes were dropped and the Prophet's concept carried through to completion."[42]

Using modern equipment such as motion pictures made it possible to present the endowment in a single ordinance room and in more than one language with far fewer than the usual number of temple workers. A committee consisting of Elders Joseph Fielding Smith, Richard L. Evans, and Gordon B. Hinckley, together with Edward O. Anderson, supervised the

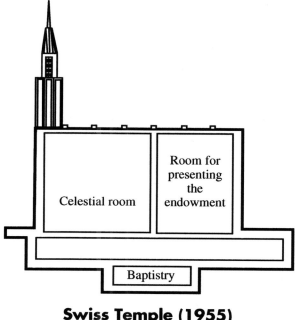

Swiss Temple (1955)

preparation of the films. Their work would "simplify, accelerate, and, in a sense, revolutionize temple work." President McKay personally spent considerable time reviewing the temple ceremonies, praying, and counseling with the committee.[43] Although scenes were shot at various locations in California and Utah, the new films were produced in the large assembly room of the Salt Lake Temple. Using immigrants and returned missionaries, the sound was dubbed in several languages. Architect Anderson recruited the help of several Southern California motion picture studios in designing the technical equipment. A one-twelfth scale working model of the ordinance room was demonstrated to the First Presidency and temple building committee, who enthusiastically approved the new concept.[44]

By April 1953, the architect's drawings of the new temple were released to the public and forwarded to Switzerland. In accordance with Swiss law the plans were placed on public display in the city hall before a building permit could be issued. A leading Protestant minister objected because the law recognized only the Catholic and Protestant churches. All others must be registered as Vereins (Associations). To comply with this requirement, a group of Saints convened the following Sunday in Basel and officially organized, then voted to authorize President Bringhurst to proceed with the temple project.[45]

The groundbreaking ceremony was set for August 5, 1953. As this date drew near, the Saints were concerned because it had been raining steadily for six weeks. Consequently, the missionaries and the Saints fasted and prayed for good weather. The morning of the groundbreaking was gloriously sunny with the magnificent snow-capped Alps in full view. The grassy temple site was on elevated ground and had a beautiful forest backdrop. When President David O. McKay and his party arrived, children from Bern presented him with an arrangement of rare Alpine edelweiss. Fifty chairs had been set up in front of the small platform because only a few were expected to attend this relatively unpublicized event. Surprisingly, however, about three hundred from various parts of Switzerland and Germany attended. Following his prayer dedicating the site, President McKay and other leaders turned the first shovels of soil. With the shovel still in his hand, President McKay was pleased to explain the purposes of the future temple to interested civic officials who were present. That night the rains resumed and continued throughout the following day. "Surely," President McKay was convinced, "the prayers for good weather during the dedicatory services were answered."[46]

Saints throughout Europe eagerly contributed to the temple's construction. Therese Leuschner, an eighty-year-old widow, had saved one hundred francs over an extended period. Because she had been able to put aside only a little bit at a time, the entire amount was given in half-franc pieces. "I will not live when this holy building will be dedicated," she believed (and she did not), but she was eager to make her donation anyway.[47]

Construction on the temple got under way in the fall. Local craftsmen were employed wherever possible. William Zimmer, a counselor in the mission presidency, redrew and rewrote the plans in German. The branch president in Basel became the contractor for the metal work on the doors and the baptismal font. The stainless steel font, when filled with water, had the appearance of being filled with molten silver.[48]

The cornerstone was laid November 13, 1954, under the direction of Stephen L Richards, First Counselor in the First Presidency. Most of the service was conducted inside the uncompleted building, the congregation being seated on rough wooden benches. At the conclusion of President Richards's address, the group moved outside. A mason in his working clothes brought out the copper box containing various historical documents and placed it in the space which had been prepared. As the masons began to brick up the opening, President Richards, using a trowel, assisted in placing the last stone, which bears an inscription, including the dates of construction.[49]

As the appointed time drew near, some feared that the temple would not be ready. Nevertheless, technicians worked around the clock for several days to have everything in order on time. As President McKay left Salt Lake City for the dedication, he rejoiced that the European Saints would no longer need to emigrate in order to receive their temple blessings. He stressed that this milestone was "but the beginning of a temple building program that would bring these blessings to every Latter-day Saint throughout the world."[50]

The first dedicatory session convened Sunday morning, September 11, 1955, in the temple's celestial room. Three hundred members of the Salt Lake Tabernacle Choir, then on a concert tour of Europe, were seated in a

Swiss Temple

semi-circle around the stand. "From the time we entered the temple," choir members recalled, "there was not a word spoken [by choir or congregation] until we left the temple at the close of the services. During much of the service there was not a dry eye in the congregation." The choir found it difficult to sing through "tears and emotion of a very sacred nature.... It was as if the Heavenly Hosts were verily a tangible part of the audience. If our mortal eyes could have been opened we might have seen them."[51] As President McKay greeted those who were present, he declared that he "felt the near presence also of a great unseen audience of former Presidents and Apostles of the Church and departed loved ones."[52] Elder Ezra Taft Benson reflected on this sacred occasion as he spoke at general conference three weeks later: "I think I have never felt in all my life the veil quite so thin" as it was during the temple's dedication. All were convinced that "the action taken by the First Presidency in extending temples into Europe had the benediction and approval of our Heavenly Father. I shall never forget that glorious event! To me it was the most important event that has transpired in Europe in 118 years since the gospel was first taken to those shores."[53]

In addition to the 1,200 inside the temple, hundreds of others filled the grounds outside. Many lined adjacent streets waiting for admission to the afternoon session, designated for missionaries and servicemen. Dedication events continued through Thursday, there being a total of ten sessions conducted in seven different languages. The opening session was recorded and was later broadcast on radio station KSL in Salt Lake City.

To accommodate those who had traveled long distances, temple ordinances commenced Friday morning, the day after dedicatory services ended. Gordon B. Hinckley, who had a key role in preparing the recordings and films for use in the temple, personally carried these materials to Switzerland. His bringing them through customs without major difficulties was regarded as an answer to prayer. Church officials had fasted and prayed that sacred items might reach the temple "unmolested."[54] Under Brother Hinckley's supervision, final preparations had been completed for presenting the temple ceremonies. In six languages, session followed session without ceasing for forty hours. Speaking through an interpreter, President McKay greeted the first three companies and commended them for their faith. Through the night, various groups waited in the temple for their turn. The faithful Saints endured this inconvenience because they were eager to receive their temple blessings.[55] By Saturday evening, some 280 had received their endowment.[56]

Mission authorities reported that the new temple created interest among nonmembers, who often referred to it as "our temple." Saints from throughout Europe devoted their vacations to working in the temple. Residents of the neighborhood, not members of the Church, rented rooms to the visitors, sometimes giving up their own beds and sleeping on the floor. Other Saints camped out in the beautiful woods behind the temple.[57] Now that the house of the Lord was accessible to them, it became a powerful influence in their lives.

A Temple in New Zealand

At about this same time, steps were being taken to obtain a temple site in the South Pacific. As early as about 1928 the president of the New Zealand Mission, John E. Magleby, told the small group of Saints in the Waikato Valley that "it would not be long until a House of God would be built in this area." He further prophesied that "the Waikato would become a gathering place and that some time in the future, the Saints in New Zealand would not need a passport to go to the temple."[58]

In 1954 President McKay appointed Wendell B. Mendenhall, who was then directing the Church's Pacific building program, to confidentially investigate possible temple sites. Elder Mendenhall looked over various properties in New Zealand, but felt that he had not yet seen the temple site. One day he felt impressed to go to Hamilton, where the Church College was then under construction. "While in the car on the way, the whole thing came to me in an instant," he recalled. "The temple should be there by the college. The Church facilities for construction were already there, and that was the center of the population of the mission. Then, in my mind, I could see the area even before I arrived, and I could envision the hill where the temple should stand. As soon as I arrived at the college and drove over the top of the hill, my whole vision was confirmed." This hill commanded a spectacular view not only of the Church college but also of the fertile Waikato River valley.

About ten days later President McKay arrived in Hamilton. Elder Mendenhall first met him in the presence of others, so nothing could be said about the question of a temple site. Elder Mendenhall described their first visit to the hill: "After we stepped from the car and were looking around, President McKay called me to one side. By the way he was looking at the hill, I could tell immediately what was on his mind. I had not said a word to him. He asked, 'What do you think?' I knew what his question implied, and I simply asked in return, 'What do you think, President McKay?' And then in an almost prophetic tone he pronounced, 'This is the place to build the temple.'"

The owners of this choice hill had previously indicated that they did not wish to sell their property. One morning following President McKay's departure from New Zealand, Elder Mendenhall again met with them. They still were not willing to sell. By afternoon, however, Elder Mendenhall had convinced them to change their minds. His account continues:

"Elder [George] Biesinger [supervisor of Church construction in New Zealand] and I had gone over the property very thoroughly and had put a valuation on it by breaking it down into various lots and acres. We met with the attorney and he overpriced the property considerably. After discussing the matter for about an hour, he said, 'Would you be willing to consider this purchase if I break this property down my way and arrive at its valuation?' And we hazarded the chance and said, 'Yes.'

"He figured the property his way, not knowing what was in our hearts or that we had our own valuation on paper in our pockets. He passed his paper to us. We looked at it. It was exactly the same figure, right to the penny, we had figured that morning before going to his office. At five-thirty that evening we had the signed papers."[59]

President McKay did not announce the new temple immediately, but at a conference meeting in Auckland he declared: "I can hardly restrain myself in telling you what we have seen in vision. There may not be a temple on that high mountain...but I think there will be some day in the future." He instructed them, though, that they would have to be personally worthy in order to benefit from temple blessings.[60] At Ipswich, Australia, he similarly counseled the Saints against going "to Zion" for temple blessings and encouraged them "to remain in their own habitat. Let a temple be built nearer to you."[61] Upon returning home from the Pacific, President McKay conferred with his counselors and with the Quorum of the Twelve in their weekly Salt Lake Temple meeting, and that afternoon an announcement of the New Zealand Temple appeared in the *Deseret News*.[62]

Planning for the new temple moved quickly, because it closely followed the pattern of the Swiss Temple. Mission President Ariel S. Ballif conducted the groundbreaking exercises (no General Authorities being present) on a warm afternoon, December 21, 1955, the first day of the Southern Hemisphere summer.[63] As soon as this service concluded, two caterpillar tractors and five dumptrucks moved onto the site and began excavating with the interested crowd looking on. Within seventy-two hours the 190-by-95-foot excavation was completed to an average depth of 19 feet. Thirty-seven "labor missionaries" gave up their Christmas holiday to prepare the roofings. They did not walk, but ran with loaded wheelbarrows "as if the temple could not be built soon enough."[64]

All of the construction was done by volunteer labor. Beginning in 1950 the Church had devised the "labor missionary" program to build badly needed chapels and schools in the Pacific. Experienced builders, responding to mission calls, acted as supervisors. Young men from the islands, also serving as missionaries, donated their labor, learning valuable skills in the process. The local Saints did their part by feeding and housing these missionaries.[65] Most of the volunteers were Maoris from New Zealand, although each of the other Pacific missions agreed to provide four workers throughout the period of construction despite having extensive building projects of their own. One group who had come from a branch 350 miles away, declined to take any days off despite heavy rains (seventy inches fell during the first year of construction). Some changed into dry clothing at noon in order to continue their work. During one weekend, half of the volunteers were not members of the Church. Of a group of fifty nonmembers who worked on the temple, forty-five were eventually baptized.[66]

Cornerstone-laying ceremonies were conducted December 22, 1956, by Elder Hugh B. Brown, an Assistant to the Twelve then on a tour of the

New Zealand Temple

Pacific missions. Among other memorabilia, the commemorative box included the names of all the labor missionaries who had worked on the temple.[67]

As time for dedication approached, the pace quickened. The work day began at 5:00 A.M. Despite these long hours, many came early and stayed late, singing hymns while they worked. Women assisted with the land-scaping and in weaving carpets—as had been done with temples in the previous century. On the day before the open house began, workers were still hanging wallpaper and laying carpet. Until 1:00 A.M. they could be seen carrying furniture into the temple. Even though the work had been done by volunteer and often unskilled labor, government inspectors found everything in excellent condition.[68]

More than five thousand gathered for the dedication of both the temple and the Church College of New Zealand in April 1958. Most were housed in eight hundred army tents. As President McKay arrived, he received the traditional Maori welcome and noted his pleasure at being able to dedicate the first temple below the Equator.

The London Temple

When President David O. McKay announced plans to construct a temple in Switzerland, he indicated that it "would be the first of several such temples to be erected for the Saints in Europe."[69] Plans for a temple near London were announced in 1953. In August of that year, President McKay visited the thirty-two-acre estate the Church had recently purchased about twenty-four miles south of London. He and Church architect Edward O. Anderson spent the day walking over the grounds until they knew specifically where the new temple should be situated. President McKay was particularly anxious to preserve the estate's beautiful formal gardens. Just a week later, following groundbreaking services for the Swiss Temple, the President returned to dedicate the London site. Only a small group was invited, and most sat on the lawn under the stately oaks during the two-hour service. President McKay spoke enthusiastically of the site's beauty, sug-gesting that being there "is like entering into a little paradise" and that the stream along the southern border of the property, Eden Brook, was appro-priately named. He indicated that the 350-year-old Elizabethan manor house and other buildings on the property would be retained and used for various purposes.[70] Formal groundbreaking would come two years later. This was a period of intensified genealogical activity among the British Saints. Many spent Saturdays poring over old parish records, copying cemetery inscriptions, or traveling to London to consult records at the General Register Office.[71]

A problem arose as plans for temple construction moved forward. A lily pond had once covered part of the plot where the temple was to be built, and now construction engineers were concerned about this swampy ground. Nevertheless, President McKay insisted that the temple be located on the spot he had selected. After much discussion, test holes were drilled to determine if the soil could carry the temple's weight. Surprisingly, rock was found at the proper depth to support the foundations. One of the engineers quipped: "You could build the City of London on that site."[72]

About a thousand gathered for the groundbreaking service on Saturday, August 17, 1955. The Salt Lake Mormon Tabernacle Choir, then in Europe on a concert tour in connection with the Swiss Temple dedication, took part. Although the weather was sunny during most of the service, a light shower of rain was falling as President McKay turned the first spade of soil.[73] The temple's construction reflected high standards of craftsmanship. Below ground level, the structure was carefully "damp-proofed" with an inch-thick layer of hard asphalt. The interior plaster was applied to "furring strips" of wood rather than directly to the brick wall in order to prevent "sweating."[74] Construction progressed to the point that the cornerstone was placed May 11, 1957, under showery skies.

The temple was completed in 1958. The ground floor measured 84 by 159 feet. The lead-covered copper spire rose to a height of 156 feet. The 34,000-square-foot structure had been erected at a cost of $1.25 million. The formal gardens with their beautiful rhododendrons, azaleas, and huge oaks were listed in a Britain-wide directory. During the two weeks scheduled for the pre-dedication open house, some 53,000 persons visited the temple. Because of high public interest three days were added, and the final total was 76,324. At certain times as many as a thousand were in line to tour the edifice. One newspaper reported: "The Mormon Temple is the only Church in Britain with a quarter-mile queue waiting to get in."[75]

Twelve thousand Saints were able to attend the six dedicatory services held Sunday, Monday, and Tuesday, September 7-9. In his dedicatory prayer, President McKay expressed appreciation for the fundamental freedoms guaranteed by the Magna Charta signed centuries earlier in the same county of Surrey where the temple was located.[76]

The first ordinances commenced the morning after the dedicatory services concluded. One of the first families sealed for eternity in the new temple was that of Derek and Muriel Cuthbert, who had been baptized just a few years before.[77] Nearly three decades later he would become the first British resident to be called as a General Authority of the Church. Saints came from all parts of Britain to enjoy the blessings of the House of the Lord. Members in the North British Mission, for example, typically rented twelve-passenger mini-buses for the 200-mile trip. At first, overnight

London Temple

accommodations were provided in the Manor House with its forty spacious rooms, some overlooking the beautiful temple grounds. Subsequently, other facilities were provided nearby for temple patrons. In 1985 the Manor House would become a Missionary Training Center for the European area.

The temple's impact, however, was not limited to Latter-day Saints. Shortly after the temple's dedication, an amateur photography club in the area sponsored a contest. Seventeen-year-old John H. Cox spent an entire day photographing the temple grounds from all angles in varying light. His pictures won the prize. When William's father told temple president Selvoy J. Boyer about the pictures, he ordered some prints. He and other temple workers subsequently ordered more than a hundred additional copies. Each time the youth came to deliver his pictures, President Boyer took time to teach him some principles of the gospel. At the dedication, President McKay had stated that many would view the temple and its grounds, be impressed, and even be baptized. Young Cox was the first known fulfillment of this prophecy, joining the Church in 1960. Eventually he became president of the London Stake.[78]

In 1961 local government officials ruled that the Church would have to pay taxes on the London Temple because it was not a place of "*public* religious worship." The Church appealed this decision, but the House of Lords, the highest court in the land, affirmed the local ruling. There was some speculation that because of this unexpected tax burden the temple might even be closed. Nevertheless, the Saints met the emergency and increased their tithe-paying, and the temple remained open.[79] Like the temples in Switzerland and New Zealand, it would continue to be a source of spiritual strength to an ever-expanding worldwide Church membership.

Chapter Ten

The Pace Quickens

The expansion in temple building which characterized the 1950s did not cease. To the contrary, during succeeding decades the pace quickened even further. Both in North America and abroad new temples were designed and earlier structures were remodeled to enhance their efficiency and effectiveness. Then, during the 1980s, previous records tumbled as new temples for many parts of the world were announced in unprecedented numbers.

Modern Temples in North America

Following the purchase of a site in Oakland, Latter-day Saints in Northern California and adjoining areas eagerly awaited the time when a temple would be constructed there. On Monday, January 23, 1961, President David O. McKay flew to San Francisco, where he met with stake presidents from the area and announced that the time had arrived for the temple's construction. He displayed the architect's sketch of the new temple, which would be surmounted by a 170-foot tower. He appointed two stake presidents, O. Leslie Stone of the Oakland Berkeley Stake and David B. Haight of Palo Alto Stake, to head the temple committee. After only

Oakland Temple

three hours in the Bay area, President McKay returned to Church head-quarters.[1]

The Oakland Temple was designed by Church architect Harold W. Burton, who had also planned the Hawaii Temple nearly a half-century earlier. The modern design had an oriental flavor, reflecting the presence of substantial Asian communities in the area. The architect even planned details of furniture, carpeting, and draperies to harmonize with motifs in the temple's design. The temple's main spire as well as the smaller spires at each of the building's four corners featured lacy, goldleafed grillwork fitted with blue glass through which interior lighting created a striking beauty at night. The temple's reinforced concrete structure was faced with white granite from the Sierras and featured two 35-foot-long sculptured panels. The sculpture facing the temple's north court portrayed the Savior commissioning his Apostles in the Old World, while the panel on the south depicted Christ's appearance to the Nephites.[2]

Unlike the Swiss, New Zealand, and London temples, which had only one ordinance room, the Oakland Temple had two, each seating two hundred and equipped for modern audiovisual presentations. This meant that two groups could receive the endowment instructions simultaneously, a new session beginning each hour. The temple was dedicated November 17, 1964, by President David O. McKay and went into service early the following month.

In 1967, the First Presidency announced that two new temples would be built at Provo and Ogden, the first to be erected in Utah in over three-quarters of a century. The Presidency explained that 52 percent of all temple work was being done in the Salt Lake, Logan, and Manti temples, which consequently were seriously overcrowded. Rather than expending funds to enlarge these temples, Church leaders concluded to build two new ones in order to reduce the amount of travel required of the Saints.

The site chosen for the Ogden Temple was the ten-acre tabernacle square the Church had owned in the downtown area since pioneer times. As early as 1921 President Heber J. Grant had personally inspected two potential sites in Ogden but concluded that the time was not right to build a temple there.[3] For years the hill just northeast of downtown Provo had been

Provo Temple

called "Temple Hill," but in 1911 Brigham Young University's Maeser Building was constructed there. In the coming decades the campus expanded to the north and east, but in 1967 seventeen acres at the mouth of Rock Canyon remained undeveloped even though they were surrounded by subdivisions. This property, easily visible from most parts of the Utah Valley, became the site for the Provo Temple.

The Provo and Ogden temples were designed by Church architect Emil B. Fetzer. Church leaders decided to build both temples from the same basic plan in order to expedite construction and to economize. Efficiency and convenience were prime concerns. Fetzer's assignment was to create a design which would accommodate large numbers of people at a reasonable cost. To achieve the desired efficiency, there would be six ordinance rooms surrounded by an exterior hallway, and the celestial room would be in the building's center. Fetzer reported that the idea for this arrangement came when he read of a park developed in Denmark, which would be completely surrounded by a roadway.[4] Increasing the number of rooms to six made it possible to begin a new endowment session every twenty minutes.

Proceedings of both temples' dedications were carried to other buildings. An overflow congregation was seated in the adjacent tabernacle during each of the six dedicatory sessions of the Ogden Temple, January 18-20, 1972. Only two sessions were required for the dedication of the Provo Temple on February 9, because several large auditoriums on the BYU campus carried the proceedings by means of closed-circuit television. Witnessing throngs leaving the 23,000-seat Marriott Center in reverent silence was an unusual experience. For the next quarter of a century the Provo Temple led the Church in the total number of endowments performed for the dead, even when the estimated participation from Brigham Young University and the Missionary Training Center was subtracted.

The Washington Temple

During the early 1970s the Saints living east of the Mississippi River and in eastern Canada constituted the largest group of Church members that did not live within one day's drive of a temple. They therefore were thrilled with the 1968 announcement that a temple would be built near Washington, D.C. The new temple would also serve members in South America. The First Presidency had approved this project as early as 1960, and the site had been secured in 1962 at a cost of $850,000. This was the "finest, most attractive, and largest undeveloped tract of its kind in the metropolitan Washington area," being situated on a wooded hill overlooking beautiful Rock Creek Park. Only eleven of the fifty-seven wooded acres were to be cleared, giving the temple a feeling of isolation from nearby city bustle.[5]

Because the Church architect was still heavily involved with the Ogden and Provo temples, a team of four prominent Utah architects received the assignment to design the Washington edifice. "We were overwhelmed to have been chosen for such a responsible task," commented Keith W. Wilcox (who would become a General Authority sixteen years later). "We considered it to be the greatest opportunity of our lives. Every architect having membership in the Church dreams of having an opportunity to design a temple."[6] They realized that because "the Washington Temple represents visually the Church in the eastern part of the United States," it needed to be a "majestic edifice." Architect Wilcox testified that he experienced "a great surge of the Spirit" as he first envisioned the six-towered design approved for the new temple. The new structure would be easily "recognized as a Mormon temple," because it embodied a "new and unique expression" of the widely recognized Salt Lake Temple. The temple with its vertical lines "visually expresses [our] relationship to Deity."[7] The previous summer, Wilcox's mother had told him: "Keith, you are going to design a temple for the Church." With a laugh he thanked her for this vote of confidence but explained that "our temples, historically, had been designed by the Church architect." Nevertheless, she told him that he should be prepared.[8] As the planning process moved forward, all four men contributed key ideas to the final design.

The estimated cost for the temple was $15 million, of which the Saints were asked to raise 4.5 million. Contributions poured in from people in varying circumstances. A Mississippi girl contributed eighty dollars in babysitting money. A wealthy businessman donated thousands in the form of stocks. Eventually members in the temple district donated more than $6 million.[9]

Washington Temple

Construction on the huge building began in 1971. Although the basic structure was of concrete, the temple's exterior was covered with beautiful white Alabama marble. In narrow, vertical bands every few feet, the translucent marble was cut to a five-eighths-inch thickness. During daylight hours these "marble windows" admitted a soft amber light to the temple's interior.

Gleaming in the morning sun, the eighteen-foot two-ton figure of the angel Moroni was hoisted by means of a spindly construction crane to the top of the temple's east center tower. This tower, 280 feet high, is the tallest on any Latter-day Saint temple. The figure was sculpted by Avard Fairbanks, who in designing it "thought of the angel Moroni coming to the world to herald the advent of the latter days."[10]

A striking feature of the temple's interior was a thirty-foot-long mural in the main lobby depicting the Second Coming. J. Willard Marriott, who donated the painting, suggested that the artist include the Washington Temple in the scene.[11] On one of the temple's seven floors there were six ordinance rooms arranged in the same efficient pattern as in the Ogden and Provo Temples. The celestial room had a vaulted ceiling thirty-five feet high. As was the case in the Los Angeles Temple, a large solemn assembly room occupied the upper floor.

"Completion ceremonies" attended by three hundred invited guests on September 9, 1974, marked the formal conclusion of the three-year construction period. Members of the First Presidency assisted in placing in the temple's northeast corner a metal box containing historical artifacts. In conducting these ceremonies, President Marion G. Romney pointed out that "we have no finer buildings in the Church than the temples," because they are God's "dwelling place" where He "reveals His presence to His faithful saints."[12] Immediately following these exercises, President Spencer W. Kimball conducted the largest press conference in the Church's history.

These events inaugurated the temple's open house. The first week was devoted to special tours for United States government officials and members of the diplomatic corps representing many other nations. There was even a tour specifically for the temple's immediate neighbors. Betty Ford, the wife of the U.S. President, participated in one of these tours. While "watching the First Lady having her photograph taken with President Spencer W. Kimball," Elder Gordon B. Hinckley recalled that the Prophet Joseph journeyed to the nation's capital and unsuccessfully petitioned the government to compensate the Saints for their sufferings in Missouri. "How far the Church has come in the respect and confidence of public officials, he thought."[13]

During the seven weeks of tours, a record total of 758,328 persons visited the temple. "I saw people change from coldness to a mellow spirit as they entered the temple, heard the explanation, saw John Scott's painting [of the Second Coming] and then proceeded through the temple," recalled President Edward E. Drury, the temple's first president. "Many left with tears in their eyes."[14] The open house also attracted widespread publicity. Favorable articles about the temple appeared not only in national periodicals but in newspapers in all fifty states and abroad.[15]

All the General Authorities except two spoke during the ten dedicatory sessions November 19-22, 1974. At the time of the groundbreaking in 1968, President Hugh B. Brown, who had carried a significant load in planning for the new temple, had asked the Lord to prolong his life so that he might be able to attend the dedication. On the morning of the temple's dedication, President Brown told his colleagues that "he had been visited during the night by President Harold B. Lee," who had died the year before. Later in the morning he greeted President Lee's widow: "I had a glorious visit with Harold last night. He is just fine. It was so good to visit with him."[16] Speaking during the dedication, President Brown declared: "I have looked forward to this for some time. In fact, I set this as a departing point for me and thought that when this was accomplished I probably would be released or assigned to another field."[17] He died just over a year later.

The Temples' Impact Enhanced

In 1975 the Church announced plans to build its first temple in the Pacific Northwest at Seattle. Concerns that the temple would adversely affect the forested environment were answered satisfactorily, and city officials concluded that the temple would be an asset to the community; they therefore granted permits for construction. Because the temple was situated not far from a small airport, the proposed height of the single spire had to be reduced, and a strobe warning light for aircraft was placed at the base of the gold-leafed statue of the angel Moroni. Various anti-Mormon groups opposed the temple's construction, and a few women went so far as to chain themselves to front gates during the temple's dedication in order to protest the Church's stand on the Equal Rights Amendment. The new temple would serve Latter-day Saints coming from as far as Alaska. Each of the four ordinance rooms seated 110, allowing a new endowment session to begin every half hour.

Many were surprised in 1978 when the First Presidency announced that a second temple would be built in the Salt Lake Valley. Even with the Provo and Ogden Temples, the increasing number of Latter-day Saints in the area had created serious overcrowding in the Salt Lake Temple. Church members in the Salt Lake Valley accepted and fulfilled the unusual request to provide all of the funds needed to build the new temple.[18] The extensive use of stained glass together with nighttime illumination made the temple a prominent landmark, easily seen from many parts of the valley. The geographical area served by the new temple was the smallest in the Church, consisting of only the south half of the Salt Lake Valley. At the time of its dedication in 1981, the Jordan River Temple had the largest capacity of any temple in the Church. Each of its six endowment rooms seated 125. Hence it was about 25 percent larger than the similarly designed Ogden and Provo temples.

During the dedicatory services of the Jordan River Temple, Elder Mark E. Petersen powerfully expounded the necessity of work for the dead. "His memory for scriptures" was impressive. "His testimony of the Savior brought tears to many eyes." Several in the audience described a "light that seemed to radiate from his face as he spoke." Elder Petersen later told his family of "the strength of the Spirit he had felt."[19]

Success with these new temples led Church leaders to rebuild and remodel several earlier temples. The interiors of the Arizona, St. George, Hawaii, and Logan Temples were thoroughly redesigned to make use of motion pictures and other modern means of presenting the endowment instructions. In some cases the original endowment rooms were retained and modified only slightly, but in other instances completely new rooms were created. The rebuilding of these temples was so extensive that they were reopened to public tours similar to open houses conducted when new temples are completed. The Arizona Temple made history in 1975 when it became the first of these structures to be reopened and then formally rededicated. At Hawaii, missionaries received some 55,000 referrals as nonmembers signed the temple's guest register. A non-Latter-day Saint teacher in Honolulu so impressed her elementary school students with the sanctity of the temple that some of them bought new shoes before attending the open house. In Hawaii's tropical climate children typically would have worn rubber sandals.[20]

These rebuilt temples had a greater capacity than before. Before its remodeling the St. George Temple normally had three endowment sessions per day, which kept workers busy. Now there were fourteen.[21] These temples accounted for 30 to 60 percent more ordinances than before their remodeling. In 1981, when a fourth lecture room was created in the Los Angeles Temple, it became the temple with the largest capacity in the Church.

Latter-day Saint temples increasingly became means of sharing the gospel, not only with Church members by means of sacred ordinances but also with nonmembers who visited these structures. As early as 1902 a "Bureau of Information" was opened on Temple Square in Salt Lake City. Over the years this became one of the most popular tourist attractions in the Intermountain West.[22] During the 1960s approximately two million persons visited the square each year. Hence, in 1968, an enlarged visitors' center opened to accommodate them. Similar centers at other temples were opened or substantially upgraded in succeeding years. In 1978 a second visitors' center opened on Temple Square to meet the needs of the expanding number of visitors. Many of these centers included large picture windows affording a good view of the adjacent temple and featured displays teaching gospel principles related to temple service.

These centers became popular means for missionaries and home teachers to introduce investigators and less-active members to key gospel teachings. While visiting the Washington Temple Visitors' Center, a family of five who had received the missionary discussions made their decision to be baptized. A woman came to the Oakland Temple to arrange a tour for a group of Campfire Girls. As she found herself in a maze of dead end streets below the temple, "she felt that some influence was trying to keep her from reaching her goal…'yet all the time, right there in front of me, huge and beautiful, was the temple.'" As she finally entered the visitors' center and was greeted by the guides, she was overcome with emotion and burst into tears as they presented their message. This experience led to contacts of full-time missionaries and the baptism of her entire family.[23]

A Growing Need for Temples Around the World

Early in the twentieth century President Joseph F. Smith had spoken of the need to make temple blessings accessible to the Saints living in distant areas. President David O. McKay echoed this same theme during the years following the century's midpoint. In subsequent decades the Church's international growth accelerated. Hence, as the Church approached its 150th anniversary, the need for temples around the world was greater than ever before.

Many Latter-day Saints still lived thousands of miles from the nearest temple and had to make substantial sacrifices to go there. A Tongan family sold their livestoc and, went without new shoes and other necessities; in addition all the children worked and saved for two years, and the father rode a bicycle, rather than driving a car even long distances, so that they could go to the New Zealand Temple and be sealed.[24] A group of eighty-four Church members from Central America had to make an eight-thousand-mile round trip through the mountains and across the deserts, changing buses—most not air-conditioned—at each national border, in order to receive their eagerly-anticipated blessings at the Arizona Temple.[25] Between forty and eighty members from Tahiti partici-pated in the annual excursion to the New Zealand Temple, even though the trip for an average family cost more than eight months' wages.[26] A unique challenge faced the Saints in Korea, where the law made it difficult for a husband and wife to leave the country at the same time. Temples located nearer to all these Saints would be a major blessing.

First Temple in South America and Asia

The announcements for the first temples on two continents came in 1975. "I have an important announcement," President Spencer W. Kimball began at the Brazil area conference, even before the opening hymn or prayer. The Saints gave him their full attention. "A temple will be built in Brazil," he announced, as a painting of the future temple was unveiled. A gasp could be heard throughout the hall. "It will be built [here] in Sao Paulo." By then tears filled the eyes of many as they wept for joy. Elder L. Tom Perry referred to this as "the greatest audience reac-tion I have ever seen."[27]

One challenge facing those building the new one-story temple was to find a suitable material for the building's exterior. Local stone was not suf-ficiently white, and the cost of importing would be prohibitive. Consequently architect Emil Fetzer decided to use a cast stone facing made of marble and quartz crystals set in white concrete. The Church had to set up its own shop on the temple site to produce this material.[28]

South American Saints sacrificed for the new temple. A widow in northern Argentina donated her home and began living in rented housing.

Sao Paulo Temple

Some coming from Bolivia by bus for the dedication in 1978 fasted—not just because they chose to, but because they had spent all their money for transportation.[29]

Like their counterparts in South America, the Saints of Asia had longed for the opening of a temple. Soon after the close of World War II, the Church had reopened its mission in Japan. After several weeks of searching for a suitable headquarters, mission officials were able to locate only a partially bombed home. Even though the building had to be rebuilt, it was chosen because of its good location near several embassies and across the street from a beautiful park. In 1949, standing in the library of the refurbished home, Elder Matthew Cowley prayed that the Lord's work might progress and that even temples might be erected in this land.[30]

Over the centuries the peoples of Asia had learned to value their families and to honor their ancestors. Hence the restored gospel's concept of vicarious service for the dead was not entirely foreign to them. "We should one day have a temple in Japan," Elder Cowley declared in 1953. "They know a little about our temple rites. At some of their places of worship they take a little panel of wood with the name of an ancestor on it and immerse it under water. I hope the day is not too far off before these people themselves can go down into the water and be immersed for their ancestors."[31] The long-awaited word came at the Tokyo area conference on August 9, 1975. When President Kimball announced that a temple would be built in Japan, "the audience broke out in applause. Then the weeping began."[32]

The downtown location of mission headquarters, with its excellent access to public transit, was chosen as the site for the new temple. Mission President Harrison T. Price, one of the elders who had been present when the mission home was dedicated, now had the assignment to supervise the demolition of this building to make way for the temple.

The congested nature of the neighborhood led to some unique features in the temple. Its basement included a sixteen-car parking garage. An apartment for the temple president, with a separate outside entrance, was

Tokyo Temple

located on one of the upper floors. Furthermore, the small size of the site, slightly less than one-half acre, meant that the temple could cover relatively little ground space and that vertical lines would need to be emphasized. One contractor expressed surprise when he learned that this building was to be a "temple." He knew that the Buddhist and Shinto religions erected many shrines and temples, and that Christian churches built chapels and cathedrals, but this was the first time he had known of a Christian group building a temple. He was told that the Tokyo Temple "would be a sacred building, a holy house, where the glorious work of salvation for the living and the dead would be carried out."[33]

As had been the case with other "international" temples, challenge accompanied the commencement of ordinance work at the Sao Paulo Temple in 1978 and at the Tokyo Temple two years later. Because of the great distance of these two areas from any other temples, relatively few local Latter-day Saints had received their own temple blessings. Hence many temple workers received their own endowment as the temple opened, and they needed more extensive training as they prepared to share these blessings with others.

The Mexico City Temple

Ever since endowments were given in Spanish at the Arizona Temple beginning in 1945, faithful Saints in Mexico had eagerly anticipated the time when they might have the benefit of a temple in their own country. On March 21, 1976, at a meeting of stake presidents, regional representatives, and mission presidents from Mexico and Central America, the First Presidency, with all three members present, announced the longawaited news: the Lord had directed that a temple be built in Mexico.[34] About two weeks later a small announcement of the new temple appeared in the *Church News*. Designed by Emil B. Fetzer, Church architect, the new temple would feature "a modern adaptation of original Mayan architectural styles."[35] The unique A-framed base of the 140-foot tower featured arched openings, inspired by Mayan doorways, through which the sky could be seen. The exterior would be covered with white cast stone, the upper two-thirds of the surface being highly ornamented.[36] After its completion, the temple would be one of three buildings to receive an international award for artistic use of precast concrete.[37]

Because of legal requirements concerning religious buildings in Mexico, approval to build the temple came only after sensitive negotiations between Church and government leaders. These were made easier because Mexican officials had come to regard the Church as an organization interested in complying with the laws of the land. Government officials were also pleased with the indigenous Mayan design, which distinguished the temple from the churches of any other denominations.[38] Three and one-half years passed before the temple project could move forward. Plans for the new temple were made public in September 1979.

The Mexico City Temple would be the largest ever built by the Church outside of the United States, and the fifth largest among all the temples. Its 128,000-square-foot interior included four ordinance rooms, each seating

Mexico City Temple

120 persons. A unique innovation was providing one foyer where people in street clothes would present their temple recommends and a second foyer where those dressed in white clothing would proceed up the escalators to the ordinance rooms. "A separate area devoted completely to those wearing temple clothing helps to maintain the sacred spirit of the temple," the architect suggested.

Ground was broken on November 25, 1979, under the direction of Elder Boyd K. Packer of the Council of the Twelve, who offered the prayer, in Spanish, dedicating the site. More than nine thousand attended the one-hour service, many having camped out overnight at the site in order to secure a favorable vantage point. Saints in the Mexico City area formed a six-hundred-voice choir to provide music for the occasion.[39]

Despite widespread poverty, the 242,000 Saints in the Mexico City Temple district raised the remarkable total of $1.5 million. Some sold family heirlooms, while others sacrificed their livelihood by dedicating crops to the temple. Because of the scarcity of heavy equipment, most of the construction was accomplished by hand labor.

Following its completion, the new temple was open to the public from November 9-19, 1983. The fact that some 120,000 visited the temple during this period was remarkable because media coverage was limited, and most of the invitations came by word of mouth. One visitor asked if he might bring some friends. The next day he came with a group of twenty-nine. He then asked if he could return the following day with a hundred. Another group of forty-seven young men training to become priests spent an hour and a half at the visitors' center after the regular tour. Among the visitors were some five thousand business, civic, and government leaders. Typically these professional people "entered with a nonchalant attitude but left deeply impressed by the sanctity of the temple."[40]

The cornerstone was laid and the temple dedicated on December 2, 1983, by Gordon B. Hinckley, second counselor in the First Presidency. Some forty thousand Saints attended the nine dedicatory sessions extending over a period of three days. Several speakers referred to the temple's dedication as a fulfillment of Book of Mormon promises of great latter-day blessings to the descendants of Lehi. "Bless thy Saints in this great land and those from other lands who will use the temple," petitioned the dedicatory prayer. "Most have in their veins the blood of Father Lehi. Thou hast kept thine ancient promise. Many thousands 'that walked in darkness have seen a great light'" (Isaiah 9:2). Some speakers referred to Elder Spencer W. Kimball's 1947 dream in which he envisioned the Lamanites' destiny. At a time when there were no wards or stakes in Mexico other than in the Mormon colonies, he "saw a temple" which would be filled with many faithful men and women.[41] It was at the dedication that Elder Ezra Taft Benson was prompted to stress a theme that would become one of the hallmarks of his presidency: "As I participated in the Mexico City Temple dedication," he later recalled, "I received the distinct impression that God is not pleased with our neglect of the Book of Mormon."[42]

While the temple was under construction, there had been a renewed emphasis on genealogical research. Many Saints wanted to do temple work for their own family members at first, rather than for persons randomly identified through name extraction.

Smaller Temples to Dot the Earth

A dramatic acceleration in temple construction came in April, 1980, when the First Presidency announced that seven new temples were to be built. These included the first temple in the southeastern United States, two more temples in South America, and four in the Pacific. (See the list of temples in Appendix B.) "They will bring the blessings of temple ordinances to an ever-increasing number of faithful Latter-day Saints," the Presidency explained. "We know that as our people meet the high moral standards required of those who would enter the temple, their marriages, family life and individual life will be strengthened."[43] Elder Gordon B. Hinckley noted that "through ancient prophets the Lord promised that in the latter days he would remember his people on the isles of the sea. We have witnessed a marvelous fulfillment of these prophecies."[44]

"There now begins the most intensive period of temple building in the history of the Church," affirmed the First Presidency.[45] Typically the Church has undertaken the erection of just one temple at a time. During the early 1880s, however, there were three under construction at once—Logan, Manti, and Salt Lake.

A century later this record was shattered. The year 1981 brought the announcement of nine additional temples—two each in the United States,

Tahiti Temple

Europe, and Latin America; plus a temple each in Korea, the Philippines, and South Africa. By 1984 ten more temples had been announced, including one in the German Democratic Republic (East Germany). Church leaders declared their intention to continue building temples so that Saints in every nation might have the same privileges to receive the blessings in the house of the Lord. Most of these new temples were located where they could make sacred blessings available to the living even though they might not contribute large numbers of ordinances for the dead.

"We are living in one of the most significant and important epochs in the history of the Church and in the history of God's work among His people," testified President Gordon B. Hinckley. "We are living in the greatest era of temple building ever witnessed.... This great impetus in temple building was given by President [Spencer W.] Kimball under revelation from the Lord, whose work this is. The sacred and important work that goes on in temples must be accelerated."[46]

The First Presidency emphasized that the new temples would be of such a quality that they would "be pleasing to all" and yet could be constructed "at a cost that will not be burdensome for members to bear. The character and beauty of the new temples will be in keeping with their sacred purpose."[47] The desired economy was achieved in two ways: These temples were comparatively small, having a floor space of from 7,000 to 27,000 square feet. (At that time, a typical stake center accommodating two wards had an area of about 25,000 square feet.) Furthermore, these temples were designed in families, thus substantially cutting the cost of planning. Architect Emil Fetzer explained that a group of temples would follow a basic plan "with perhaps some slight modifications to make outward appearance fit the local culture."[48] Though small, these plans were quite efficient. Hence the new temples sometimes had a greater capacity than earlier, larger structures.

The Saints viewed the construction of certain temples as the fulfillment of prophecy. In 1936 President Heber J. Grant stopped in Boise, Idaho. About fifteen local businessmen came to visit him at the home of stake president Ezra Taft Benson. They indicated they would donate any land in Boise the Church might choose as a temple site. President Grant declined their kind offer because the number of members in the area at that time did not justify a temple there. "I'll make you a counter proposition," he said, "If all of you will join the Church and volunteer your services as missionaries, we'll build a temple in this valley as soon as the numbers justify it." He then prophesied that "someday you will have a temple in this valley."[49] At the cornerstone-laying ceremony of the Idaho Falls Temple, President Grant's counselor, J. Reuben Clark, affirmed that "as surely as we are here we shall build other temples in Idaho."[50]

In 1959 Elder Harold B. Lee met at Guatemala City with over sixteen hundred Church members and leaders. He regarded being with this large group of "distinctive Lamanite people" as a "most thrilling experience." He was impressed that this was a significant Lamanite center and that "a temple for the Latin American people should be built here."[51]

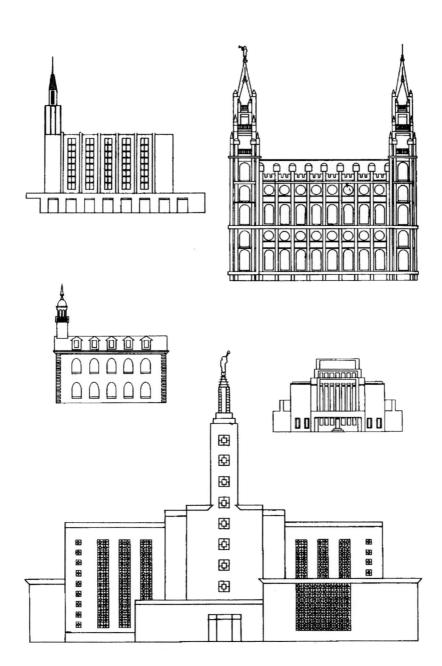

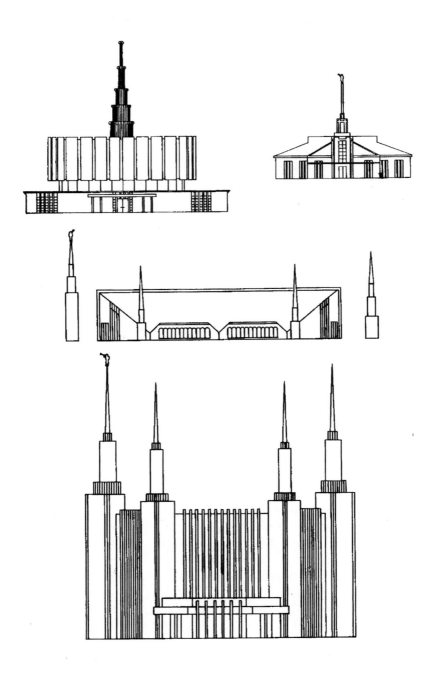

In the 1960s, Korean mission president Spencer J. Palmer purchased a choice hilltop property in a Seoul suburb. He felt this was what the Lord wanted him to do. "Wouldn't this be a beautiful location for a temple?" he remarked to an associate. Many years later Elder Boyd K. Packer was appointed to select the Korean Temple site. After looking at several possible locations, he chose the land earlier purchased by President Palmer. "He felt that the mind and will of the Lord was that it be the location of the first temple to be built on the continent of Asia." When a subway system was built in conjunction with the 1988 Seoul Olympics, one of the lines ended at the bottom of the hill, affording inexpensive and convenient access to the temple. Furthermore, a supply of fresh water was discovered directly under the hill.[52]

Reporting on the condition of the Saints in Asia in 1970, Elder Ezra Taft Benson noted that the Church had only one building in all the Philippines. Nevertheless "in our lifetime," he declared, "we shall see stakes and chapels, converts in great numbers, local leaders with power and ability, and perhaps even a temple erected among these good people."[53] Within just over a decade, all of these prophecies had been fulfilled.

Construction of several of these temples encountered unexpected delays for a variety of reasons. In Stockholm, the government asked the Church to suspend construction for over a year so that anything of value might be removed from ancient Viking graves discovered on the site. Environmentalists were concerned that the Chicago Illinois Temple would disrupt migration patterns of birds from a nearby nature preserve. Increased traffic was another concern of neighbors in Chicago, Denver, and Dallas. Church officials shared these concerns and therefore took measures to allay them, such as improving communication with those who had expressed concerns.

"The adversary has not been unmindful" of the quickening pace of temple construction, testified President Gordon B. Hinckley. "The building and dedication of these sacred edifices has been accompanied by a surge of opposition from a few enemies of the Church as well as criticism from a few within." Nevertheless, noted President Hinckley, the Lord has promised that his work will not be destroyed (D&C 10:43). "We have been strengthened, and we have moved forward under the promise of the Lord."[54] "Oh, that we had the power, the gift of tongues, the spirit of persuasion, to portray to those who criticize us the beauty, the peace, the spirit which comes of Christ, all of which are felt in these holy places," President Hinckley wished as he spoke at the Atlanta Temple dedication.[55]

Those involved in the difficult process of finding a site for the Denver Temple were convinced that they had witnessed the hand of the Lord guiding them. When the preferred location proved not to be available, they turned to two other sites. In each case, approval was blocked by citizens who were concerned that an increase in traffic would alter the character of their neighborhood. By this time the originally preferred site had become available. Church officials, having benefited from experience in dealing with opposition, were able to gain the support of the temple's neighbors. As the building was completed, however, there were some objections to the planned nightly floodlighting. Church officials therefore decided to turn off the lights at 11:00 P.M. By then the neighbors had come to appreciate the temple's beauty and asked that the lights be left on all night.[56]

As these smaller temples were still in the planning stage, the design of some was modified so that all (except Sydney and Freiberg) would include a spire surmounted by a statue of the angel Moroni. Heretofore, only selected larger temples (Salt Lake, Los Angeles, Washington, Seattle, Jordan River, and Mexico City) had included the familiar figure of the herald angel. Architect Fetzer explained that these statues "symbolize the Savior's charge to take the gospel throughout the world."[57] Elder Thomas S. Monson had earlier taught that "the Moroni statue which appears on the top of several of our temples is a reminder to us all that God is concerned for all His people throughout the world, and communicates with them wherever they may be."[58] President Devere Harris and officials of the Idaho Falls Temple district believed that their temple's tower was ideal for a statue of the angel. The First Presidency concurred, and a helicopter was brought in to place the ten-foot figure atop the temple.[59] Seven- or ten-foot figures of the angel for the new temples were made of fiberglass, which was stronger, more weather resistant, and less expensive than steel. Two Latter-day Saints, Karl Quilter and LaVar E. Wallgren, had just developed the difficult technique of shaping fiberglass into works of art.[60]

In many areas where these new temples were being built, the Saints were less able to contribute financially. Nevertheless, they demonstrated in other ways their eagerness for their temple. When sisters were requested to hand-crochet seven altar cloths for the Buenos Aires Argentina Temple, they went to work and provided sixty-four. Some two thousand braved the elements to attend the groundbreaking service for the Manila Philippines Temple even though a typhoon was about to hit the area. Later, twenty-seven thousand attended the open house for this temple despite two more typhoons which struck forty-eight hours apart.[61]

The ceremonial placing of cornerstones, explained President Gordon B. Hinckley, was "in harmony with a tradition that goes back to ancient times." When buildings were made of stone, the large pieces of the foundation with importing blocks at each corner had to be in place before the superstructure could be commenced.[62] Paul likened this to the Church being "built up on the foundation of the apostles and prophets, Jesus Christ himself being the chief corner stone" (Ephesians 2:20). Thus, for example, the laying of the cornerstones marked the commencement of construction on the Kirtland, Nauvoo, and Salt Lake temples. As reinforced concrete became the common building material, the cornerstone ceremony became more symbolic and typically occurred somewhere in the midst of construction. A space was left in the wall to receive a sealed metal box containing relevant historical memorabilia. The ceremony usually featured dignitaries placing this box and then assisting in covering it with a commemorative plaque. By the 1980s, the cornerstone laying occurred only an hour or so prior to the first dedicatory session.

Especially thrilling was the dedication in 1985 of the temple at Freiberg, in the German Democratic Republic. A decade earlier, Elder Thomas S. Monson of the Quorum of Twelve had been impressed to offer a prayer of dedication on that land and its people. On that occasion he prayed: "Let this be the beginning of a new day for the members of Thy church in this land," and asked that their desire for temple blessings be fulfilled.[63] After President Henry J. Burkhardt repeatedly requested permission to organize a temple excursion to Switzerland, government officials suggested the possibility of the Church building a temple in the GDR itself. With the full cooperation of the government, the temple was designed and constructed. Even though the government-employed

Freiberg Temple

workmen were not Church members, they took a personal pride in this project.[64]

Although there were only about 4,000 Latter-day Saints in the German Democratic Republic, a total of 89,871 persons visited the newly completed temple, some waiting in the rain up to three hours. "While recognizing the different political philosophies under which we live," President Gordon B. Hinckley expressed "sincere appreciation to the officials of the government of that nation for their help in making possible this sacred edifice for the blessing of our brethren and sisters in that land." During the dedication "there was a solemn stillness," wrote one of the German Saints who was present, "and there was not a dry eye. The sun was shining after a long time.... You could sense gladness and enthusiasm and the wish for a never-ending harmony.... Tears, laughter, and gladness; everything was present."[65]

Only four years after the dedication of this temple, great political changes took place in Germany. The Iron Curtain, including the Berlin

Wall, came down, and shortly, East and West Germany were reunited.

The dedications of these temples were spiritual highlights for the Saints scattered around the world. Because of the smallness of the Tokyo Temple's celestial room, only about thirty-five singers comprised the dedication choir. Elder Mark E. Petersen recorded that "it seemed that there was a far larger choir singing than was present, and various people thought there must have been an angelic choir singing with our little choir because of the beauty of the music and the volume that was heard. The Spirit was so strong that everybody burst into tears, including the members of the choir, who literally sang through their tears."[66]

Because of illness Presidents Spencer W. Kimball and Ezra Taft Benson were unable to be present at many of these temple dedications so they assigned their counselor, Gordon B. Hinckley, to preside. Thus, even before becoming president of the Church in 1995, President Hinckley had dedicated twenty-two temples, more than any other person in the Church's history. (See Appendix B.) Despite turmoil in surrounding areas at the time the Johannesburg South Africa Temple was dedicated, President Hinckley noted that there was peace in the house of the Lord as people with different roots "mingled together as brothers and sisters."[67] He conducted the twenty-four dedicatory sessions for the Boise Temple and reported a great outpouring of the Spirit of the Lord in each.

The dedication of all these temples was an evidence of the Church's substantial growth worldwide. Not only did they make available the gospel's highest blessings but they also reflected the spiritual readiness of the Saints who built them. Elder Stephen L Richards described the erection of temples as a "monument" to the Saints' faith and an evidence of the "high spirituality that comes from the Gospel of Jesus Christ."[68] In contrast to the fifteen temples in service when Spencer W. Kimball became President of the Church, there would be a total of forty-seven when all the temples he announced were completed.

The Hong Kong temple was one of the most unique erected by the Church. Because real estate is so difficult to secure in this crowded city, the building had to serve more that just one function. Temple facilities occupied only the top three floors of the seven story structure, with the baptismal font in the basement. The other floors, accessible from a separate entrance, included offices, a chapel, and residences for the temple and mission presidents.

Temples Throughout the World

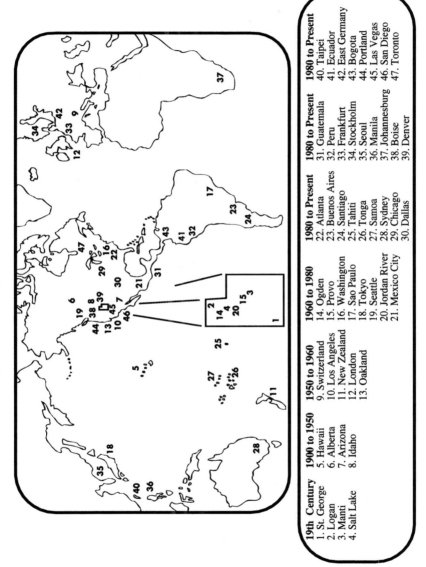

19th Century	1900 to 1950	1950 to 1960	1960 to 1980	1980 to Present	1980 to Present	1980 to Present
1. St. George	5. Hawaii	9. Switzerland	14. Ogden	22. Atlanta	31. Guatemala	40. Taipei
2. Logan	6. Alberta	10. Los Angeles	15. Provo	23. Buenos Aires	32. Peru	41. Ecuador
3. Manti	7. Arizona	11. New Zealand	16. Washington	24. Santiago	33. Frankfurt	42. East Germany
4. Salt Lake	8. Idaho	12. London	17. Sao Paulo	25. Tahiti	34. Stockholm	43. Bogota
		13. Oakland	18. Tokyo	26. Tonga	35. Seoul	44. Portland
			19. Seattle	27. Samoa	36. Manila	45. Las Vegas
			20. Jordan River	28. Sydney	37. Johannesburg	46. San Diego
			21. Mexico City	29. Chicago	38. Boise	47. Toronto
				30. Dallas	39. Denver	

The timing of the temple's dedication was significant—just over one year before the British colony of Hong Kong would revert to mainland Chinese jurisdiction. In the dedicatory prayer, President Gordon B. Hinckley petitioned, "May the blessings of freedom continue to be enjoyed by those who live here and, in a particular way, we pray that future events may be conducive to the growth and strengthening of Thy work."[69]

In 1994 the Church announced the construction of yet another unusual temple. The shell of the old stake tabernacle in Vernal, Utah, would be restored to its original appearance and temple facilities would be constructed inside. "This is the first time an older building has been restored for use as a temple."[70]

With the multiplication of temples, "a different type of sacrifice will be required of the people," declared Derek Metcalfe, managing director of the Temple Department. "In the past, going to the temple has for many members of the Church been a once-in-a-life-time experience. Some members have saved money for years, at considerable sacrifice, to travel to the nearest temple. As more temples are built worldwide, the sacrifice will be one of time, as members attend local temples with far greater frequency."[71]

Prophecies of Future Temples

As great as has been the recent expansion in temple building, prophetic statements indicate that this will be eclipsed by even more growth. In 1856 President Brigham Young declared: "To accomplish this work there will have to be not only one temple but thousands of them, and thousands and tens of thousands of men and women will go into those temples and officiate for people who have lived as far back as the Lord shall reveal."[72] President Joseph F. Smith concurred. In 1906, at the time when he prophesied that a temple would be built in Europe, he also spoke of the time "when temples of God...will be erected in the diverse countries of the earth, for the gospel must be spread over all the world."[73]

Not only will there be more temples, but they will be kept busier than at present. "The time will come," announced President Lorenzo Snow, "when there will be temples established over every portion of the land, and we will go into these temples and work for our kindred dead night and day."[74] Similarly, President Spencer W. Kimball urged: "We should so organize ourselves and the work that it will go forward in leaps and bounds. In the Book of Revelation [7:15], John saw that some time in the future (and it is still in the future to us), those who are faithful and have cleansed their lives will work night and day in the holy temples. Evidently there will be then a constant succession of groups going through the temple somewhat like it was in the days of the Nauvoo Temple." At the rededication of the Arizona Temple he stated that he looked forward to the time "when the temples will be used around the clock and throughout the year. We have been promised hundreds of temples and hundreds of thousands of people who want to go to the temples."[75]

Perhaps the most often-discussed future temples are those to be built in Jerusalem and at the New Jerusalem. "Judah must return," specified the Prophet Joseph Smith, "Jerusalem must be rebuilt, and the temple, and water come out from under the temple, and the waters of the Dead Sea be healed...all this must be done before the Son of Man makes His appearance."[76] (Compare Ezekiel 47:1-8.) This temple will be unique, taught Elder Orson Pratt, because "it will contain the throne of the Lord, upon which he will, at times, personally sit and reign over the House of Israel for ever." Many have wondered who will build this significant temple. Elder Pratt was convinced that it would be erected "by those who believe in the true Messiah."[77] Because the "ordinances of salvation will be performed," concluded Elder Mark E. Petersen, this requires "revealed direction and authorized priesthood. Only through them can any acceptable temple be built and operated."[78] Some have supposed that the temple would be built by the Jews themselves. Elder Bruce R. McConkie concurred. He cited Zechariah's prophecy (6:15) that those "from far off" would build the temple, and concluded: "Surely they are the Jews who have been scattered afar," but insisted that they will be "Jews who have come unto Christ...and who have learned anew about temples."[79]

Several latter-day leaders have spoken of the great temple of the New Jerusalem to be built in Independence, Jackson County, Missouri. The precise design of this structure has not yet been revealed. Two descriptions hark back to Joseph Smith's reference to twenty-four temples. Speaking in the domed Salt Lake Tabernacle, Orson Pratt shared his idea of what the temple would look like. It would be "much larger, very much larger" than any existing Latter-day Saint building. It would not consist of one large hall as in the Tabernacle, but there will be twenty-four separate "compart-ments." "When we build these 24 rooms in a circular form and arched over the center, we shall give the names to all these different compartments just as the Lord specified through Joseph Smith."[80] Another description was given more recently by Elder Alvin R. Dyer. He envisioned "a temple complex such as has never been known." At its center will be the great temple of the New Jerusalem in which the Lord will make his appearance, and from which he will govern all the earth.[81]

Regardless of the design, this temple will be a glorious edifice. "A cloud of glory [will] rest upon that temple by day, the same as the cloud rested upon the tabernacle of Moses," testified Elder Orson Pratt. "Not only that, but a flaming fire will rest upon the temple by night." He continued, "you will have no need of any artificial light, for the Lord God will be the light thereof…and his glory will be there, and you will see it and you will hear his voice."[82]

Temple work will accelerate even further during the Millennium. "When the Savior comes," foresaw Elder Wilford Woodruff, "a thousand years will be devoted to this work of redemption; and Temples will appear all over this land of Joseph—North and South America—and also in Europe and elsewhere."[83]

Those laboring in the temples during the Millennium will enjoy a distinct advantage. Speaking at the Logan Temple dedication, President John Taylor testified: "Communications from the heavens will be received in regard to our labors, how we may perform them, and for whom."[84] "Before this work is finished," President Brigham Young explained, the elders "will become pillars in the Temple of God, to go no more out: They will eat and drink and sleep there; and they will often have the occasion to say—'Somebody came into the Temple last night [and] gave us the names of a great many of our forefathers that are not on record…for hundreds of years back. He said to me, You and I are con-nected in one family: there are the names of your ancestors; take them and write them down.'"[85]

With this kind of guidance, President Joseph F. Smith explained, we will not be working "by chance." One of his counselors, President Anthon H. Lund, amplified this thought: During the Millennium "the veil will be much thinner between the spirit world and this; and we will work for the dead, not only in faith that those for whom we labor will accept the Gospel, but with an actual knowledge that they are longing for the work to be done."[86] Elder Joseph Fielding Smith concurred: "Those who will be living during the Millennium will be in daily communication with resurrected beings who will supply names of every soul who is entitled to a place in the celestial kingdom—so temple work can be done for them."[87] Nevertheless, cautioned Elder Smith, this help will not come until "after we have done all that we are able."[88] Hence, as Elder Melvin J. Ballard put it, "Man's extremity is God's opportunity. The Lord never helps us while we can help ourselves." Then the authorities from "the other side" will "make known all who have received the Gospel in the spirit world, and everyone entitled to have their work done.... We can speed that day," Elder Ballard concluded, "by doing now the work that we can do."[89]

This vicarious service, cautioned Elder Wilford Woodruff, "will require the whole of the millennium, [even] with Jesus Christ at the head." Nevertheless, he insisted, "the ordinances of salvation will have to be attended to for the dead who have not heard the gospel, from the days of Adam down, before Christ can present this world to the Father, and say, 'it is finished.'"[90]

Chapter Eleven

"The Hearts of the Children"

The prophet Isaiah declared that the Lord reveals his truths "precept upon precept" and "line upon line; here a little, and there a little" (Isaiah 28:10). This is the way the Saints' understanding of their temple responsibilities unfolded. From the Master's example and teachings they learned that baptism was essential (Matthew 3:13-16; John 3:5). From the writings of Peter they learned that between the Savior's death and resurrection he taught the gospel to the spirits in prison (1 Peter 3:18-20; 4:6). The New Testament also taught that the early Christians performed the saving ordinance of baptism in behalf of the dead (1 Corinthians 15:29).

The first latter-day revelation dealing with vicarious salvation for the dead came early in 1836. As the Prophet Joseph Smith beheld a glorious vision of the celestial kingdom, he saw that his brother Alvin would inherit that kingdom, even though he had died prior to the restoration of authorized saving ordinances. On that occasion the Lord declared that "all who have died without a knowledge of this gospel, who would have received it if they had been permitted to tarry, shall be heirs of the celestial kingdom of God" (D&C 137:7). Just over two months later, one week following the dedication of the Kirtland Temple, the ancient prophet Elijah appeared and restored the priesthood keys by which authoritative acts may be bound on earth and in heaven and by which "the hearts of the children" may be turned to their fathers (Malachi 4:5-6; D&C 110:13-16). The Prophet Joseph Smith explained that the word *turn* in Malachi's prophecy might better be translated "bind" or "seal."[1]

At this time there were no genealogical societies other than those concerned with maintaining pedigrees of royalty and nobility. Elder Joseph Fielding Smith pointed out that the first organized effort to collect and preserve genealogical data of the "common people" came with the incorporation of the New England Historic and Genealogical Society in 1844, just eight years after Elijah's appearance. The following decades brought the formation of many more such organizations.[2] "No person can deny," President Heber J. Grant insisted, "that from the time of Elijah's visit, restoring the keys that he held, turning the hearts of the children to their fathers, there has come into the hearts of people all over the world a desire to know something about their ancestors."[3]

Meanwhile, saving ordinances in behalf of the dead were restored beginning in 1840. In the fall of that year the Saints at Nauvoo were permitted to resume the New Testament practice of baptisms for the dead.[4] The Prophet Joseph Smith instructed the Saints that "the greatest responsibility in this world that God has laid upon us is to seek after our dead,"[5] and that those who neglect it "do it at the peril of their own salvation."[6] In 1842 the Prophet warned that "the earth will be smitten with a curse unless there is a welding link of some kind or other between the fathers and the children," and he explained that this link was to be established through temple ordinances (D&C 128:18). At this time endowments for the dead had not yet been instituted, so the amount of time involved in performing vicarious ordinances was relatively little. Furthermore, because almost all ordinances were received in behalf of close relatives, with whom the Saints had been personally acquainted, no time-consuming genealogical research was required. To obtain these blessings for themselves and their deceased ancestors, the Nauvoo Saints sacrificed to complete the temple, even though they knew they would have to leave it behind almost immediately.

The Scope Broadens

As the pioneers settled in the Rocky Mountains, they had to devote almost all of their time to simply surviving in the desert. This resulted in a temporary lull in vicarious temple service.[7] Nevertheless, President Brigham Young continued to teach this important responsibility and even suggested that it extended back more generations than the Saints had previously realized. In 1852 he challenged them to be prepared "to go into the Temples of God to officiate for our fathers and our grandfathers—for our ancestors back for hundreds of years, who are all looking to see what their children are doing upon the earth."[8] To this end, President Young believed the Lord was prompting the people to trace their lineage "from father to father, father to father, until they get the genealogy of their forefathers as far as they possibly can."[9] By the authority of the priesthood, President Young testified, "we shall be connected with our fathers, by the ordinance of sealing until we shall form a perfect chain from father Adam down to the closing up scene."[10]

The inauguration of endowments for the dead resulted in a major expansion of the Saints' temple responsibility. While baptisms and sealings could be performed in only a few moments, hours were required to receive the endowment in behalf of each deceased individual. As early as 1856 Brigham Young had spoken of the Saints receiving endowments in behalf of their progenitors,[11] but this service had to be done in a temple. In 1873 President Young explained that the Saints could "officiate in the ordinances so far as baptism and sealing are concerned...but no one can receive endowments for another until a temple is prepared in which to administer them."[12] Thus this service was not instituted until the Lord's house was complete at St. George in 1877.

President Young had stressed the responsibility of the Saints to officiate for their own blood relatives. For example, a man, upon becoming converted to the gospel, may think that his wife should officiate in behalf of his female ancestors. "Well, now," Brother Brigham countered, "the wife is not a blood relation, consequently she is not in reality the proper person." However, he explained, if the man has no sister, daughter, or other qualified female relatives in the Church, his wife "can be appointed the heir" and be authorized to officiate.[13] Even though the Saints were responsible for performing ordinances in behalf of their own blood relatives, there would be situations requiring others to assist.

A new precedent was set following the opening of the St. George Temple when Elder Wilford Woodruff sensed the urgency of performing ordinances in behalf of his deceased relatives. Because none of Elder Woodruff's family had accompanied him to St. George, the Lord authorized him to obtain help from the Saints there "and it should be acceptable unto him."[14] "We can assist one another in the temples by doing ordinance work not only for our own lineage, but for the lineage of others," Elder Theodore M. Burton later explained. "It is true that our personal responsibility is to see that the work is done for our own ancestry, but there is nothing in the scriptures that prohibits us from obtaining aid from others or from giving aid to our brothers and sisters to speed this work."[15]

Beginnings of the Genealogical Society

During the later nineteenth century many of the Saints, especially those whose own parents were not faithful, increasingly came to feel that they should be "adopted," or sealed to prominent Church leaders, as a means of assuring eventual exaltation.[16] Concerned about this growing practice, President Wilford Woodruff on April 5, 1894, met with his counselors and the Twelve "upon the subject of endowments & adoption" and on that occasion received a revelation from the Lord.[17] A few days later he made the following statement in general conference: "When I went before the Lord to know who I should be adopted to (we were then being adopted to prophets and apostles), the Spirit of God said to me, 'Have you not a father, who begot you?' 'Yes, I have.' 'Then why not honor him? Why not be adopted to him?'"

President Woodruff then instructed: "We want the Latter-day Saints from this time to trace their genealogies as far as they can, and to be sealed to their fathers and mothers. Have children sealed to their parents, and run this chain through as far as you can get it.... This is the will of the Lord to his people."[18]

At the Salt Lake Temple's dedication President Woodruff declared: "There is a mighty work before this people. The eyes of the dead are upon us.... The spirits on the other side rejoice far more than we do" because they appreciate even more clearly the importance to them of the work about to be accomplished.[19] President Woodruff later testified: "You...hold the keys to the destiny of your fathers, your mothers, your progenitors. From generation to generation you hold the keys to their salvation."[20]

Elder George F. Richards taught: "We will have to account to [God] for the way we have done or have neglected to do this important work.... We will meet our kindred dead, and we will have to account to them also.... We are indebted to our ancestors...for that which we have inherited." If we have neglected our responsibility to them, they may say: "If you did not think enough of us to make a search to find us out and do this work for our salvation and progress, on whom may we depend?"[21]

In November 1894, just a few months after President Woodruff's announcement on being sealed to our own forefathers, a group of top Church leaders met and organized the Genealogical Society of Utah (renamed Genealogist Society of the Church in 1944 and known as the Family History Department since 1987, although some legal contracts still use the original name) with the purpose of establishing and maintaining a genealogical library for the use of Church members and others, and of disseminating information on genealogical matters.[22]

Growth of the Society

From this early beginning, the Church's Genealogical Society has grown in stature and holdings to become recognized internationally as one of the major genealogical organizations of the world. In 1911, Nephi Anderson, an early leader in the Church's genealogical activities, envisioned remarkable future growth:

> I see the records of the dead and their histories gathered from every nation under heaven to one great central library.... Branch libraries may be established in the nations, but in Zion will be the records of last resort and final authority. Trained genealogists will find constant work in all nations having unpublished records, searching among the archives for families and family connections. Then, as temples multiply, and the work enlarges to its ultimate proportions, this Society, will have in its care some elaborate, but perfect system of exact registration and checking, so that the work in the temples may be conducted without confusion or duplication. And so throughout the years, reaching into the Millennium of peace, this work of salvation will go on, until every worthy soul that can be found from earthly records will have been searched out and officiated for; and then the unseen world will come to our aid, the broken links will be joined, the

tangled threads will be placed in order, and the purposes of God in placing salvation within the reach of all will have been consummated.[23]

A Rekindled Interest in Temple Service

As temples were dedicated at Logan, Manti, and especially Salt Lake City during the closing years of the nineteenth century, the Saints increasingly had ready access to the house of the Lord. Statistics of temple activity clearly reflect a boost when each new temple opened its doors. The Genealogical Society increasingly promoted temple activity through its classes and publications. Beginning in 1910, for example, the Utah Genealogical and Historical Magazine appeared quarterly, with Elder Joseph Fielding Smith as editor. The publication in 1912 of Elder James E. Talmage's scholarly and insightful work *The House of the Lord* further broadened the Saints' interest in this sacred service. The announcement in 1918 of President Joseph F. Smith's vision of the Savior's ministry in the spirit world (D&C 138) provided additional impetus.

To accommodate the increasing numbers coming to the temple, more endowment sessions had to be scheduled. When the Salt Lake Temple first opened there was only one session per day, but by 1920 this number had increased to four. During that decade, evening sessions were scheduled for the first time to meet the needs of people who were employed or otherwise unable to attend during the day. During the 1920s, Elder George F. Richards of the Council of the Twelve, and president of the Salt Lake Temple, headed a committee which standardized and streamlined temple procedures in order to achieve greater efficiency and to enhance the impact of temple ceremonies.

Elder James E. Talmage explained that our vicariously administering ordinances "in behalf of departed spirits" in no way interferes with "the right of choice and the exercise of free agency on their part. They are at liberty to accept or reject the ministrations in their behalf." Furthermore, he insisted, "though baptism be duly administered to a living man in behalf of a dead ancestor, that spirit will derive no immediate advancement nor any benefit therefrom if he has not yet attained faith in the Lord Jesus Christ or if he be still unrepentant."[24] It is up to the person in the spirit world to develop faith and repent of his sins. "Then," Elder Talmage explained,

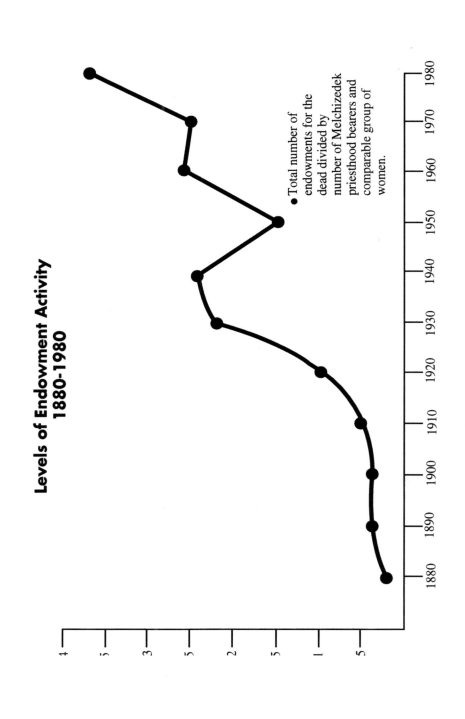

**Levels of Endowment Activity
1880-1980**

● Total number of
endowments for the
dead divided by
number of Melchizedek
priesthood bearers and
comparable group of
women.

"when he yearns for baptism, and sorrows deeply that he had no chance to be baptized in the flesh, it will be made known to him that one of his descendants...has been a savior on Mt. Zion in his behalf."[25] President Wilford Woodruff was convinced that "there would be very few souls for whom the people perform ordinances in the temples of God, who, when they heard the Gospel preached to them beyond the veil, would not accept of the vicarious work."[26]

A significant expansion in the Saints' temple work came when they were permitted to officiate for individuals other than their own or their personal friends' direct ancestors. A 1924 genealogical handbook explained that Saints "residing in missions" far from temples can arrange to have saving ordinances performed in behalf of their departed kindred. Thus "persons who desire to perform Temple ordinances in behalf of the dead, but have not names of their own kindred, or friends, for that purpose, can be provided with names from lists [received from the missions] that are on file in the Temple Recorder's office."[27]

A particularly potent stimulus to temple activity was the personal example of President Heber J. Grant. Speaking at general conference in 1928 he declared: "For years I felt that I was too busy to find a day or an evening in which to go to the temple. A little over a year ago I made up my mind that by planning my affairs...I could go to the temple at least once every week and have ordinances performed in behalf of some of my loved ones who had passed away. By making up my mind that I could do this I had no difficulty whatever in going through the temple once a week during the entire year."[28] Not only did he attend personally, but he also sent letters to his family inviting them to set aside a "temple night" each Thursday. As many as twenty relatives responded. During 1930, members of the Grant family accounted for 913 baptisms, 986 endowments, 764 sealings of couples, and 1,767 sealings of children to parents.[29] "You can be Saviors upon Mt. Zion by laboring in the temples," President Grant admonished. "To my mind, one of the greatest and grandest and most glorious of all the labors that anyone can be engaged in is laboring for the salvation of the souls of their loved ones, their ancestors who have gone before, who had not the privilege of listening to the Gospel and embracing it."[30]

Efforts to Eliminate Duplication

As interest in temple activity expanded, the likelihood of more than one person performing ordinances for a given individual increased. Many Church members were inclined to gather all the names they could of people that might even remotely be related to them and have temple ordinances performed. Because such "name gathering" significantly expanded the probability of duplication, genealogical leaders discouraged this practice. As early as 1919, Latter-day Saints were instructed that they were entitled to perform temple ordinances only in behalf of the surname lines of their four grandparents. A 1924 handbook explained that individuals had to limit their temple work to these four family lines because branching out beyond them "involves the probability of repeating Temple ordinances that individuals representing other families may have a better right to have performed. Every possible precaution should be taken to prevent such undesirable repletion."[31] Over three decades earlier Elder Lorenzo Snow, the recently appointed president of the Salt Lake Temple, insisted that "in the performance of work for the dead, the rights of heirship (blood relationship) should be sacredly regarded."[32] In 1929 Elder Joseph Fielding Smith declared: "It is our duty as individuals to seek after our immediate dead—those of our own line. This is the greatest individual responsibility that we have."[33]

The Genealogical Society was responsible for procuring and organizing the records that identified persons for whom ordinances were performed in the temples. The Society therefore took the initiative in solving the growing problem of duplication. Beginning in 1922, volunteers called as "genealogical missionaries" copied data by hand onto index cards from the records of each temple. Soon nearly a half million cards had been produced, and the society had created a phonetic system for filing them. This project led to the creation of the Temple Records Index Bureau in 1924. Beginning three years later, the "TIB" checked all records for accuracy and duplication before clearing names for temple ordinance work.

With this endowments index in place, the Saints once again were permitted and encouraged to research all of their ancestral lines. In 1936, Archibald F. Bennett, secretary of the Genealogical Society, instructed: "It is incumbent on every aspirant for Celestial exaltation to trace back his lineage, obtaining complete or sufficient information regarding every member of every family group on all ancestral lines...so that all may be joined together in the bonds of sealing in this Celestial family organization, so that every ordinance necessary for them to obtain a fulness of happiness hereafter may be administered in their behalf in the temples of the Lord."[34] "Temple work begins with genealogy," Elder John A. Widtsoe declared. "Every family should be steadily engaged in securing their pedigrees. When the names of our dead have been secured, the work to be done for them, should be done promptly."[35] To expedite the completion of all ordinances needed to unite parents and their children, the familiar family group sheet was introduced in 1942, and the Genealogical Society required that all names for temple work be submitted on this form.

Microfilms and Genealogy

The coming of microfilms accelerated the process of fulfilling Nephi Anderson's prophecy of a great central genealogical library having branches around the world. The Genealogical Society filmed vital records all over the world, making available information which otherwise would likely have remained inaccessible. This project began in the eastern United States just before the outbreak of World War II. Expansion overseas had to wait until the years immediately following the close of the conflict.

Microfilming resumed even before the war ended. In March 1945 the Church began filming 365 English parish registers which had been brought to Salt Lake City for this purpose. Then, during 1947 Archibald F. Bennett spent four months in Europe conferring with government and religious officials. He was successful in obtaining permission for the Society to microfilm records in twelve countries. George Fudge, who in later years would become director of the Church's genealogical program worldwide, inaugurated this work in England. At first he had only a used camera with no light meter and had to work alone. During the first three months he filmed nearly a quarter of a million pages. Soon new equipment was purchased, and two other cameramen were employed to work under his direction.[36] In 1950 twenty-two full-time microfilmers were at work in the United States, Finland, Sweden, Norway, Denmark, Germany, Holland, and Switzerland. In later decades microfilming was carried on not only in Europe and North America but also in Latin America, the South Pacific, the Far East, and even behind the Iron Curtain.

In the aftermath of war, local archivists were generally eager to cooperate with the microfilmers in order to ensure that a copy might be preserved in case the original records were destroyed. Furthermore, the Society presented each library or church with a positive copy of the material microfilmed, allowing the public to have access to this information without having to handle the already fragile originals. In 1966 the Church would begin storing microfilm originals in its Granite Mountain Record Vault near Salt Lake City.

The advent of the microfilm also made the establishment of branch libraries practical, the first one opening in 1964. Microfilm copies of materials in the main library could be circulated inexpensively as needed. Four years later some 140,000 patrons used the facilities of the main library in Salt Lake City, while 212,000 utilized the branches.[37] By the end of 1980 the society's library included 1,024,000 hundred-foot rolls of microfilm, equivalent to 4,927,000 volumes of three hundred pages each. At that time it was acquiring records from thirty-six countries.[38] Branch libraries numbered in the hundreds.

Regular Temple Attendance and Genealogical Research Encouraged

In 1943 the First Presidency reported that there were in excess of one hundred thousand men for whom vicarious baptisms had been performed but who had not yet received the endowment or sealing ordinances. Most of these names had been submitted by Saints living in the missions far away from any temple. This provided Church leaders with the opportunity to stress the value of regular temple attendance. The Priesthood Committee of the Twelve recommended that during the coming year every Melchizedek priesthood bearer attend the temple regularly, "at least once a month, better once a week.... Attention should be given at first to the names of our own lines," counseled the Twelve, "but failing this," priesthood brethren were encouraged to perform ordinances for those whose names had been sent from missions.[39]

Such a time-consuming service was truly unselfish. Speaking at the cornerstone laying of the Swiss Temple, President Stephen L Richards declared: "We are charged with the responsibility to carry forward this altruistic, Christlike vicarious service for our kindred who have gone before. It involves untold work and expense. It contemplates unending research for genealogical information. While it is not given to us to see the exact manner in which all this service may be performed for the myriads who have gone beyond, we have faith that ways will be opened that that noble task may be accomplished."[40] Nearly three decades later, President Gordon B. Hinckley would reflect the same sentiments: "What a remarkable and wonderful thing it is that those who are living may administer the blessings of earthly ordinances in behalf of those who have gone beyond and who lived without an opportunity to hear the gospel or accept it."[41]

With such encouragement the Saints steadily increased their temple attendance, especially following the opening of the Los Angeles Temple in 1956. In 1960 more than one million endowments for the dead were performed for the first time during a single year. Unfortunately, however, the Saints' genealogical research was not keeping pace with this growth. By the mid1970s, more than three million endowments for the dead were being performed annually, but less than one million names were being supplied by individual Latter-day Saints. The difference was being made up through the "Records Tabulation" program in which staff members of the Genealogical Department at Church headquarters extracted all the names from selected parish and civil records in countries where most of the Saints' ancestors were concentrated.

Still, Church leaders desired to stimulate the Saints' own genealogical research. Over the years the Genealogical Society had sponsored classes, published instructions, and in other ways sought to stimulate Church members' involvement in genealogical activity. In 1965 Church leaders challenged individuals to fill out family group forms for the seven families in the first three generations of their pedigrees. Church officials hoped that this practical experience with actual genealogical forms would spark an interest in further family research and would also generate names for temple work.[42] During the following year, those who had accomplished this assignment were challenged to complete the eight family group forms corresponding to the fourth generation of their pedigrees.

Church leaders reminded the Saints that they were still responsible to seek out their own direct ancestors and see that the needed ordinances were performed for them. "Be it known," declared Elder Mark E. Petersen in 1976, "that each living person is responsible to assist in the salvation of his own deceased relatives. Our own salvation is largely dependent upon it.... If we go to the temple, and not for our own dead, we are performing only a part of our duty because we are also required to go there specifically to save our own dead relatives.... We must disabuse our minds of the idea that merely 'going to the temple' discharges our full responsibility, because it does not."[43]

That same year President Spencer W. Kimball emphasized that "the spirit world is filled with the spirits of men and women who are waiting for you and me to get busy in their behalf. They ask, 'Why do you keep me waiting?'...We are their offspring, and upon us rests the full responsibility to do their temple work." On another occasion President Kimball stressed: "I feel the same sense of urgency about temple work for the dead as I do about missionary work for the living, since they are basically one and the same."[44]

Computers Expedite Research

The computer became an invaluable tool in genealogical research. In 1961, when Genealogical Society employees began extracting names for temple work, this information was entered into a computer, which automatically alphabetized and printed it. This "Records Tabulation" program generated hundreds of thousands of additional names.

In 1969 the "Name Tabulation" program enabled Church members to submit names of individual ancestors for computer processing. Theretofore only names grouped into families had been accepted for temple work. This greater freedom allowed the Saints to accelerate their genealogical activity, so many more names were made available. Still, the goal was to organize individuals into family groups.

Despite the Saints' increased genealogical activity, the majority of names for temple work were still being supplied by genealogical employees at Church headquarters. To shift this responsibility back to the Saints themselves, the Church introduced a new two-fold emphasis in 1978. First, the four-generation assignment should be completed by families rather than by individuals. These broader groups would work together to verify the accuracy of genealogical data and then submit this information for at least the first four generations of their pedigree. This information became the basis of a new "Ancestral File" compiled by the Genealogical Department.[45]

Second, because duplication of ancestral lines compounds, and because genealogical records are much more difficult to locate beyond the fourth generation, the General Authorities emphasized that research beyond this point could best be facilitated by the Church as a whole. Instead of separate individuals searching endless hours through the same records for their respective ancestors, volunteers would copy all names from the original records and enter them into the computer. This "Extraction Program" quickly provided enough names for temple work to relieve genealogical department employees of this responsibility. These names, Elder J. Thomas Fyans explained, were then alphabetized by the computer in "telephone book" fashion for easy reference.[46] All the data entered into the computer became part of a rapidly growing "International Genealogical Index" (originally known as the Computer File Index). The Saints' involvement in this "Extraction Program" would help achieve the goal of each temple district supplying its own names for temple ordinance work.

The "Personal Ancestral File" (PAF), introduced in 1986, represented a significant new use of the computer. This software program, designed for use on personal computers, enables individuals to organize and analyze their genealogical information. PAF can then automatically print pedigree charts as well as family-group records. It also allows individuals to share genealogical data with others, and to submit the results of their personal research directly on computer diskette to the Churchwide Ancestral File.

Since their beginning, Family History Centers (formerly called branch genealogical libraries), relied primarily on microfilms to enable local patrons to conduct their research. A significant change came when computers were introduced to locate information more rapidly.

In April 1990, the First Presidency announced "FamilySearch," a computer program on compact discs "designed to help simplify the task of family history research and hasten the work of redeeming the dead." By means of these discs, each holding about 5,000,000 names or the equivalent of 320,000 pages, massive amounts of genealogical information could be made available at the 1,500 Family History Centers. Elder David B. Haight enthusiastically explained that FamilySearch can "guide you from one small fragment of sketchy information to full screens of information."[47]

At the outset, FamilySearch included three major resources: (1) The main Family History Library's catalog "describes the content of some 1.6 million rolls of microfilm and 230,000 books" gathered by the Family History Department. The computer enables the researcher to search the catalog not only for books according to authors and titles, but also for information by location, family names, or other key descriptive words. (2) The International Genealogical Index gives birth or marriage dates and places,

Sources of Names for Temple Work

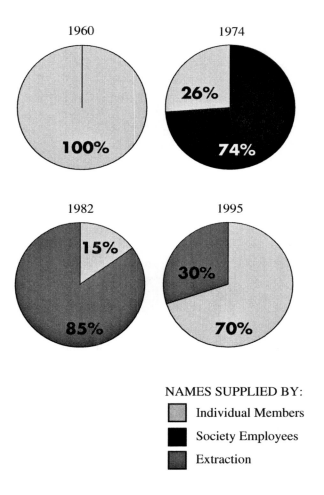

1960

100%

1974

26%

74%

1982

15%

85%

1995

30%

70%

NAMES SUPPLIED BY:

Individual Members

Society Employees

Extraction

names of parents or spouse, as well as information on temple ordinances completed. (3) The Ancestral File contains information on family groups submitted by Church members as part of the "four generation" and other programs since 1979. The Ancestral File has "made the world a smaller place," observed Elder Haight, "because it has put total strangers with common ancestry in touch with each other."[48] The foregoing information is updated regularly and other major databases are being incorporated as they become available. If Church members find useful information in any of these sources, they will be able to make printed copies, or to "download" the data on diskettes which they can use to transfer the information to their own personal computers.[49]

Elder Boyd K. Packer looked forward to the time when the computer would make clearing names for temple ordinances as easy as making an airplane reservation.[50] In 1990, the First Presidency also announced another computerized program, "TempleReady." In the past, clearing names for temple ordinances had taken as long as several months. Elder Scott explained, however, that "you will be able to clear ancestors' names for temple ordinances in your own meetinghouse yourself, without the need to request headquarters approval. When you verify that no previous ordinance has been performed, you can go immediately to the temple to perform these ordinances." With the aid of such powerful tools, individual Church members by the mid 1990s were once again the major source of names being sent to temples.

Reflecting on the impressive capacity of the computer and related technology to facilitate the work, Elder Packer declared:

> When the servants of the Lord determine to do as He commands, we move ahead. As we proceed, we are joined at the crossroads by those who have been prepared to help us. They come with skills and abilities precisely suited to our needs. And, we find provision; information, inventions, help of various kinds, set along the way waiting for us to take them up. It is as though someone knew we would be traveling that way. We see the invisible hand of the Almighty providing for us.[51]

In like spirit, Elder Haight testified, "These marvelous new technological developments have been revealed in this dispensation in greater fullness and greater plainness than ever before in the history of the world as far as we know so that his purposes might be speedily brought to pass.

Percentage of Endowments Performed for the Dead (by Periods)

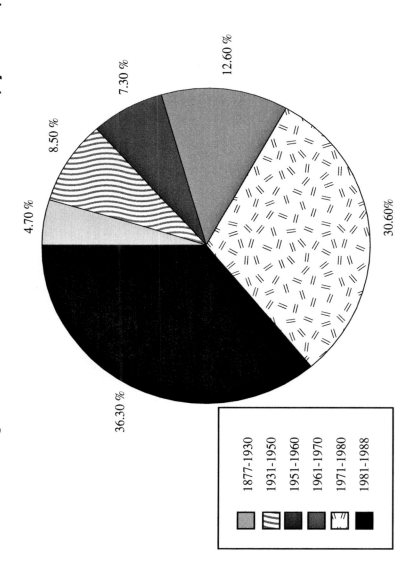

12.60 %

7.30 %

8.50 %

4.70 %

30.60%

36.30 %

	1877-1930
	1931-1950
	1951-1960
	1961-1970
	1971-1980
	1981-1988

Church, in establishing family history centers, is now bringing these marvelous developments directly to you."[52] Thus such modern tools as the microfilm and the computer have made almost limitless what can be accomplished in uniting families and providing for them the ordinances of exaltation.

The Saints' Continuing Responsibility

While stressing the need to provide names for temple work, Church leaders also emphasized the Saints' responsibility to preserve their spiritual heritage through writing personal journals and family histories. "How happy we are," noted President Spencer W. Kimball, "as we find our grandparents' journals and follow them through their trials and joys and gain for our own lives much from the experiences and faith and courage of our ancestors. Accordingly, we urge our young people to begin today to write and keep records of all the important things in their own lives and also the lives of their antecedents."[53] Church leaders emphasized that Latter-day Saints were to keep a personal or family "book of remembrance," which should be a sacred history of spiritual, ecclesiastical, or other significant experiences. It also should include a record of temple ordinances performed for all members of their immediate as well as directline ancestral families.[54] "That record," Elder John A. Widsoe instructed, "should be the first stone...in the family altar. It should be a book kept and used in the family circle; and when the child reaches maturity and gets out to make another household, one of the first things that the young couple should take along should be the records of their families, to be extended by them as life goes on. It does no harm if there is duplication.... There is strength, and inspiration, and a joy in having such a record near at hand."[55]

Genealogical research and temple work is for everyone, stressed President Thomas S. Monson. The Saints "need not be specialists, they need not be in their 80s, they need not be exclusively genealogists in order to understand the responsibility which rests upon each member of the Church to seek out his kindred dead and to perform the work which must necessarily be performed in their behalf.... I believe there is an 'iron curtain' which we have hidden behind through the years—feeling that genealogy is for a select few and not for the general membership of the Church."[56] To make it easier for more to become involved, genealogical leaders made an effort to simplify name submission procedures and requirements. Even the name of the program was changed in 1987 from "genealogy" to "family history."[57] These efforts brought a great increase in the number of names submitted by the Saints for their "family files."

At the same time as the Saints were responding to the challenge to compile family histories, they were also increasing their service in the temples. As many new temples opened around the world during the 1980s, the volume of vicarious ordinances expanded. Referring to the increasingly international scope of temple service, President Hinckley declared: "If there is any work in all the world that demonstrates the universality of God's love, it is the selfless work that goes on in these sacred houses."[58] An important milestone was reached in 1988 when the one hundred millionth endowment for the dead was performed.

Divine Assistance Promised

Identifying distant ancestors is a demanding challenge. Needed records are often difficult to find or may no longer exist. "Each member will trace his genealogy clear back," affirmed President George Q. Cannon as early as 1880. "When you get stopped, the Lord will reveal further information to you."[59] Elder John A. Widtsoe similarly promised: "If those who wish to secure genealogies will work in the temples for those whose names they can obtain, the Lord will open the way to obtain more names."[60] To those Saints who had become discouraged thinking that they had exhausted all available records, Elder Boyd K. Packer counseled: "You have forgotten revelation. Already we have been directed to many records through that process. Revelation comes to individual members as they are led to discover their family records in ways that are miraculous indeed.... When we have done all that we can do, we shall be given the rest. The way will be opened up."[61]

Many Latter-day Saints gratefully acknowledge the fulfillment of these promises. One day, for example, a close friend of the author was browsing through a secondhand bookstore in England. For some reason his attention was attracted to a particular ordinary-appearing book, even though it was on such a high shelf that he could not even read the title. Only after he climbed up and took it down did he discover that it was a very detailed history of the Scottish parish from which the Cowan family came. Truly, the promises made to the fathers are being fulfilled, and the hearts of the children are being turned to the fathers.

Chapter Twelve

Temples Bring Blessings

When we perform vicarious ordinances in the temple we not only benefit those for whom we are officiating but we also can receive many important blessings that will enrich our own lives. Understanding these personal benefits from temple worship will help us know how best to make necessary preparations in order to gain the most from our temple experience.

The House of the Lord

Many ancient peoples regarded temples as the optimum place to go in order to receive revelation from God and to be close to him.[1] This view was consistent with the Lord's promises to reveal himself in the tabernacle (Exodus 25:8, 22) and with his references to the temple as "my house" (Mark 11:17). Latter-day revelations describe temples in the same terms (D&C 109:5, 124:27-28) and promise that those who enter worthily may commune with God (D&C 97:15-17). President Wilford Woodruff shared a challenging thought at the Salt Lake Temple dedication: "We will find many glorious temples in the heavens, and the Lord wishes us to imitate them as far as we can. It is our duty to build good temples and to make them glorious and beautiful that God himself and the Son of God with his angels may visit us there."[2]

President Brigham Young viewed temples as "the house of the Lord" in a very personal and intimate way. Speaking at the cornerstone-laying ceremony for the Salt Lake Temple in 1853, he asked: "Shall [the Son of Man] have a house on the earth which he can call his own? Shall he have a place where he can lay his head, and rest over night, and tarry as long as he pleases, and be satisfied and pleased with his accommodations?"[3]

Elder John A. Widtsoe similarly affirmed: "The temple is a house or home of the Lord. Should the Lord visit the earth, he would come to his temple. We are of the Lord's family. We are his children begotten in our pre-existent life. Hence, as the earthly father and mother and their family gather in the family home, so the worthy members of the Lord's family may gather as we do in the house of the Lord."[4]

The presence of God's Spirit, as well as his personal visits in temples, results in an abundance of divine power being concentrated there. This influence then radiates outward from these sacred structures to bless the whole area. President Stephen L Richards testified that "the power emanating from temples is far greater than we realize."[5] "Spiritual power is generated within temple walls," explained Elder Widtsoe, "and sent out to bless the world. Light from the house of the Lord illumines every home within the Church fitted for its reception by participation in temple privileges. The path from the temple to the home of man is divinely brilliant. Every home penetrated by the temple spirit enlightens, cheers, and comforts every member of the household. The peace we covet is found in such homes. Indeed, when temples are on earth, the whole world shares measurably in the issuing light."[6]

Elder George Q. Cannon testified that the construction of temples "lessens the power of Satan on the earth, and increases the power of God and Godliness, [and] moves the heavens in mighty power in our behalf."[7] Elder Marion G. Romney likewise described temples as "great fortresses for righteousness in the world" without which the Saints would not have been able to survive. The devil is absolutely opposed to such sources of divine power.[8]

Some early Saints hesitated when Brigham Young asked them to help to build the temple, because such action had always intensified persecution:

"I do not like to do it, for we never began to build a Temple without the bells of hell beginning to ring." Nevertheless, President Young responded fearlessly, "I want to hear them ring."[9]

One morning, President Marriner W. Merrill of the Logan Temple noticed a large group of people occupying the temple grounds. "They presented rather a strange appearance, not only in dress but in a mode of travel." President Merrill asked the group's leader who they were. "I am Satan and these are my people.... I don't like the work that is going on in this temple and feel that it should be discontinued. Will you stop it?" When President Merrill emphatically refused, Lucifer disclosed his strategy: "I will take these people, my followers, and will distribute them throughout this temple district, and will instruct them to whisper in the ears of the people persuading them not to go to the temple, and thus bring about a cessation of your temple work."[10]

God has promised that he will never allow Satan to tempt us beyond our power to resist (1 Corinthians 10:13). The temptations of the devil are countered by inspiration from God, and we are free to choose which of these two influences to follow. This principle may also be applied to the building of temples. "It depends upon us," taught Bishop Edward H. Hunter, "whether the progress of temple building is fast or slow. Satan works hard to stop the building of temples [so] we need to be righteous."[11] The Lord, and not Satan, is in charge of temple building. Speaking at the Swiss Temple dedication in 1955, Elder Spencer W. Kimball testified that "as the Lord gave directions to David and Solomon in the building of that temple, and as He gave directions to the Prophet Joseph Smith in those temples.... He has directed the present Prophet of the Lord in the erection of these temples."[12]

Sacred Temple Ordinances

"The temple in itself, just the mere building, is not of very great importance, any more than other great buildings in the world," Elder Rudger Clawson pointed out. "The thing that gives the temple special value is the fact that holy ordinances are performed therein."[13] The fact that temples, ancient and modern, have been identified as "the house of the Lord," Elder Dallin H. Oaks explained, "obviously involves something far more significant than the mere inscription of his sacred name on the structure. The scriptures speak of the Lord's putting his name in a temple because he gives authority for his name to be used in the sacred ordinances of that house."[14]

At the heart of our temple experience is the holy endowment. The term *endowment* commonly refers to a substantial gift of money which is given to a university or charitable institution in such a way as to have continuing benefit. The temple endowment is a spiritual gift from God, and its benefits continue eternally. "To endow is to enrich," taught Elder Boyd K. Packer, "to give to another something long lasting and of much worth." He explained that temple ordinances endow one with divine power, with eternally significant knowledge, and with marvelous promises and challenges.[15] On the occasion when the Prophet Joseph Smith gave the first endowment, he stated that he had spent the day with a group of trusted associates "instructing them in the principles and order of the Priesthood," communicating priesthood keys "and all those plans and principles by which any one is enabled to secure the fulness of those blessings which have been prepared for the Church of the First Born, and come up and abide in the presence of the Eloheim in the eternal worlds."[16] Elder James E. Talmage's description of the endowment as a course of instruction setting forth the high standards by which we may return to the presence of God was echoed by Elder John A. Widtsoe: "The temple endowment relates the story of man's eternal journey, sets forth the conditions upon which progress in the eternal world depends, requires covenants or agreements of those participating to accept and use the laws of progress, gives tests by which our willingness and fitness for righteousness may be known, and finally points out the ultimate destiny of those who love truth and live by it."[17]

Elder Widtsoe regarded this broadened vision as one of the greatest gifts we receive in the endowment: "The mighty perspective of eternity is unraveled before us in the holy temples; we see time from its infinite beginning to its endless end." We are able to see ourselves in relation to the universe and God's purposes for us. We are therefore "better able to value and to weigh, to separate and to organize the common, ordinary duties of...life, so that the little things shall not oppress [us] or take away [our] vision of the greater things that God has given us."[18]

"The endowment is a concept of glory that is to be had from no other source," testified Elder Stephen L Richards. "It is by and through this endowment that man shall attain to that status of glory that God has set for him."[19]

Like the children of Israel, explained President George Q. Cannon, the Latter-day Saints have been anxious to build temples. In them "we have received promises, endowments and keys by which we can go to God as the ancients did, exercise faith before Him, and obtain the promises they received. It is for this purpose that temples have been built."[20]

Thus the object of the temple endowment is to help us attain our eternal potential. Elder Harold B. Lee testified that "the temple ceremonies are designed by a wise Heavenly Father who has revealed them to us in these last days as a guide and a protection throughout our lives, that you and I might not fail to merit exaltation in the celestial kingdom where God and Christ dwell."[21] President Brigham Young identified how temple in-structions can assist us in reaching the celestial kingdom: "Your endowment is to receive all those ordinances in the house of the Lord, which are necessary for you, after you have departed this life to enable you to walk back to the presence of the Father, passing the angels who stand as sentinels...and gain your eternal exaltation."[22]

In the temple we covenant to live by those principles which will assure our eventual exaltation. "The ordinances of the endowment embody certain obligations on the part of the individual," emphasized Elder James E. Talmage, "such as covenant and promise to observe the law of strict virtue and chastity, to be charitable, benevolent, tolerant and pure; to devote both talent and material means to the spread of truth and the uplifting of the race; to maintain devotion to the cause of truth; and to seek in every way to con-tribute to the great preparation that the earth may be made ready to receive her King—the Lord Jesus Christ."[23]

"The House of the Lord is a house of purity," explained President Gordon B. Hinckley. "Those who serve therein dress in spotless white. They participate in sacred ordinances. They are instructed in the eternal plan of the Lord. They make covenants enjoining personal morality and rectitude, unselfishness and service."[24] "These are the covenants of exalta-tion," affirmed Elder A. Theodore Tuttle. "Teach your children that only by receiving these ordinances and making these covenants can they be exalted and become like our Heavenly Father."[25]

Remembering and keeping these specific covenants is one way in which the endowment is a protection.[26] Then, explained Elder Boyd K. Packer, the sacred garment received in the temple "represents [these] sacred covenants. It fosters modesty and becomes a shield and protection to the wearer."[27]

The Lord has often employed symbols to more effectively teach great eternal truths. Consider, for example, the concepts represented in baptism by immersion, in the laying on of hands, and in ancient sacrifices. Such is also the case with the temple endowment. "One man may explain or show a symbol to another, and this is a common, everyday practice," remarked Elder John A. Widtsoe, "but no man can reveal to another the sublime, deep inner meaning of those symbols presented in the House of the Lord, for it is an individual matter and every man must seek and obtain it for himself, and that alone, with God's help only."[28] "We live in a world of symbols," Elder Widtsoe stressed. "No man or woman can come out of the temple endowed as he should be, unless he has seen, beyond the symbol, the mighty realities for which the symbols stand."[29] Thus, like the Master's parables, the temple endowment has various levels of understanding. What we gain from it depends on our spiritual receptivity.

The sealing of families is the end product of our temple service. "When we organize families according to the order that the Lord has revealed," noted Elder Boyd K. Packer, "we organize them in the temples. Temple marriage, that sealing ordinance, is a crowning blessing that you may claim in the holy temple."[30] Scriptures in the Bible support the importance of family relationships. In the Garden of Eden, God provided a companion for Adam (Genesis 2:20-24). During his earthly ministry, the Savior taught the continuing nature of the marriage relationship (Mark 10:6-9). The Apostle Paul stressed that "neither is the man without the woman, neither the woman without the man, in the Lord" (1 Corinthians 11:11).

Latter-day revelation defines the characteristics which must be present for a valid celestial marriage: it must be a covenant "for time and all eternity" rather than just for the time the couple is "in the world"; it must be performed by the Lord's authorized servants; and it must be "sealed by the Holy Spirit of Promise," indicating that the ordinance has been received worthily (D&C 132:7, 15, 18). "In my judgment," concluded Elder Bruce R. McConkie, "there is no more important single act that any Latter-day Saint ever does in this world than to marry the right person in the right place by the right authority."[31] Speaking at the Jordan River Temple's cornerstone laying, President Ezra Taft Benson reflected on the far-reaching impact of sacred temple ordinances: "The saints in this temple district will be better able to meet any temporal tribulation because of this temple. Faith will increase as a result of the divine power associated with the ordinances of heaven and the assurance of eternal associations.... This valley will be preserved, our families will be protected, and our children will be safeguarded as we live the gospel, visit the temple, and live close to the Lord."[32]

Temple Worship

"Many view the temple as for the benefit of the dead only," observed Elder Joseph Fielding Smith, "but the temples are built for the blessing and benefit of the living who receive not only their own blessings within these sacred walls, but are clothed upon with great power when they administer in behalf of their dead."[33] There are important ways in which temple attendance blesses us beyond the direct benefits of sacred ordinances.

Many of these benefits arise from the unselfish nature of temple service. Elder John A. Widtsoe pointed out that "as the Lord gave His life to prove His love for His brothers and sisters, the human family, we may show the spirit of love more vigorously than we have done if we will make the small sacrifices necessary to seek out our genealogies [and] take time to go to the temple ourselves for the dead. All such service may entail sacrifice, but sacrifice lifts us toward the likeness of God, the likeness of our Elder Brother Jesus Christ."[34] "Teach members of the Church," admonished Elder Joseph Fielding Smith, "that doing temple work will bring them the fulness of the glory of God."[35] The benefits of such service may be immediate. Elder David B. Haight was convinced that those who labored unselfishly in behalf of others with no thought of remuneration were "physically and spiritually refreshed and renewed."[36] On the other hand, lamented Elder Widtsoe, "those who have had their own endowments but who do not work for the dead fail to receive the refreshing of their souls that comes by repeated communion with the Spirit of God so abundantly manifested in the temple." He was sure that "temple repetition is the mother of daily blessings."[37]

Divine assistance with personal needs is another outcome of temple worship. Elder Widtsoe promised: "To the man or woman who goes through the temple, with open eyes, heeding the symbols and the covenants, and making a steady, continuous effort to understand the full meaning, God speaks his word, and revelations come.... At the most unexpected moments, in or out of the temple, will come to him, as a revelation, the solution of the problems that vex his life." Elder Widtsoe taught that those who go to the temple should "have a strong desire to have God's will revealed to them."[38] Elder Boyd K. Packer also testified that help comes to those facing crucial decisions. "In the temple we can receive spiritual perspective. There, during the time of the temple service, we are 'out of the world.' A large part of the value of these occasions is the fact that we are doing something for someone that they cannot do for themselves. As we perform the endowment for someone who is dead, somehow we feel a little less hesitant to pray fervently to the Lord to assist us.... There is something cleansing and clarifying about the spiritual atmosphere of the temple."[39]

Those who regularly attend the temple "will reap a blessing of harmony in their lives," promised President Gordon B. Hinckley. "They will draw nearer unto the Lord, and He will draw nearer unto them."[40]

Preparation is Paramount

"The temple occupies a unique and peculiar place in our theology," indicated President Gordon B. Hinckley. "It is not a house of public worship, of which we now have many thousands across the world. Temples, on the other hand, are dedicated as special houses of God, in which are performed some of the most sacred and elevating ordinances associated with the gospel of Jesus Christ."[41] President Hinckley noted that many thousands have visited temples during their open house periods. "These visitors have been respectful and reverent as they have partaken of the spirit of these sacred structures. As they have felt of that spirit and learned something of the purposes for which the temples have been built, these who have been our guests have recognized why, following dedication, we regard these buildings as sanctified and holy, reserved for sacred purposes and closed to the public."[42]

Many have criticized what they regard as the secrecy surrounding dedicated temples which are not open to the public. In response, Elder Harold B. Lee insisted: "Anyone may come here if he is properly recommended. The whole world may come if they will accept the gospel and live according to its precepts." Therefore Elder Lee concluded that "we say the ordinances are sacred as contrasted with just being secret."[43] These safeguards are consistent with restrictions in former dispensations concerning who was permitted to enter the inner rooms of the tabernacle. "If 'secret' means that others are permanently prevented from knowing of them, then secret is the wrong word. These things are sacred. It was never intended that knowledge of these temple ceremonies would be limited to a select few who would be obliged to ensure that others never learn of them. It is quite the opposite, in fact. Those who have been to the temple have been taught an ideal. Someday every living soul and every soul who has ever lived shall have the opportunity to hear the gospel and to accept or reject what the temple offers."[44]

Because of the spiritual nature of temple ordinances, personal preparation is essential in order to benefit fully from them. "The endowment you are so anxious about, you cannot comprehend now," the Prophet Joseph Smith insisted. "Strive to be prepared in your hearts, be faithful in all things...we must be clean every whit." On another occasion the Prophet emphasized that the endowment was to be received "only by the spiritual minded."[45] "The endowment which was given by revelation can best be understood by revelation," instructed Elder Widtsoe, "and to those who seek most vigorously, with pure hearts, will the revelation be the greatest."[46]

In universities, advanced courses typically specify prerequisites for those who wish to enroll. Elder ElRay L. Christiansen, who for many years served as president of the Salt Lake Temple, expanded on this principle. "These ordinances of the priesthood are administered, and their purpose taught, in what might be termed 'closed revelation,' that is, they are not revealed to the unprepared world.... Those who enter the temple hungering and thirsting,' as it were, have revealed to them knowledge and understanding of their relationship to God, and they learn what they need to do to gain the greatest gift of God—eternal life and exaltation with their loved ones. Thus, one might in reverence refer to the temple as the single 'university of the Lord.'"[47]

Not only must the individual be prepared for temple worship but the sanctity of the temple itself must be protected. The Lord instructed that if his people "do not suffer any unclean thing to come into [the temple], that it be not defiled, my glory shall rest upon it; yea, and my presence shall be there, for I will come into it, and all the pure in heart that shall come into it shall see God" (D&C 97:15-16; see also 94:8 and 110:7-8). Speaking at the Idaho Falls Temple dedication, President George Albert Smith told the Saints that they were fortunate to come out of the world into this "little bit of heaven." On the same occasion his counselor, David O. McKay, charged the Saints "to enter the temple as they would the presence of God."[48]

Bishops and stake presidencies therefore have an important responsibility to be sure that those recommended for the temple are prepared and worthy. Elder M. Russell Ballard insisted that "teaching and preparing the members of the Church to be worthy of the temple blessings rests upon the shoulders of the priesthood. There is no substitute, in my opinion, for inspired local leaders."[49] "Members of the Church might well cherish the great privilege of going before the bishop for an interview" to receive their temple recommend, taught Elder Boyd K. Packer, and experience the "deep personal satisfaction" of declaring that their lives are in order.[50] As part of his dedicatory prayer for the Swiss Temple, President David O. McKay petitioned, "may all who enter this Holy Temple come with clean hands and pure hearts that Holy Spirit may ever be present to inspire, to comfort, and to bless."[51]

References

The following abbreviations are used in the references below:

BYU	Brigham Young University (Provo, Utah)
CA	Church Archives, Historical Department of The Church of Jesus Christ of Latter-day Saints, Salt Lake City, Utah
CN	*Church News*: A weekly supplement to the *Deseret News*, Salt Lake City, Utah; also called *Church Section* during certain years
DN	*Deseret News*, Salt Lake City, Utah
GHMA	*Genealogical and Historical Magazine of the Arizona Temple District*
HC	*Joseph Smith, History of the Church of Jesus Christ of Latter-day Saints*, Century 1, B.H. Roberts, ed., 7 vols. (Salt Lake City: Deseret Book Co., 1952-1962)
IE	*Improvement Era*
JD	George D. Watt, et. al., eds., *Journal of Discourses*, 26 vols. (London: Latter-day Saints Book Depot, 1854-1886)
JH	Journal History of the Church, Manuscript in Church Archives
MS	Manuscript
PGRS	*Proceedings of the First [Second, etc.] Priesthood Genealogy Research Seminar* (held on the campus of Brigham Young University)
SLC	Salt Lake City
Star	*The Latter-day Saints' Millennial Star*
TMH	N.B. Lundwall, comp., *Temples of the Most High* (Salt Lake City: Bookcraft, 1968)
TPJS	Joseph Fielding Smith, comp., *Teachings of the Prophet Joseph Smith* (Salt Lake City: Deseret Book Co., 1940)
UGHM	*Utah Genealogical and Historical Magazine*
WWJ	Scott G. Kenney, ed., *Wilford Woodruff's Journal*, 9 vols. (Midvale, Utah: Signature Books, 1983)

Chapter 1. Background from Former Dispensations

1. JD 4:192.

2. John A. Widtsoe, "Temple Worship," UGHM 12 (April 1921): 52.

3. Joseph Fielding Smith, *Doctrines of Salvation*, Bruce R. McConkie, comp., 3 vols. (SLC: Bookcraft, 1954-56), p. 237.

4. Hugh Nibley, "The Idea of the Temple in History," *Star* 120 (August 1958): 228-37, 247; this article was republished in pamphlet form by BYU Press in 1963 under the title "What Is a Temple?"

5. James E. Talmage, *The House of the Lord* (SLC: Bookcraft, 1962), p. 17.

6. Mark E. Petersen, *Moses, Man of Miracles* (SLC: Deseret Book Co., 1977), p. 96.

7. Boyd K. Packer, *The Holy Temple* (SLC: Bookcraft, 1980), pp. 94, vii.

8. See "Holy of Holies" in *The Oxford English Dictionary* (Oxford, England: The Clarendon Press, 1933).

9. Bruce R. McConkie, *Mormon Doctrine*, 2nd ed. (SLC: Bookcraft, 1966), pp. 103-4.

10. Bible Dictionary in Latter-day Saint edition of the King James Version of the Bible (1979), p. 708.

11. George Arthur Buttrick, ed., *The Interpreter's Dictionary of the Bible* (New York: Abingdon Press, 1962), 4:540.

12. Sidney B. Sperry, "Some Thoughts Concerning Ancient Temples and Their Functions," IE 58 (November 1955): 814.

13. Joseph Fielding Smith, "Was Temple Work Done in the Days of the Old Prophets?" IE 52 (November 1955): 794.

14. Brigham Young, January 1, 1877, in JD 18:303.

15. HC 4:211; see also TPJS p. 172.

16. Joseph Fielding Smith, "Was Temple Work Done?" p. 794.

17. See "Priestly Vestments" in the *Encyclopedia Judaica* (Jerusalem, Israel: Keter Publishing House Ltd., 1972), vol. 13, p. 1063; see also Moshe Levine, *The Tabernacle: Its Structure and Utensils* (Tel Aviv, 1969), pp. 124-40.

18. See Hugh Nibley, *Message of the Joseph Smith Papyri: An Egyptian Endowment* (SLC: Deseret Book Co., 1975).

19. See Yigael Yadin, "The Temple Scroll," in David Noel Freedman, ed., *New Directions in Biblical Archaeology* (Garden City, NY: Doubleday,

1969), pp. 156-66; Jacob Milgrom, "The Temple Scroll," *Biblical Archaeologist*, September 1978, vol. 41 no. 13, pp. 105-20.

20. Asher S. Kaufman, "Where the Ancient Temple of Jerusalem Stood," *Biblical Archaeology Review*, March-April 1983, vol. IX no. 2, pp. 42-59.

21. Smith, *Doctrines of Salvation*, 2:165.

22. Heber C. Kimball, 19 July 1863, JD 10:241.

23. Quoted in Nibley, *Message of the Joseph Smith Papyri*, pp. 279-80.

24. See, for example, Nibley, "The Early Christian Prayer Circle," *BYU Studies* 19 (Fall 1978): 41-78.

25. Gospel of Philip, 69:14-25, 70:17-20, 86:3-7; see R. McL. Wilson, trans., The Gospel of Philip (New York: Harper & Row, 1962), pp. 45-46, 62.

26. Talmage, *House of the Lord*, p. 91.

27. Sperry, "Ancient Temples," p. 827.

Chapter 2. The Kirtland Temple and the Restoration of Temple Worship

1. Orlen C. Peterson, "A History of the Schools and Educational Programs of the Church...in Ohio and Missouri, 1831-1839" (master's thesis, BYU, 1972), p. 23.

2. HC 1:334-335; Milton V. Backman Jr., *The Heavens Resound* (SLC: Deseret Book Co., 1983), pp. 266-67.

3. Peterson, "A History of the Schools," pp. 23-24.

4. HC 1:352; Lucy Mack Smith, *History of Joseph Smith*, ed. Preston Nibley (SLC: Bookcraft, 1958), p. 230.

5. Brigham Young, April 6, 1853, JD 2:31.

6. Lauritz G. Petersen, "The Kirtland Temple," *BYU Studies* 12 (Summer 1972): 404-9; Clarence L. Fields, "History of the Kirtland Temple" (master's thesis, BYU, 1963), p. 28.

7. Orson Pratt, May 5, 1870, JD 13:357; see also 14:273.

8. Truman O. Angell Autobiographical Sketch, MS, Harold B. Lee Library, BYU, p. 3, quoted in Marvin E. Smith, "The Builder," IE 45 (October, 1942): 630.

9. Roger D. Launius, *The Kirtland Temple: A Historical Narrative* (Independence, Missouri: Herald House, 1986), p. 40.

10. Benjamin F. Johnson, *My Life's Review* (Independence, Missouri:

Zion's Printing and Publishing Co., 1947), p. 28.

11. HC 1:349.

12. Heber C. Kimball, JD 10:165.

13. HC 1:400.

14. Heber C. Kimball's journal quoted in HC 2:2.

15. Nicolas G. Morgan, comp., *Eliza R. Snow an Immortal* (SLC: Nicolas G. Morgan Foundation, 1957), p. 59.

16. HC 2: 167.

17. Backman, *The Heavens Resound*, pp. 151-53.

18. Backman, *The Heavens Resound*, p. 285.

19. HC 2:379-82.

20. HC 2:392.

21. Orson Pratt, October 9, 1875, JD 18:132.

22. HC 2:410-26.

23. Morgan, *Eliza R. Snow*, p. 63; see also Lael Woodbury, "Origin and Uses of the Sacred Hosanna Shout," in *Sperry Lecture Series 1975* (Provo: BYU Press, 1975), pp. 18-22.

24. HC 2:428.

25. Reported by George A. Smith in JD 11:10.

26. HC 2:428; Backman, *The Heavens Resound*, p. 300.

27. Morgan, *Eliza R. Snow*, p. 63.

28. Brigham Young, April 6, 1853, JD 2:31.

29. Bruce R. McConkie, *Mormon Doctrine*, 2nd ed. (SLC: Bookcraft, 1966), p. 831.

30. Harold B. Lee, "Correlation and Priesthood Genealogy," address at Priesthood Genealogical Research Seminar, 1968 (Provo: BYU Press, 1969), p. 60.

31. Boyd K. Packer, *The Holy Temple* (SLC: Bookcraft, 1980), p. 129.

32. Brigham Young, January 1, 1877, JD 18:303.

33. Packer, *The Holy Temple*, p. 43.

34. Eliza R. Snow, *Biography and Family Record of Lorenzo Snow*, pp. 20-21, quoted in B.H. Roberts, *A Comprehensive History of the Church* (Provo: BYU Press, 1965), 1:406 fn.

35. HC 1:199; Richard and Pamela Price, *The Temple of the Lord* (Independence, Missouri: the authors, 1982), pp. 20-25.

36. HC 1:358-59.

37. HC 1:359-62.
38. T. Edgar Lyon, "The Sketches on the Papyri Backing," IE 71 (May 1968): 19-23.
39. HC 3:41-42.
40. George Q. Cannon, December 3, 1871, JD 14:319-20.
41. John Tayor, June 18, 1883, JD 24:197; George Q. Cannon, December 3, 1871, JD 14:3 19-20.
42. HC 3:33-39.
43. E. Cecil McGavin, "The Kirtland Temple Defiled," IE 43 (October 1940): 594-95.

Chapter 3. The Nauvoo Temple and the Restoration of Temple Ordinances

1. HC 4:179; see also D&C 124:132.
2. Andrew F. Ehat and Lindon W. Cook, eds., *The Words of Joseph Smith* (Provo, Utah: Religious Studies Center, BYU, 1980), p. 49.
3. HC 4:206, 231; TPJS p. 179.
4. HC 4:425-26.
5. "A Most Glorious Principle," in *Children of the Covenant* (SLC: Genealogical Society of Utah, 1937), pp. 129-30.
6. Wilford Woodruff, April 9, 1857, JD 5:85.
7. HC 4:186, 205.
8. J. Earl Arrington, "William Weeks, Architect of the Nauvoo Temple," *BYU Studies* 19 (Spring 1979): 340.
9. HC 6:196-97.
10. Arrington, "Weeks," p. 342.
11. *Times and Seasons* 2:259-60.
12. HC 4:329-30.
13. HC 4:426.
14. HC 4:446-47, 454, 486.
15. *The Wasp*, Nauvoo, Illinois, August 4, 1842, quoted in Don F. Colvin, "A Historical Study of the Mormon Temple at Nauvoo, Illinois" (master's thesis, BYU, 1962), pp. 69-71.
16. HC 5:182.
17. HC 4:205.

18. DN, October 14, 1863, cited in Colvin, "A Historical Study," p. 68.

19. *History of Relief Society, 1842-1966* (SLC: General Board of the Relief Society, 1966), p. 18.

20. *The Women's Exponent* 37 (March 1909): 41, cited in Colvin, "A Historical Study," p. 55.

21. E. Cecil McGavin, *The Nauvoo Temple* (SLC: Deseret Book Co., 1962), pp. 33-34.

22. Brigham H. Roberts, *A Comprehensive History of The Church of Jesus Christ of Latter-day Saints* (Provo: BYU Press, 1965), 2:472.

23. James E. Talmage, *The House of the Lord*, (SLC: Bookcraft, 1962), pp. 99-100.

24. Lisle G Brown, "The Sacred Departments for Temple Work in Nauvoo: The Assembly Room and the Council Chamber," *BYU Studies* 19 (Spring 1979): 363.

25. Lucius N. Scovil letter in *DN Semi Weekly*, February 15, 1884, p. 2, quoted in BYU Studies 19 (Winter 1979): 159 fn.

26. HC 5:1-2.

27. Heber C. Kimball to Parley P. Pratt, June 17, 1842, Parley P. Pratt papers, CA; quoted in Stanley B. Kimball, *Heber C. Kimball: Mormon Patriarch and Pioneer* (Urbana: University of Illinois Press, 1981), p. 85.

28. John A Widtsoe, *Evidences and Reconciliations*, G. Homer Durham, comp. (SLC: Bookcraft, 1960), pp. 111-13.

29. L. John Nuttall diary, February 7, 1877, quoted in *BYU Studies* 19 (Winter 1979): 159 fn.

30. *Times and Seasons* 5 (September 15, 1844): 651.

31. DN *Weekly* 44 (March 19, 1892): 406.

32. *Star* 5 (March 1845): 151.

33. HC 7:323-24.

34. HC 7:417-18.

35. HC 7:456-57.

36. Matthias F. Cowley, ed., *Wilford Woodruff, History of His Life and Labors* (SLC: Deseret News, 1909), p. 158.

37. Andrew F. Ehat, ed., "They Might Have Known That He Was Not a Fallen Prophet—The Nauvoo Journal of Joseph Fielding," *BYU Studies* 19 (Winter 1979): 158.

38. HE 7:567.

39. HC 7:579.
40. Quoted in Brown, "Sacred Departments," p. 374.
41. Kimball, *Heber C. Kimball*, p. 118.
42. Cowley, ed., *Wilford Woodruff*, pp. 247-48.
43. CN December 22, 1973, p. 5; May 21, 1977, p. 14.

Chapter 4. Temples in the Tops of the Mountains

1. Matthias F. Cowley, *Wilford Woodruff: History of His Life and Labors* (SLC: Deseret News, 1909), p. 255.
2. Ibid., pp. 619-20.
3. Brigham H. Roberts, *A Comprehensive History of the Church* (Provo: BYU Press, 1965), 3:386.
4. HC 4:608.
5. James R. Clark, comp., *Messages of the First Presidency*, 6 vols. (SLC: Bookcraft, 1965-75), 1:333.
6. C. Mark Hamilton, *The Salt Lake Temple: A Monument to a People* (SLC: University Services, Inc., 1983), p. 48.
7. Leonard J. Arrington, *Great Basin Kingdom* (Cambridge, Mass.: Harvard University Press, 1958), pp. 109-12.
8. *Deseret News Weekly*, April 19, 1851, p. 1.
9. Brigham Young, October 9, 1852, in JD 1:218-20.
10. James E. Talmage, *The House of the Lord* (SLC: Bookcraft, 1962), p. 142; see also JD, 1:162.
11. James H. Anderson, "The Salt Lake Temple," *The Contributor* 14 (April 1893): 250-58; WWJ, 4:195-99.
12. Brigham Young, April 6, 1853, in JD 2:33; James H. Anderson, "Salt Lake Temple," pp. 252-59.
13. Parley P. Pratt, April 7, 1853, in JD 1:14.
14. Anderson, "Salt Lake Temple," p. 257.
15. Brigham Young, April 6, 1853, in JD, 1:132-33.
16. Andrew Jenson, *Encyclopedic History of the Church* (SLC: Deseret News), 1941, p. 161; Roberts, *Comprehensive History*, 4:12-14; JH July 7, 1852, p. 1, MS, CA. Elder Roberts' statement that the endowment was given in 1852 for the first time since the expulsion from Nauvoo is in error.

17. JH May 5, 1855, pp. 1-2.
18. Marvin E. Smith, "The Builder," IE 45 (October 1942): 630.
19. Historian's Private Journal, recorded by Wilford Woodruff, MS. F 348, No. 4, CA, entry for August 22, 1862; see also WWJ August 23, 1862, 6:71.
20. Ibid.
21. WWJ, 1870 summary, 6:586.
22. Brigham Young, August 24, 1872, in JD 15:138.
23. Brigham Young, October 6, 1863, in JD, 10:254.
24. Brigham Young, September 4, 1873, in JD, 16:186-87; WWJ July 13, 1865, 6:232.
25. Clark, *Messages of the First Presidency*, 2:278-80.
26. Daniel Tyler, "Temples," *Juvenile Instructor* 15 (August 15, 1880): 182.
27. Stanley B. Kimball, *Heber C. Kimball Mormon Patriarch and Pioneer* (Urbana: University of Illinois Press, 1981), p. 201.
28. John Taylor, November 9, 1881, in JD, 23:14.
29. Statement by David H. Cannon, Jr., October 14, 1942, quoted in Kirk M. Curtis, "History of the St. George Temple" (master's thesis BYU, 1964), pp. 24-25.
30. H. Donl Peterson, *Moroni: Ancient Prophet, Modern Messenger* (Bountiful, Utah: Horizon Publishers, 1983), p. 76.
31. Juanita Brooks, "The St. George Temple," MS, Brooks Papers, Utah State Historical Society, p. 3.
32. Tyler, "Temples," p. 182; Janice Force DeMille, *The St. George Temple First 100 Years* (Hurricane, Utah: Homestead Publishers, 1977), pp. 21-23.
33. DeMille, *St. George Temple*, pp. 26-29; TMH, p. 78.
34. Brooks, "St. George Temple," p. 3.
35. Southern Utah Mission Historical Record, 1873-77, MS, CA, p. 78.
36. DeMille, *St. George Temple*, pp. 39-41.
37. WWJ, November 10, 1876, 7:291.
38. Ibid., p. 297.
39. Maggie Cragun interview, "The Dedication of the St. George Temple," Juanita Brooks papers, Utah State Historical Society; Brigham Young, January 1, 1877, in JD, 18:304.
40. WWJ, January 9, 1877, 7:321.

41. Brigham Jarvis to Susa Young Gates, November 8, 1926, Susa Young Gates papers, Utah State Historical Society.
42. WWJ, January 14, February 12, and March 21, 1877, 7:322, 327, and 340; see also Ensign 7 (March 1977): 94.
43. G. Homer Durham, ed., *Discourses of Wilford Woodruff* (SLC: Bookcraft, 1969), p. 159. WWJ, February 23, 1877, 7:329.
44. WWJ, March 1, 1877, 7:330-32.
45. Martha Cragun Cox, "Autobiography," holograph, CA, p. 150.
46. Wilford Woodruff, September 16, 1877, in JD 19:229.
47. WWJ, August 19 and 21, 1877, 7:367-69.

Chapter 5. A New Generation of Temples

1. Orson Pratt, October 26, 1879, in JD 24:25.
2. Orson Pratt, May 20, 1877, in JD 19:19-20.
3. Erastus Snow, November 20, 1881, in St. George Stake Historical Record, MS, CA.
4. Brigham Young, February 14, 1853, in JD 1:277-78.
5. James E. Talmage, *The House of the Lord* (SLC: Bookcraft, 1962), pp. 110-11.
6. Paul L. Anderson, "William Harrison Folsom: Pioneer Architect," *Utah Historical Quarterly* 43 (Summer 1975): 240-59; Laurel B. Andrew, *The Early Temples of the Mormons* (Albany: State University of New York Press, 1978), pp. 175-76.
7. Truman O. Angell Jr. to John Taylor, May 8, 1878, and William H. Folsom to John Taylor, May 20, 1878, MSS, CA.
8. TMH, p. 87.
9. Henry Sudweeks diary, p. 46, Harold B. Lee Library, BYU; Wilford Woodruff in *Deseret Evening News,* December 13, 1877, p. 3.
10. Cache Valley Stake Historical Record, Book A, quoted in Nolan Porter Olsen, *Logan Temple: The First 100 Years* (Providence, Utah: the author, 1978), pp. 6-7, and in Melvin A. Larkin, "The History of the L.D.S. Temple in Logan, Utah" (master's thesis, Utah State Agricultural College, 1954), p. 14.
11. WWJ, May 8, 1884, 8:247; Olsen, *Logan Temple*, pp. 10-12; Larkin, "History," pp. 14-15.

12. Olsen, *Logan Temple*, pp. 24-26.

13. Brigham Young and John Taylor, May 18, 1877, in JD 19:33-35.

14. Quoted in Olsen, *Logan Temple*, p. 34; WWJ, September 17, 1877, 7:374.

15. Boyd K. Packer, *The Holy Temple* (SLC: Bookcraft, 1980), p. 248.

16. Leonard J. Arrington and Melvin A. Larkin, "The Logan Tabernacle and Temple," *Utah Historical Quarterly* 41 (Summer 1973): 308.

17. Juvenile Instructor 19 (February 1884): 95.

18. Arrington and Larkin, "Logan Tabernacle," p. 306.

19. Olsen, *Logan Temple*, pp. 129-30.

20. Larkin, "History," 133-35.

21. Quoted in Olsen, *Logan Temple,* pp. 140-41.

22. Franklin D. Richards, May 17, 1884, in JD 25:231.

23. TMH, p. 100.

24. Melvin Clarence Merrill, *Marriner Wood Merrill and His Family* (n.p.: the author, 1937), pp. 78-79.

25. Nuttall diary, May 19, 1884; John Taylor, May 18, 1884, in JD 25: 185-87.

26. Nuttall diary, May 22, 1884.

27. Quoted in *Star* 50 (August 13, 1888): 521.

28. Daniel Tyler, "Temples," *Contributor* 16 (November 30, 1880): 160; Glen R. Stubbs, "A History of the Manti Temple" (master's thesis, BYU, 1960), pp. 17-18.

29. Moses F. Farnsworth (Manti Temple Recorder) to George Teasdale, July 2, 1888, in Star 50 (August 13, 1888): 521; Barbara Lee Harris, "A Folk History of the Manti Temple: A Study of the Folklore and Traditions Connected with the Settlement of Manti, Utah, and the Building of the Temple" (master's thesis BYU, 1968), pp. 55-56.

30. *Star* 39 (June 11, 1877): 373.

31. *Star* 41 (May 12, 1879): 295.

32. Thomas Weston Welch, "Early Mormon Woodworking at Its Best: A Study of the Craftsmanship in the First Temples in Utah" (master's thesis, BYU, 1983), p. 11.

33. Stubbs, "History of Manti Temple," pp. 38-42.

34. Ibid., p. 47.

35. Welch, "Early Mormon Woodworking," p. 85.

36. Welch, "Early Mormon Woodworking," pp. 81-85; Stubbs, "History of

Manti Temple," p. 67.

37. Stubbs, "History of Manti Temple," p. 50.

38. WWJ, May 13-18, 1888, 8:496-500.

39. "The Dedication of the Manti Temple," *Star* 50 (June 18, 1888): 385-92; for dedicatory prayer see TMH, pp. 103-12.

40. Star 50 (June 25, 1888): 401.

41. Franklin D. Richards in Star 50 (June 25, 1888): 403.

42. "Spiritual Manifestations at the Manti Temple," *Star* 50 (August 13, 1888): 521-22.

43. "Dedication of the Manti Temple," Star 50 (June 25, 1888): 405.

44. Franklin D. Richards in Star 55 (June 19, 1893): 431.

45. "A String of Pearls for Those Who Have Intelligence to Appreciate Them," *Young Woman's Journal* 1 (April 1890): 213-14.

Chapter 6. The Salt Lake Temple Completed

1. Mark E. Petersen, PGRS, August 1, 1973 (Provo: BYU, 1974), p. 510.

2. Heber C. Kimball, April 6, 1863, in JD, 10:165.

3. Heber J. Grant message in GHMA 19 (April 1942): 3-4.

4. *The Scoutmaster's Minute* (SLC: Young Men's Mutual Improvement Association General Board, 1948), p. 10.

5. Truman O. Angell Jr. to John Taylor, April 28, 1885, and Truman O. Angell Sr. to John Taylor, March 11, 1885, in Charles Mark Hamilton, "The Salt Lake Temple: An Architectural Monograph" (doctoral dissertation, Ohio State University, 1977), pp. 68-73.

6. Orson F. Whitney, *Life of Heber C. Kimball* (SLC: Bookcraft, 1945), p. 397.

7. Leonard J. Arrington, Great Basin Kingdom (Cambridge, Mass.: Harvard University Press, 1958), p. 362.

8. TMH, pp. 87-94.

9. Leonard J. Arrington and Wayne K. Hinton, "The Logan Tabernacle and Temple," *Utah Historical Quarterly* 41 (Summer 1973): 312-13; Melvin A. Larkin, "The History of the L.D.S. Temple in Logan, Utah," (master's thesis, Utah State Agricultural College, 1954), pp. 143-55.

10. James H. Anderson, "The Salt Lake Temple," *Contributor* 14 (April 1893): 269-70.

11. Ibid., p. 270.

12. Ibid., p. 271.
13. WWJ, April 6, 1892, 9:192-94; James E. Talmage, *House of the Lord* (SLC: Bookcraft, 1962), pp. 149-52.
14. Hamilton, "The Salt Lake Temple," p. 105.
15. DN, April 15, 1892.
16. Truman O. Angell Sr., "A Descriptive Statement of the Temple Now Being Erected in Salt Lake City..." *Star* 36 (May 5, 1874): 273-75.
17. Hamilton, "The Salt Lake Temple," pp. 94-97.
18. Duncan M. McAllister, *Description of the Great Temple* (SLC: Bureau of Information, 1912), pp. 7-10; Anderson, "Salt Lake Temple," p. 276.
19. Truman O. Angell Sr., descriptions of the Salt Lake Temple, DN, August 17, 1854, and *Star* 36 (May 1874): 273-75, quoted in James E. Talmage, *House of the Lord* (SLC: Bookcraft, 1962), p. 145, and Wallace Alan Raynor, *The Everlasting Spires: A Story of the Salt Lake Temple* (SLC: Deseret Book Co., 1965), p. 175.
20. Harold B. Lee in CR, October 1964, p. 86.
21. Anderson, "Salt Lake Temple," p. 274.
22. WWJ October 10, 1892, 9:222.
23. William Hurst diary as cited in Joseph Heinerman, *Temple Manifestations* (Manti, Utah: Mountain Valley Publishers, 1974), p. 116.
24. Anderson, "Salt Lake Temple," p. 282.
25. McAllister, "Temples of the Latter-day Saints: Purposes for Which They Are Erected," *Liahona the Elder's Journal* 24 (February 22, 1927): 417; John R. Winder, "Temples and Temple Work," *Young Woman's Journal* 14 (February 1903): 51.
26. Anderson, "Salt Lake Temple," p. 278.
27. First Presidency circular letter, March 18, 1893, in James R. Clark, comp. *Messages of the First Presidency*, 6 vols. (SLC: Bookcraft, 1965-75): 3:241-44.
28. Anderson, "Salt Lake Temple," p. 292.
29. Talmage, *House of the Lord*, p. 159.
30. Frank T. Pomeroy, "Temples of Our Lord, Ancient and Modern," GHMA 2 (April 1925): 34.
31. WWJ, 1893 summary, 9:279.
32. WWJ, April 6, 1893, 9:246.
33. Quoted in *Saviors on Mount Zion* (SLC: Deseret Sunday School

Union, 1950), pp. 142-43.
34. George Q. Cannon, quoted in *Our Lineage* (SLC: Genealogical Society of Utah, 1934), p. 20.
35. Lucile C. Tate, *LeGrand Richards: Beloved Apostle* (SLC: Bookcraft, 1982), pp. 10-11.
36. Anderson, "Salt Lake Temple," p. 301.
37. Brigham H. Roberts journals, 1890-93, entries for April 19 and 20, MSS, Ms 1430, box 3, folder 6, in the Special Collections of the Harold B. Lee Library at BYU, 1893; Anthon H. Lund journal, April 20, 1893, MS F 288, No. 1, HDC.
38. Lund journal, April 18, 1893.
39. Roberts journal, April 21, 1893
40. Quoted in Lund journal, April 19, 1893.
41. Roberts journal, April 24, 1883.
42. *Deseret News Weekly*, August 19, 1893, p. 267.
43. *Instructor* 95 (August 1960): 257.
44. Talmage, *House of the Lord*, pp. 193-94.
45. Boyd K. Packer, *The Holy Temple* (SLC: Bookcraft, 1980), p. 4.
46. LeRoi C. Snow, "An Experience of My Father's," IE 36 (September 1933): 677, 679.
47. Ibid.

Chapter 7. Temples in a New Century

1. Joseph F. Smith in CR, April 1901, p. 69.
2. Quoted Serge F. Ballif, CR, October 1920, p. 90.
3. Jonathan E. Layne diary, June 19, 1887, quoted in Melvin S. Tagg, "The History of The Church of Jesus Christ of Latter-day Saints in Canada, 1830-1963" (doctoral dissertation, BYU, 1963), p. 215.
4. TMH, p. 165.
5. "The Alberta Temple," in *History of the Mormon Church in Canada* (Lethbridge: Lethbridge Stake, 1968), pp. 70-71.
6. C. Frank Steele, "Latter-day Saint Settlements in Canada," *Instructor* 83 (September 1948): 412.
7. "A Temple in Canada," IE 16 (November 1912): 85; Edward J. Wood journal, entry for October 4, 1912, quoted in Tagg, "Canada," p. 218.

8. TMH, p. 166.

9. Paul L. Anderson, "First of the Modern Temples," *Ensign* 7 (July 1977): 8.

10. Hyrum Pope remarks, "Dedication Proceedings of the Alberta Temple, August 26-29, 1923," pp. 228-29, MS, CA.

11. Anthony W. Ivins's remarks at the Alberta Temple dedication, UGHM 15 (July 1924): 98-99.

12. Edward J. Wood in CR, October 1915, p. 66; JH, September 19, 1915, p. 5, cited in Tagg, "Canada," p. 222.

13. W. McD. Tait, "The Mormon Temple in Canada," *Canadian Magazine* 42 (1914): 490.

14. Tagg, "Canada," pp. 228-30.

15. "*Summary of Alberta Dedication Addresses*," Susa Young Gates papers, Utah State Historical Society; Tagg, "Canada," p. 233.

16. Heber J. Grant in CR, October 1923, p. 3.

17. Tagg, "The Life of Edward J. Wood, Church Patriot" (master's thesis, BYU, 1959), pp. 107-24.

18. Mission Annual Reports, 1927, p. 256, MS in CA; William R. Sloan, "Northwestern States Temple Caravan," UGHM 22 (January 1931): 8-12; C. Frank Steel, "Pilgrims of the Light," IE (October 1932): 710-11; Edward J. Wood, "Alberta Temple," IE (April 1936): 235, 263.

19. R. Lanier Britsch, *Unto the Islands of the Sea* (SLC: Deseret Book Co., 1986), p. 150.

20. Ibid., p. 153.

21. Reed Smoot in CR, October 1920, pp. 136-37.

22. Joseph F. Smith, in CR, October 1915, p. 8.

23. John A. Widtsoe, "The Temple in Hawaii: A Remarkable Fulfillment of Prophecy," IE 19 (September 1916): 955-58, and "Was Brigham Young a Prophet?" IE 50 (November 1947): 745, 786.

24. Samuel E. Woolley in CR, October 1917, p. 80; Widtsoe, "Temple in Hawaii," p. 954.

25. Hyrum C. Pope, "About the Temple in Hawaii," IE 23 (December 1919): 149-50; remarks by Romania Woolley (widow of Temple contractor Ralph E. Woolley) Nov. 27, 1969, recording in BYU Hawaii Campus Library.

26. Remarks by Romania Woolley, Feb. 17, 1970, recording in CA.

27. J. Leo Fairbanks, "The Sculpture of the Hawaii Temple," *Juvenile Instructor* 56 (November 1921): 575-83.
28. Albert L. Zobell Jr., "Hawaii," IE 66 (November 1963): 948.
29. Castle H. Murphy to Hawaiian Temple jubilee, November 14, 1969, Castle H. Murphy papers, Harold B. Lee Library Special Collections, BYU.
30. Rudger Clawson, "Dedication of Hawaiian Temple," UGHM 11 (January 1920): 11.
31. Ibid.
32. TMH, pp. 151-58.
33. Britsch, *Islands of the Sea*, p. 158.
34. Susa Young Gates, "Sandwich Island Genealogy," UGHM 10 (October 1919): 148.
35. Murphy to Hawaiian Temple jubilee.

Chapter 8. Continued Expansion

1. James W. LeSueur, "The Arizona Temple," UGHM 18 (January 1927): 1; see also Frank T. Pomeroy, "Arizona Temple: Intimate Description of Sacred Temple," GHMA 4 (July 1927): 10; and LeSueur, "The Arizona Temple," IE 30 (October 1927): 1-2.
2. DN August 21, 1920, p. 4.
3. "The Arizona Temple," GHMA 15 (April 1939): 4-5; DN December 3, 1921, Section 3, VII.
4. Gusse Thomas Smith, "The Mormon Temple at Mesa," GHMA 5 (January 1928): 4.
5. LeSueur, "The Story Told by the Frieze of the Temple," GHMA 4 (July 1927): 19ff.; Rae Rose Kirkham, "Shrine of Mormonism," *Arizona Highways* 12 (December 1936): 6, 24; Joseph Miller, "The Arizona Temple, Shrine of Mormonism," *Arizona Highways* 19 (November-December 1943): 36-37.
6. "The Dedication of the Arizona Temple," GHMA 4 (October 1927): 3; Francis M. Gibbons, *Heber J. Grant: Man of Steel, Prophet of God* (SLC: Deseret Book Co., 1979), p. 189.
7. "The Dedication of the Arizona Temple," GHMA 12 (October 1927): 3.
8. DN October 29, 1927, Section 3, IX.

9. "Manifestations in the Arizona Temple," GHMA 12 (July 1935), quoted in TMH, p. 191.

10. UGHM 29 (July 1938): 54-63.

11. Nolan P. Olsen, *Logan Temple: The First 100 Years* (Logan, Utah: the author, 1978), pp. 176-77.

12. Twelve to the Saints in California, JH August 7, 1847.

13. Brigham H. Roberts, *A Comprehensive History of the Church* (SLC: Deseret News Press, 1930), 6:493.

14. DN March 6, 1937, p. 1.

15. Heber J. Grant to J. Reuben Clark, March 6, 1937; see also February 22, 1937, First Presidency Letterbooks, MS, CA.

16. First Presidency to David P. Howells, March 17, 1937, First Presidency Letterbooks, MS, CA.

17. Harold W. Buron and W. Aird Macdonald, "The Oakland Temple," IE 67 (May 1964): 380-81.

18. Eugene Hilton, "Temple Hill," in *Triumph*, a souvenir book commemorating the opening of the East Bay Inter Stake Center in January, 1959 (published by the Hayward, Oakland-Berkeley, and Walnut Creek stakes of The Church of Jesus Christ of Latter-day Saints, 1959), pp. 10, 19.

19. Francis M. Gibbons, *David O. McKay: Apostle to the World, Prophet of God* (SLC: Deseret Book Co., 1986), p. 164.

20. Quoted in Delbert V. Groberg, *The Idaho Falls Temple* (SLC: Publishers Press, 1985), p. 15; see also MS, CA.

21. Groberg, *The Idaho Fall Temple*, p. 63.

22. Paul L. Anderson, "Mormon Moderne: LDS Architecture 1925-1945," in *Journal of Mormon History* 9 (1982): 79-84.

23. DN, April 5, 1939, p. 7; TMH, p. 202.

24. Groberg, *Idaho Falls Temple*, pp. 82-109.

25. Carl W. Buehner, in *Speeches of the Year*, October 19, 1960 (BYU, 1961), pp. 3-4.

26. Fred Schwendiman, "The Temple in Idaho Falls," IE 45 (June 1942): 378, 402.

27. Anderson, p. 82; D. Michael Quinn, *J. Reuben Clark, the Church Years* (Provo, Utah: BYU Press, 1983), pp. 142-43.

28. *Church Section*, September 29, 1945, pp. 1-16; IE 48 (October 1945): 562-65.

Chapter 9. Postwar Progress

1. Lorin F. Jones, interview, 1964, tape recording in possession of the author.
2. Eduardo Balderas, "Northward to Mesa," *Ensign* 2 (September 1972): 30-33.
3. Ibid., p. 31.
4. CN, November 10, 1945, p. 1; Ivie H. Jones, "Historia Lamanita," *Liahona* (January 1946), pp. 7-11.
5. Report by President Lorin F. Jones of the Spanish-American Mission, Mission Annual Reports, 1945, MS, CA.
6. CN, November 10, 1945. p. 8.
7. Report by Alma Sonne, General Authorities' Mission Tour Reports, 1945, MS, CA.
8. CN, November 30, 1946, p. 9.
9. Balderas, "Northward to Mesa," pp. 32-33.
10. Related August 23, 1982, by Harold Wright, President of the Arizona Temple.
11. CN, December 18, 1965, p. 11.
12. Balderas, "Northward to Mesa," p. 33.
13. *Los Angeles Times*, in JH, January 17, 1949, p. 5; DN in JH, January 18, 1949, p. 4; IE 52 (March 1949): 132.
14. Chad M. Orton, *More Faith Than Fear: The Los Angeles Stake Story* (SLC: Bookcraft, 1987), p. 180.
15. George Albert Smith, Diary, November 8, 1949, MS, Western Americana Collection, University of Utah; Edward O. Anderson, "The Los Angeles Temple," IE 56 (April 1953): 225-26, and 58 (November 1955): 804.
16. Edward O. Anderson, "Los Angeles Temple," IE 58 (November 1955): 803; CN, December 5, 1953, p. 9.
17. CN, December 13, 1950, pp. 1-2.
18. Anderson, "Los Angeles Temple," IE 56 (April 1953): 226.
19. CN, September 26, 1951, pp. 1-2; *California Intermountain News*, September 27, 1955.
20. California Intermountain News, September 27, 1955, p. 12.
21. Ibid., p. 46.
22. Carl W. Buehner, *Do Unto Others* (SLC: Bookcraft, 1957), p. 152.

23. CN, May 8, 1954, pp. 1, 8; Buehner, *Do Unto Others*, p. 153.

24. *California Intermountain News*, September 27, 1955, pp. 3, 45.

25. CN, December 19, 1953, pp. 6-12.

26. Francis M. Gibbons, *David O. McKay: Apostle to the World, Prophet of God* (SLC: Deseret Book Co., 1986), pp. 342-43, 357-58.

27. Statement by Benjamin L. Bowring to Anna Mae Robinson, CA.

28. Buehner, *Do Unto Others*, p. 157.

29. *California Intermountain News*, September 27, 1955, p. 39.

30. Albert L. Zobell Jr., "Los Angeles," IE 66 (November 1963): 953.

31. Joseph Gibby to the author, September 23, 1988.

32. *California Intermountain News*, March 15, 1956, pp. 1-6.

33. Gibbons, *David O. McKay*, p. 234.

34. Alberta Temple dedications proceedings, MS, CA, p. 242.

35. Frederick W. Babbel, *On Wings of Faith* (SLC: Bookcraft, 1972), pp. 61-62.

36. CN, September 17, 1955, p. 2.

37. CN, July 23, 1952, p. 2; July 30, 1952, p. 1; April 11, 1953, p. 7.

38. Samuel E. Bringhurst, "Acquisition of Property and Construction of Swiss Temple," CN, September 17, 1955, pp. 4, 10.

39. Quoted in Marba C. Josephson, "A Temple Is Risen to Our Lord," IE 58 (September 1955): 624-25.

40. Bringhurst, "*Swiss Temple*," p. 10.

41. Edward O. Anderson, "Inspirational Events Associated with the Building of New Temples," MS, CA.

42. Edward O. Anderson, "The Making of a Temple," *Star* 120 (September 1958): 278.

43. Gibbons, *David O. McKay*, pp. 328-29, 342.

44. Dale Z. Kirby, "History of The Church of Jesus Christ of Latter-day Saints in Switzerland" (master's thesis, BYU 1971), p. 127.

45. Bringhurst, "Acquisition," p. 10.

46. Clare Middlemiss, *Cherished Experiences* (SLC: Deseret Book Co., 1967), pp. 38-39; CN, August 15, 1953, pp. 3-6.

47. Josephson, "A Temple Is Risen," pp. 685-86.

48. Kirby, "Switzerland," p. 130.

49. CN, November 20, 1954, p. 4.

50. CN, September 10, 1955, p. 2.

51. Warren John "Jack" Thomas, *Salt Lake Mormon Tabernacle Choir Goes to Europe 1955* (SLC: Deseret News Press, 1957), p. 153.

52. CN, September 17, 1955, p. 2.

53. CR, October 1955, p. 107.

54. CN, September 10, 1955, p. 2; Kirby, "Switzerland," pp. 134-35.

55. CR, October 1955, p. 8.

56. CN, September 24, 1955, p. 2.

57. CN, September 24, 1955, p. 2, September 8, 1956, p. 4; Kirby, "Switzerland," pp. 139-40.

58. Wendell B. Mendenhall, New Zealand Temple dedication proceedings, April 20-23, 1958, MS, CA; Brian W. Hunt, "History of The Church of Jesus Christ of Latter-day Saints in New Zealand" (master's thesis, BYU, 1971), p. 116.

59. Allie Howe, "A Temple in the South Pacific," IE 58 (November 1955): 811-13; Wendell B. Mendenhall in CR, April 1955, p. 5.

60. *Te Karere: The Messenger* 51 (January 1957): pp. 4-5.

61. CN, February 12, 1955, p. 3.

62. Gibbons, *David O. McKay,* p. 349.

63. CN, December 31, 1955, pp. 8-9.

64. David W. Cummings, *Mighty Missionary of the Pacific* (SLC: Bookcraft, 1961), p. 58.

65. Gordon W. Allred, "The Great Labor of Love," IE 61 (April 1958): 226-29, ff.

66. Cummings, *Mighty Missionary*, p. 71.

67. CN, January 5, 1957, pp. 6-7, 10.

68. Cummings, *Mighty Missionary*, p. 75.

69. CN, April 11, 1953, p. 7.

70. CN, August 8, 1953, pp. 3, 12; August 22, pp. 2, 4.

71. Derek A. Cuthbert, *The Second Century: Latter-day Saints in Great Britain* (the author, 1987), p. 23.

72. Anderson, "The Making of a Temple," p. 282; CN, September 20, 1954, p. 12; Leland R. Grover interview, February 13, 1987.

73. Ibid., September 3, 1955, pp. 6-7; *Star* 117 (October 1955): 303-6.

74. Anderson, "The Making of a Temple," pp. 282-87.

75. Cuthbert, *Second Century*, p. 30.

76. CN, September 13, 1958, p. 3.

77. Cuthbert, *Second Century,* p. 34.
78. CN, January 8, 1977, p. 6.
79. V. Ben Bloxham, et al., *Truth Will Prevail: The Rise of The Church of Jesus Christ of Latter-day Saints in the British Isles* (Solihull, England: The Church of Jesus Christ of Latter-day Saints, 1987), p. 405.

Chapter 10. The Pace Quickens

1. CN, January 28, 1961, p. 3.
2. CN, November 21, 1964, p. 12.
3. *Salt Lake Tribune*, May 17, 1921, in JH, May 15, 1921, p. 1.
4. Doyle L. Green, "Two Temples to Be Dedicated," *Ensign* 2 (January 1972): 9-11.
5. CN, November 23, 1968, p. 3.
6. CN, June 8, 1974, p. 6.
7. CN, April 12, 1969, p. 3; June 8, 1974, p. 6; "To Build a Temple," *Ensign* 4 (August 1974): 15-19.
8. CN, June 8, 1974, p. 11.
9. Frank Miller Smith, "Monument to Spirituality: Sacrifice, Dreams, and Faith Build the Washington Temple," *Ensign* 4 (August 1974): 8.
10. CN, July 10, 1971, p. 5.
11. Robert O' Brien, *Marriott, The J. Willard Marriott Story* (SLC: Deseret Book Co., 1977), p. 318.
12. CN, September 14, 1974, p. 3.
13. CR, October 1974, p. 142.
14. CN, November 9, 1974, p. 3; November 23, 1974, p. 12.
15. CN, September 28, 1974, p. 9; November 23, 1974, p. 15.
16. Russell Marion Nelson, *From Heart to Heart* (SLC: the author, 1979), p. 188.
17. Eugene E. Campbell and Richard D. Poll, *Hugh B. Brown, His Life and Thought* (SLC: Bookcraft, 1976), p. 319.
18. CN, June 9, 1979, p. 2.
19. Peggy Petersen Barton, *Mark E. Petersen: A Biography* (SLC: Deseret Book Co., 1985), p. 180.
20. CN, June 17, 1978, p. 7.
21. CN, February 26, 1977, p. 3.

22. Richard O. Cowan, *The Church in the Twentieth Century*, (SLC: Bookcraft, 1985), pp. 38, 286.

23. CN, August 18, 1973, p. 14.

24. Spencer J. Palmer, *The Expanding Church* (SLC: Deseret Book Co., 1978), pp. 225-26.

25. CN, March 13, 1976, p. 14; see also Boyd K. Packer, *The Holy Temple* (SLC: Bookcraft, 1980), pp. 21-23.

26. CN, February 28, 1981, p. 3.

27, CN, March 8, 1975, p. 3; April 19, 1975, p. 3.

28. CN, December 31, 1977, pp. 3-4.

29. *Ensign,* October 1978, p. 59; CN, November 11, 1978, p. 10.

30. Recorded remarks by Harrison T. Price, August 14, 1983, in possession of author.

31. Marba C. Josephson, comp., *Matthew Cowley Speaks* (SLC: Deseret Book Co., 1954), p. 120.

32. CN, August 23, 1975, p. 6.

33. Adney Y. Komatsu, in CR, October 1983, p. 37.

34. Agricol Lozano H., *Historia de la Iglesia en Mexico* (Mexico City: The Church of Jesus Christ of Latter-day Saints, 1980), pp. 179-81.

35. CN, April 3, 1976, p. 2.

36. CN, September 1, 1979, p. 3.

37. CN, May 26, 1985, p. 6.

38. Lozano H., *Historia,* pp. 176-77.

39. CN, December 15, 1979, p. 4.

40. CN, December 4, 1983, p. 3.

41. CN, December 11, 1983, p. 3. For a description of Elder Kimball's vision, see Richard O. Cowan, *The Church in the Twentieth Century* (SLC: Bookcraft, 1985), pp. 224-25.

42. CR, October 1984, p. 4.

43. *Ensign* 10 (May, 1980): 102.

44. CR, October 1983, p. 72.

45. *Ensign* 10 (May 1980): 99.

46. CR, October 1985, pp. 70-71.

47. CN, April 5, 1980, p. 3.

48. CN, July 12, 1980, p. 3.

49. Sheri L. Dew, *Ezra Taft Benson: A Biography* (SLC: Deseret Book Co., 1987), p. 117.

50. Delbert V. Groberg, *The Idaho Falls Temple*: *The First LDS Temple in Idaho* (SLC: Publishers Press, 1985), p. 104.

51. L. Brent Goates, *Harold B. Lee, Prophet and Seer* (SLC: Bookcraft, 1985) p. 291.

52. Spencer J. Palmer as interviewed by James S. Palmer, February 13, 1988.

53. Ezra Taft Benson, "The Future of the Church in Asia," IE 73 (March 1970): 15.

54. CR, October 1985, p. 71.

55. CN, June 5, 1983, p. 3.

56. *The* [BYU] *Daily Universe*, October 28, 1986, p. 7, and November 10, 1986, p. 6.

57. CN, July 24, 1983, p. 12.

58. CN, May 19, 1973, p. 3.

59. CN, September 11, 1983, p. 3.

60. CN, September 4, 1983, pp. 8-9, 13.

61. *Ensign* 14 (November 1984): 106-7, and 16 (May 1986): 14.

62. CR, October 1984, p. 67.

63. CR, October 1985, p. 44.

64. CN, June 9, 1985, p. 3.

65. CR, October 1985, p. 72; CN, June 30, 1985, p. 5, and July 14, 1985, pp. 3, 12.

66. Barton, *Petersen,* p. 187.

67. CR, October 1985, p. 73.

68. GHMA 22 (October 1945): 59.

69. CN, June 1, 1996, p. 4.

70. *Ensign* (May 1980), p. 102.

71. Brigham Young, June 22, 1856, in JD 3:372 also JD 10:254.

72. HC, February 19, 1994, p. 3.

73. Joseph F. Smith, August 19, 1906, trans. from *Der Stern* 38: 332, MS, CA.

74. Lorenzo Snow in *Star* 61 (August 31, 1899): 546.

75. *Ensign* 7 (January 1977): 7; CN, April 19, 1975, p. 3.

76. HE 5:337.

77. Orson Pratt, May 20, 1877, in JD, 19:19-20.

78. CN, August 7, 1971, p. 16.

79. Bruce R. McConkie, *The Millennial Messiah, The Second Coming of*

the Son of Man (SLC: Deseret Book Co., 1982), pp. 279-80.

80. Orson Pratt, October 26, 1879, in JD, 24:24.
81. Alvin R. Dyer, "Center Place of Zion," BYU devotional address, February 6, 1967, p. 8.
82. Orson Pratt, August 1, 1880, in JD, 21:330-31.
83. Wilford Woodruff, September 16, 1877, in JD, 19:230.
84. John Taylor, May 18, 1884, in JD, 25:185.
85. Brigham Young, August 15, 1852, in JD, 6:295.
86. Joseph F. Smith in IE 5 (December 1901): 146-47; Anthon H. Lund in CR, October 1903, p. 82.
87. Joseph Fielding Smith, "Heirs to Exaltation," UGHM 26 (April 1935): 60; see also *Doctrines of Salvation*, 3 vols. (SLC: Bookcraft, 1954-56), 2:251-52.
88. Joseph Fielding Smith, *Answers to Gospel Questions,* 5 vols. (SLC: Deseret Book Co., 1957-66): 4:168.
89. Melvin J. Ballard, "The Inspiration of Temple Work," UGHM, 23 (October 1932): 148-49.
90. Wilford Woodruff, September 5, 1869, in JD, 13:327.

Chapter 11. "The Hearts of the Children"

1. HC, 6: 183-84.
2. Joseph Fielding Smith, *The Way to Perfection* (SLC: Deseret Book Co., 1931), pp. 168-69.
3. CR, October 1919, p. 23.
4. See the more complete discussion in Chapter 3.
5. HC, 6:313, April 7, 1844.
6. HC, 4:426, October 2, 1841.
7. See the discussion in Chapter 4.
8. Brigham Young, August 15, 1852, in JD, 6:296.
9. Brigham Young, August 24, 1872 in JD, 15:138.
10. Brigham Young, September 4, 1873, in JD, 16:186.
11. Brigham Young, June 22, 1856, in JD, 3:372.
12. Brigham Young, September 4, 1873, in JD, 16:187.
13. Brigham Young, September 4, 1873, in JD, 16:188.
14. G. Homer Duram, ed., *Discourses of Wilford Woodruff* (SLC:

Bookcraft, 1946), p. 159; see discussion in Chapter 4.

15. Theodore M. Burton, *God's Greatest Gift* (SLC: Deseret Book Co., 1977), p. 247.

16. Gordon Irving, "The Law of Adoption," *BYU Studies* 14 (Spring, 1974): 291-314.

17. WWJ, April 5, 1894, 9:296.

18. Quoted in James R. Clark, comp., *Messages of the First Presidency*, 6 vols. (SLC: Bookcraft, 1965-75), 3:251-60.

19. Wilford Woodruff, quoted in *Family Exaltation and You* (SLC: The First Presidency, 1973), p. 14.

20. CR, October 1897, p. 47.

21. CR, April 1942, p. 24-25.

22. Merrill S. Lofthouse, "A Glance Backward—Historical Sketch of the Genealogical Society," IE 72 (July 1959): 14-17.

23. Ibid., p. 15.

24. James E. Talmage, *The House of the Lord* (SLC: Bookcraft. 1962) p. 81.

25. James E. Talmge. "Genealogy and Work for the Dead," UGHM 10 (April 1919): 58.

26. IE 44 (November 1941): 696.

27. Genealogical Society of Utah, *Handbook of Genealogy and Temple Work*, 1924, p. 267, 28; CR, April 1928, p. 8.

29. Rachel G. Taylor, "Temple Work Should Be Done," IE 44 (November 1941): 696; Archibald F. Bennett, "The Great Awakening in Genealogy and Temple Work," DN, December 20, 1930, p. 2.

30. IE 44 (November 1941): 694, 696.

31. Genealogical Society of Utah, *Handbook of Genealogy and Temple Work*, 1924, p. 265.

32. Lorenzo Snow, letter of instructions to members in the Salt Lake Temple District, June 23, 1893, cited in CN, December 5, 1964, p. 15.

33. Joseph Fielding Smith "Thoughts on Temple Work and Salvation," UGHM 20 (January 1929): 40.

34. Archibald F. Bennett, "Genealogy: Partner of Temple Work," IE 39 (April 1936): 246.

35. John A. Widtsoe, "The Urgency of Temple Service," UGHM 28 (January 1937): 5.

36. CN, March 3, 1945, p. 5; January 26, 1946, p. 1; October 25, 1947, p. 1.

37. CN, January 18, 1964, pp. 8-9; April 26, 1969, p. 12.
38. CN, April 11, 1981, p. 22.
39. First Presidency circular letter, September 13, 1943, quoted in IE 46 (November 1943): 698; "Church Service—Temple Work," IE 46 (September 1943): 552.
40. CN, November 20, 1954, p. 12.
41. Gordon B. Hinckley, "Temples and Temple Work," *Ensign* 12 (February 1982): 4.
42. CN, March 13, 1965, p. 3.
43. Mark E. Petersen, "The Message of Elijah," *Ensign* 6 (May 1976): 15-16.
44. Spencer W. Kimball, "Temple Work for the Dead as Urgent as Missionary Work," PGRS, August 4, 1977, p. 4; CR, April 1978, p. 4.
45. CN, July 7, 1979, p. 3.
46. CR, October 1978, pp. 39-40.
47. CR April 1991, p. 101.
48. Ibid.
49. CN, 19 May 1990, p. 3.
50. Boyd K. Packer and Howard W. Hunter, *That They May Be Redeemed* (SLC: The Church of Jesus Christ of Latter-day Saints), 1977.
51. CR, April 1991, p. 33.
52. Ibid., p. 103.
53. Spencer W. Kimball, "The Angels May Quote from It," New Era 5 (October 1975): 5-6.
54. *Priesthood Genealogy Handbook*, 1974, pp. 6-7.
55. John A. Widtsoe, CN, October 31, 1942, p. 7.
56. Thomas S. Monson, "The Key of Faith," PGRS 1969, pp. 15-16.
57. CN, August 15, 1987, p. 3.
58. Gordon B. Hinckley, CR, October 1985, pp. 72-73.
59. George Q. Cannon, October 31, 1880, in JD 22:130; see also *Gospel Truth*, Jerreld L. Newquist, comp. (SLC: Deseret Book Co., 1974) 2:107.
60. John A. Widtsoe, "Fundamentals of Temple Doctrine," UGHM 13 (July 1922): 135.
61. Boyd K. Packer, "The Redemption of the Dead," *Ensign* 5 (November 1975): 99.

Chapter 12. Temples Bring Blessings

1. See the more complete discussion in Chapter 1.
2. Quoted in Archibald F. Bennett, *Saviors on Mount Zion* (SLC: Deseret Sunday School Union, 1950), p. 210.
3. Brigham Young, April 6, 1853, in JD, 2:33.
4. John A. Widtsoe, "Looking Toward the Temple," IE 65 (October 1962): 708.
5. Quoted in Marion G. Romney, "Temples—The Gates to Heaven," *Look to God and Live* (SLC: Deseret Book Co., 1971), p. 236.
6. Widtsoe, "The House of the Lord," IE 39 (April 1936): 228.
7. Nolan Porter Olsen, *Logan Temple, The First 100 Years* (Logan, Utah: the author, 1978), p. 34.
8. Romney, *Look to God and Live*, p. 236.
9. Brigham Young, March 3. 1861, in JD, 8:355.
10. Quoted in CN, December 12, 1936, p. 8.
11. *Star* 15 (July 16, 1853): 453.
12. Spencer W. Kimball, Dedication Proceedings, Swiss Temple, Sept. 11-15, 1955, MS, CA.
13. Rudger Clawson, "The Temple of the Lord," UGHM 9 (October 1918): 155.
14. CR, April 1985, p. 103.
15. Boyd K. Packer, *The Holy Temple* (SLC: Bookcraft, 1980), p. 153.
16. HC 5:1-2.
17. Widtsoe, *Program of the Church* (SLC: Church Department of Education, 1937), p. 178; James E. Talmage, *The House of the Lord* (SLC: Bookcraft, 1962), pp. 99-100.
18. Widtsoe, CR, April 1922, pp. 97-98.
19. Stephen L Richards, in GHMA 22 (October 1945): 59.
20. Cannon, DN *Weekly,* November 5, 1892, p. 619.
21. Harold B. Lee, IE 70 (June 1967): 144.
22. Brigham Young, April 6, 1853, in JD, 2:31.
23. Talmage, *House of the Lord*, p. 100.
24. CR, October 1985, p. 73.
25. CR, April 1984, p. 33.
26. Joseph Fielding Smith, UGHM 21 (1930): 104.

27. Packer, *The Holy Temple*, p. 75.
28. Widtsoe, *Power from on High* (SLC: Genealogical Society, 1937), pp. 48-49.
29. Widtsoe, "Temple Worship," UGHM 12 (April 1921): 62.
30. Packer, *The Holy Temple*, p. 8.
31. CR, October 1955, p. 13.
32. CN, August 22, 1981, p. 8.
33. Joseph Fielding Smith in "Summary of Addresses Given at the Alberta Temple Dedication," Susa Young Gates papers, Utah State Historical Society.
34. CR, April 1943, p. 38.
35. Joseph Fielding Smith, "Duties of Priesthood in Temple Work," UGHM 30 (January 1939): 3-4.
36. David B. Haight, PGRS, August 1, 1974 (Provo: BYU, 1975), p. 5.
37. Widtsoe, "Beginnings of Modern Temple Work," IE 30 (October 1927): 1079; "The House of the Lord," IE 39 (April 1936): 228.
38. Widtsoe, "Temple Worship," pp. 63-64.
39. Packer, *The Holy Temple*, pp. 180-81.
40. CR, October 1985, p. 74.
41. CR, October 1983, p. 71.
42. CR, October 1984, p. 67.
43. Harold B. Lee, "Preparing to Meet the Lord," IE 68 (February 1965): 123.
44. Packer, *The Holy Temple*, pp. 28-29.
45. HC 2:309; 5:2.
46. Widtsoe, "Temple Worship," p. 63.
47. CR, April 1968, p. 134.
48. GHMA 22 (October 1945): 52-54; Delbert L. Groberg, *The Idaho Falls Temple* (SLC: Publishers Press, 1985), p. 233.
49. CR, April 1986, p. 16.
50. Packer, *The Holy Temple*, p. 54.
51. CN, September 17, 1955, p. 5.

Appendix A:

Chronology of Key Events

Key milestones are indicated with bold print, Temple dedications are italicized.

1830	Apr. 6	Church organized
1831	Aug. 3	Temple site in Independence dedicated
1832	Dec. 27	Revelation (D&C 88) commands Saints in Kirtland to build the House of the Lord
1833	June	Construction begins on Kirtland Temple
	June 25	Plan for the City of Zion prepared
	July 20	Mob attacks Saints at Independence
	July 23	Kirtland Temple cornerstones laid
1836	Jan. 21	Revelation given in Kirtland Temple (D&C 137) that the dead might yet inherit the celestial kingdom
	Mar. 27	*Kirtland Temple dedicated*
	Apr. 3	**Heavenly messengers restore keys**
1838		Apostasy in Kirtland; Prophet and others flee to northern Missouri
	July 4	Cornerstones laid for Far West Temple
1839	Apr. 26	Twelve suspend further work on Far West Temple
1840	Aug. 15	**Baptism for the dead taught;** soon afterwards baptisms would commence in Mississippi River
1841	Jan. 19	Revelation given that ordinances belong in temple (D&C 124)
	Apr. 5	**First couple sealed for eternity**
	Apr. 6	Cornerstones laid for Nauvoo Temple
	Nov. 8	Nauvoo Font dedicated in temple basement
1842	Mar. 17	Relief Society organized
	May 4	**Endowments given in Prophet's office**
1843	July 12	Revelation on eternal marriage recorded (D&C 132)
1844	June 27	Joseph and Hyrum Smith martyred

1845	May 24	Nauvoo Temple capstone placed, temple walls completed
	Nov. 30	Attic rooms of Nauvoo Temple dedicated, ordinances begin
1846	Jan. 25	**Sealing of children to parents performed for first time**
	Feb. 4	Exodus to the West interrupts regular temple activity
	Apr. 30	*Nauvoo Temple dedicated in private ceremony*
	May 1	Public dedication of Nauvoo Temple
1847	July 24	Pioneers enter Salt Lake Valley
	July 28	President Brigham Young designates site for Salt Lake Temple
1848	Oct. 9	Nauvoo Temple destroyed by fire
1851		Endowments once again given on regular basis
1853	Feb. 14	Salt Lake Temple site dedicated
	Apr. 6	Cornerstones laid for Salt Lake Temple
1855	May 5	Endowment House dedicated
1865-66		Sealings and baptisms for the dead resumed after lull
1871	Nov. 9	Ground broken for St. George Temple
1877	Jan. 1	Completed portions of St. George Temple dedicated by Erastus Snow
	Jan. 11	**First endowments for the dead**
	Apr. 6	*St. George Temple dedicated*
	Apr. 25	Manti Temple site dedicated by President Brigham Young
	May 18	Ground broken for Logan Temple
	Aug. 29	President Brigham Young dies
	Sept. 17	Cornerstones laid for Logan Temple
1879	Apr. 14	Cornerstones laid for Manti Temple
1884	May 17	*Logan Temple dedicated*
1888	May 17	*Manti Temple dedicated privately*
	May 21	*Manti Temple dedicated publicly*
1892	Apr. 6	Capstone laid on Salt Lake Temple
1893	Apr. 6	*Salt Lake Temple dedicated*
1898	Sept. 2	Savior appears to President Lorenzo Snow in Salt

		Lake Temple
1902		"Bureau of Information" opens on Temple Square
1904		Church begins repurchasing lands in Missouri
1913	July 27	Alberta Temple site dedicated by President Joseph F. Smith
1915	June 1	President Smith dedicates site for temple in Hawaii
1919	Nov. 27	*Hawaii Temple dedicated*
1923	Aug. 26	*Alberta Temple dedicated*
1927	Oct. 23	*Arizona Temple dedicated*
1937		Temple site obtained in Los Angeles; Nauvoo Temple property repurchasing begins
1938	Sept. 12	St. George Temple reopens after extensive remodeling
1942		Family group form introduced
1945	Sept. 23	*Idaho Falls Temple dedicated*
	Nov. 6	**First non-English endowments given**
1947		Permission secured to microfilm records in twelve European countries
1952	Apr. 17	**Decision to build temples abroad**
1955	Sept. 11	*Swiss Temple dedicated*
1956	Mar. 11	*Los Angeles Temple dedicated*
1958	Apr. 20	*New Zealand Temple dedicated*
	Sept. 7	*London Temple dedicated*
1960		One million endowments given during a single year for the first time
1962		Nauvoo Restoration, Inc., excavates temple site
1964		Branch genealogical libraries inaugurated
	Nov. 17	*Oakland Temple dedicated*
1966		Granite Mountain Storage Vault constructed
1968		New visitors' center opens on Temple Square
1969		**"Name Tabulation" computerized system for submitting individual names inaugurated**
1972	Jan. 18	*Ogden Temple dedicated*
	Feb. 9	*Provo Temple dedicated*

1974	Nov. 19	*Washington Temple dedicated*
1975	Apr. 15	*Arizona Temple first to be rededicated*
1978		**"Name extraction" introduced into stakes**
	Oct. 30	*Sao Paulo Temple dedicated in Brazil*
1980		Construction of seven new temples announced
	Oct. 27	*Tokyo Temple dedicated*
	Nov. 17	*Seattle Temple dedicated*
1981		Construction of nine additional temples announced
	Nov. 16	*Jordan River Temple in Salt Lake Valley dedicated*
1983	Dec. 2	*Mexico City Temple dedicated*
1984		Whitney Store in Kirtland dedicated as visitors' center
1985	June 29	*Freiberg Germany Temple dedicated*
1986		Personal Ancestral File developed for use on home computers
1987		Name "Family History" replaces "Genealogy"
	Aug. 28	*Frankfurt Germany Temple dedicated*
1988		One hundred millionth endowment for the dead performed
1989	Aug. 19	*Portland Oregon Temple dedicated*
	Dec. 16	*Las Vegas Nevada Temple dedicated*
1990		FamilySearch introduced in fifteen hundred family history centers (formerly known as branch genealogical libraries); TempleReady introduced to clear names locally for temple work
	Aug. 25	*Toronto Ontario Temple dedicated*
1993	Apr. 25	*San Diego California Temple dedicated*
1994	Jan. 22	Ground broken for Hong Kong Temple
	Feb. 13	Plans announced to renovate stake tabernacle in Vernal, Utah, as a temple
1996	May 26	*Hong Kong Temple Dedicated*
1997	June 1	*St. Louis Temple dedicated:* 50 now in service

Appendix B: Latter-day Saint Temples

	Temple	Announced	Groundbreaking/ Site Dedication	Cornerstone Laid	Dedicated	By Whom
	Independence	July 1831	3 Aug. 1831	3 Aug. 1831		
	Kirtland	27 Dec. 1832	5 June 1833	23 July 1833	27 Mar. 1836	Joseph Smith
	Far West	26 Apr. 1838	4 July 1838	4 July 1838		
	Nauvoo	Aug. 1840	18 Feb. 1841	6 Apr. 1841	30 Apr. 1846*	Joseph Young
					1 May 1846	Orson Hyde
	Endowment House		Apr. 1854		5 May 1855	Heber C. Kimball

OPERATING TEMPLES

	Temple	Announced	Groundbreaking/ Site Dedication	Cornerstone Laid	Dedicated	By Whom
1	St. George	31 Jan. 1871	9 Nov. 1871	1 Apr. 1874	1 Jan. 1877*	Erastus Snow
					6 Apr. 1877	Daniel H. Wells
2	Logan	25 Oct. 1876	18 May 1877	17 Sept. 1877	11 Nov. 1975**	Spencer W. Kimball
					17 May 1884	John Taylor
3	Manti	25 June 1875	25 Apr. 1877	14 Apr. 1879	13 Mar. 1979**	Spencer W. Kimball
					17 May 1888*	Wilford Woodruff
					21 May 1888	Lorenzo Snow
4	Salt Lake	28 July 1847	14 Feb. 1853	6 Apr. 1853	14 June 1985**	Gordon B. Hinckley
					6 Apr. 1893	Wilford Woodruff
5	Hawaii	3 Oct. 1915	1 June 1915		27 Nov. 1919	Heber J. Grant
6	Alberta	5 Oct. 1912	27 July 1913	19 Sept. 1915	13 June 1978**	Spencer W. Kimball
					26 Aug. 1923	Heber J. Grant
7	Arizona	3 Oct. 1919	28 Nov. 1921	12 Nov. 1923	23 Oct. 1927	Heber J. Grant
					15 Apr. 1975**	Spencer W. Kimball
8	Idaho Falls	3 Mar. 1937	19 Dec. 1939	19 Oct. 1940	23 Sept. 1945	George Albert Smith
9	Swiss	22 July 1952	5 Aug. 1953	13 Nov. 1954	11 Sept. 1955	David O. McKay
10	Los Angeles	6 Mar. 1937	22 Sept. 1951	11 Dec. 1953	11 Mar. 1956	David O. McKay
11	New Zealand	17 Feb. 1955	21 Dec. 1955	22 Dec. 1956	20 Apr. 1958	David O. McKay
12	London	1 Aug. 1953	23 Aug. 1953	11 May 1957	7 Sept. 1958	David O. McKay
13	Oakland	23 Jan. 1961	26 May 1962	25 May 1963	17 Nov. 1964	David O. McKay
14	Ogden	14 Aug. 1967	8 Sept. 1969	7 Sept. 1970	18 Jan. 1972	Joseph Fielding Smith
15	Provo	14 Aug. 1967	15 Sept. 1969	21 May 1971	9 Feb. 1972	Joseph Fielding Smith
16	Washington	15 Nov. 1968	7 Dec. 1968	9 Sept. 1974	19 Nov. 1974	Spencer W. Kimball
17	Sao Paulo	1 Mar. 1975	20 Mar. 1976	9 Mar. 1977	30 Oct. 1978	Spencer W. Kimball
18	Tokyo	9 Aug. 1975	27 May 1978	27 Oct. 1980	27 Oct. 1980	Spencer W. Kimball
19	Seattle	15 Nov. 1975	9 June 1979	3 Nov. 1979	17 Nov. 1980	Spencer W. Kimball
20	Jordan River	3 Feb. 1978	7 Mar. 1981	15 Aug. 1981	16 Nov. 1981	Marion G. Romney
21	Atlanta Georgia	2 Apr. 1980	19 Feb. 1981	1 June 1983	1 June 1983	Gordon B. Hinckley
22	Apia Samoa	2 Apr. 1980	18 Feb. 1981	4 Aug. 1983	5 Aug. 1983	Gordon B. Hinckley
23	Nuku'alofa Tonga	2 Apr. 1980	30 May 1981	9 Aug. 1983	9 Aug. 1983	Gordon B. Hinckley
24	Santiago Chile	2 Apr. 1980	13 Feb. 1981	15 Sept. 1983	15 Sept. 1983	Gordon B. Hinckley
25	Papeete Tahiti	2 Apr. 1980		27 Oct. 1983	27 Oct. 1983	Gordon B. Hinckley
26	Mexico City	3 Apr. 1976	25 Nov. 1979	2 Dec. 1983	2 Dec. 1983	Gordon B. Hinckley

27	Boise Idaho	31 Mar. 1982	18 Dec. 1982	25 May 1984	Gordon B. Hinckley
28	Sydney Australia	2 Apr. 1980	13 Aug. 1982	20 Sept. 1984	Gordon B. Hinckley
29	Manila Philippines	1 Apr. 1981	25 Aug. 1982	25 Sept. 1984	Gordon B. Hinckley
30	Dallas Texas	1 Apr. 1981	22 Jan. 1983	19 Oct. 1984	Gordon B. Hinckley
31	Taipei Taiwan	31 Mar. 1982	26 Aug. 1982	17 Nov. 1984	Gordon B. Hinckley
32	Guatemala City	1 Apr. 1981	12 Sept. 1982	14 Dec. 1984	Gordon B. Hinckley
33	Freiberg Germany	9 Oct. 1982	23 Apr. 1983	29 June 1985	Gordon B. Hinckley
34	Stockholm Sweden	1 Apr. 1981	17 Mar. 1984	2 July 1985	Gordon B. Hinckley
35	Chicago Illinois	1 Apr. 1981	13 Aug. 1983	9 Aug. 1985	Gordon B. Hinckley
36	Johannesburg S. Africa	1 Apr. 1981	27 Nov. 1982	24 Aug. 1985	Gordon B. Hinckley
37	Seoul Korea	1 Apr. 1981	9 May 1983	14 Dec. 1985	Gordon B. Hinckley
38	Lima Peru	1 Apr. 1981	11 Sept. 1982	10 Jan. 1986	Gordon B. Hinckley
39	Buenos Aires Argentina	2 Apr. 1980	20 Apr. 1983	17 Jan. 1986	Thomas S. Monson
40	Denver Colorado	31 Mar. 1982	19 May 1984	24 Oct. 1986	Ezra Taft Benson
41	Frankfurt Germany	1 Apr. 1981	1 July 1985	28 Aug. 1987	Ezra Taft Benson
42	Portland Oregon	7 Apr. 1984	20 Sept. 1986	19 Aug. 1989	Gordon B. Hinckley
43	Las Vegas Nevada	7 Apr. 1984	30 Nov. 1985	16 Dec. 1989	Gordon B. Hinckley
44	Toronto Canada	7 Apr. 1984	10 Oct. 1987	25 Aug. 1990	Gordon B. Hinckley
45	San Diego California	7 Apr. 1984	27 Feb. 1988	25 Apr. 1993	Gordon B. Hinckley
46	Orlando Florida	17 Feb. 1990	20 June 1992	9 Oct. 1994	Howard W. Hunter
47	Bountiful Utah	18 Feb. 1990	2 May 1992	8 Jan. 1995	Howard W. Hunter
48	Hong Kong	3 Oct. 1992	22 Jan. 1994	26 May 1996	Gordon B. Hinckley
49	Mt. Timpanogos Utah	3 Oct. 1992	9 Oct. 1993	13 Oct. 1996	Gordon B. Hinckley
50	St. Louis Missouri	29 Dec. 1990	30 Oct. 1993	1 June 1997	Gordon B. Hinckley
51	Vernal Utah	13 Feb. 1994	13 May 1995	2 Nov. 1997	Gordon B. Hinckley
52	Bogota Columbia	7 Apr. 1984	26 June 1993		
53	Hartford Connecticut	3 Oct. 1992		(replaced by 61 and 62)	
54	Preston England	19 Oct. 1992	12 June 1994		
55	Madrid Spain	4 Apr. 1993	11 June 1996		
56	Guayaquil Ecuador	31 Mar. 1982	10 Aug. 1996		
57	Santo Domingo DR	4 Dec. 1993	18 Aug. 1996		
58	Cochabamba Bolivia	13 Jan. 1995	10 Nov. 1996		
59	Recife Brazil	13 Jan. 1995	15 Nov. 1996		
60	Nashville Tennessee	2 Nov. 1994			
61	Boston Massachusetts	30 Sept. 1995	13 June 1997		
62	White Plains New York	30 Sept. 1995			
63	Venezuela	30 Sept. 1995			
64	Monterrey Mexico	27 Dec. 1995			
65	Billings Montana	31 Aug. 1996			
66	Albuquque New Mexico	4 Apr. 1997			
67	Campinas Brazil	4 Apr. 1997			
*	*private dedication*				
**	*rededication*				

Appendix C:

Temple Ordinances Summary

(Based on multiple sources; figures are given in thousands.)

	FOR THE LIVING			FOR THE DEAD		
Decade Ending	Endow- ments	Couples Sealed	Baptisms	Endow- ments	Couples Sealed	Children Sealed
1850	5.5	1.7	15.7	0	.17	*
1860	9.2	5.3	*	0	.012	0
1870	23.0	16.4	29.3	0	4.06	0
1880	19.8	19.1	213	44.9	34.7	2.5
1890	21.3	4.4	440	178	55.6	19.7
1900	26.6	12.7	517	324	86.7	66.5
1910	36.5	17.6	684	417	93.7	97.6
1920	45	22.8	1,689	835	193	289
1930	56	26	3,660	2,855	554	775
1940	69.9	32.6	5,313	4,944	1,262	2,115
1950	96.5	44.4	3,416	3,512	1,032	2,470
1960	158	71.6	7,167	7,351	2,188	6,192
1970	274	121	12,773	12,635	1,833	12,515
1980	433	202	30,797	30,581	9,358	32,944
1990	447	235		49,345		
TOTAL	1,721	833	66,714	113,023	16,695	57,486

*Statistical summaries indicate that one child was sealed in the decade ending 1850 and three baptisms were performed in the decade ending 1850.

Index

Elijah, restores sealing keys in Kirtland Temple, 32, 55, 202-3

Endowment: antiquity of, 1-2; Talmage description, 53; given in Nauvoo, 53-55, 59-61; given at various places in Salt Lake Valley, 63-64, 67; given in Endowment House, 69-70; written text prepared, 78; definition of, 224

Endowment, for the dead: only in temples, 72; inaugurated in the St. George Temple, 204; must be in temples, 204

Endowment House: on Temple Square, 68-70; successive ordinance rooms, 82; key dates, 262

Ensign Peak, endowments given on, 63-64

Ephraim City, contends for temple site, 91

Eternal marriage, *See* Marriage, eternal

European temples, *See* individual temples

Evans, Richard L., supervises preparation of temple films, 159-60

Evening sessions, expanded, 207

Excursions: to Alberta Temple, 126; to Arizona Temple, 138; to London Temple, 169-70; to distant temples, 181

Ezekiel's vision of future temple, 13-15

— *F* —

Fairbanks, Avard: Hawaii Temple friezes, 130; Moroni statue for Washington Temple, 176

Fairbanks, J. Leo, Hawaii Temple friezes, 130

Family Group Form, 211

Family History Centers, 215

Family History Department, 206

FamilySearch, 215

Far West, Missouri: temple in, 39-40; property purchased, 43

Far West Temple, key dates, 262

Fetzer, Emil B.: designs Ogden and Provo temples, 174; uses cast stone of temple exteriors, 181; designs Mexico City Temple, 184-85; on planning in groups, 189; on meaning of Moroni statues, 193

Fetzer, John and Henry, create design for Idaho Falls Temple, 142-43

Fielding, Joseph, on Nauvoo Temple, 59

Films used in temple ordinances, 159- 60

Fire: Nauvoo Temple destroyed by, 62; Logan and St. George temples damaged by, 138

Folsom, William H., Manti Temple architect, 83, 91-92

Font: at Solomon's Temple, 10; for vicarious baptisms belongs in temple, 48; in Nauvoo Temple, 50-51; proper location of, 55; in Swiss Temple, 161, *See also* Laver

Ford, Betty, tours Washington Temple, 177

Fordham, Elijah, carves font for Nauvoo Temple, 51

Fornander, Abraham, compiles Polynesian genealogies, 132

Four-generation assignment, 214

Fox, Ruth May, writes hymn for Hawaii Temple dedication, 131

Frankfurt Germany Temple, key dates, 263

Franklin, Benjamin, ordinance performed for, 79

Freiberg GDR Temple: 194-95; key dates, 263

Friezes: Alberta Temple, 124; Hawaii Temple, 130; Arizona Temple, 135; Oakland Temple, 172

Fudge, George, inaugurates microfilming in England, 212

Funds: Kirtland Temple, 28; St. George Temple, 74-75; Logan Temple, 86; Manti Temple, 93; Salt Lake Temple, 109-10; Hawaii Temple, 128-29; Arizona Temple, 134; Los Angeles Temple, 153; Swiss Temple, 161; Washington Temple, 175; Mexico City Temple, 186

Future temples, prophecies of, 198-201

Fyans, J. Thomas, on computerized indexes, 215

— *G* —

Garfield, James A., attends school in Kirtland Temple, 41

Garment: worn by ancient priests, 13; source of protection, 226

Gates, Saga Young, on compiling Hawaii genealogies, 132

Genealogical Society: beginnings and growth

— S —